ENGLISH
PLACE-NAMES

Kenneth Cameron

B. T. BATSFORD LTD. LONDON

To my Mother
and to the memory of my Father

First published 1961
Second Edition 1963
Third Edition 1977

ISBN 0 7134 0841 3

Made and printed in Great Britain by
WILLIAM CLOWES AND SONS LTD, LONDON AND BECCLES

For the Publishers B. T. BATSFORD LTD.
4 Fitzhardinge Street, London W1H 0AH

PREFACE

IT is impossible to write a book of this kind without constant reference to the numerous published works on English place-names, particularly to the volumes of the English Place-Name Society and to Professor Eilert Ekwall's *The Concise Oxford Dictionary of English Place-Names*. In these works the meaning suggested for each of the names is based on the evidence of the early spellings which are given, so that the reader may check the proposed etymology against the material provided. No one, except Ekwall himself, has a personal collection of early place-name spellings for the whole of the country, from which a general book could be written, so that a writer on the subject is almost entirely dependent on these major works for this material. It is impossible in such a book as this to indicate in individual detail and by means of footnotes my indebtedness to other scholars, but I hope that this debt will be made eminently clear by the acknowledgements which follow.

Ekwall's outstanding position in the field of English place-names is universally recognized, and his *Dictionary* is the standard reference book for all interested in the meanings of the names of our cities, towns, villages and hamlets. *Most* of the names included here will in fact be found in the *Dictionary*, and a comparison will immediately show the debt I owe to it. A selection of his other important studies is given in the Bibliography, and from these the reader will readily gather his unique importance as a place-name scholar. I can only add my own tribute to Ekwall's work, for my personal debt to it is very great, as is that of all other present-day students of place-names.

The publications of the English Place-Name Society, of course, include all the names in the respective counties found in the *Dictionary*, and countless others. In fact, the more recent volumes of the Society contain all the names marked on the Six-inch Ordnance Survey maps, and so provide an almost complete collection of the place-names of the counties dealt with, for, in addition, they consider many names now no longer in current use, but which are of importance to scholars in other fields of study. The Society's volumes are, therefore, indispensable to all interested in the study of place-names. A full list of the counties so far surveyed is given in the Bibliography, but it may be of interest to note that the next volumes to be published are those for Gloucestershire, that the research on Cheshire, Berkshire and Staffordshire is nearly complete, while that on Suffolk, Leicestershire, Rutland, Lincolnshire and Hampshire is well advanced. My own personal debt to the work of the editors of the Society's publications, both here and in general, is great: to the late Sir Allen Mawer, Sir F. M. Stenton, Mr. J. E. B. Gover, Dr. P. H. Reaney, Professor A. H. Smith, Professor Bruce Dickins, Miss A. M. Armstrong, and Mrs. M. Gelling. Professor Smith's *English Place-Name Elements*, which contains a detailed analysis of the meanings and uses of the words from which our place-names are composed, is deserving of especial mention. It is not only a remarkable compilation but also an impressive piece of scholarship, and the reader will be well repaid, particularly by an examination of the discussion of such words as *bȳ, tūn, þorp, hām*, which can be treated only generally in this book. Professor Smith has also given examples for each of the elements and the lists for some are in fact almost complete. The task which the English Place-Name Society has undertaken is tremendous and is deserving of the support of all interested in the derivations of place-names and in the light they throw on the early history of our counties.

There are also works on other English counties. Examples of names in Dorset, Kent, Lancashire and the Isle of Wight have been included from the volumes of Dr. A. Fägersten, Dr. J. K. Wallenberg, Professor Ekwall and Dr. H. Kökeritz, while the discussion of the names of the Hundreds and Wapentakes owes much to the excellent studies of Professor O. S. Arngart (formerly Anderson). To the list of eminent Swedish scholars must be added the names of Dr. R. Forsberg and Dr. R. Tengstrand, who have produced two of the most important studies in recent years on particular aspects of place-name research, and that of the late Professor R. E. Zachrisson, especially for his analysis of the influence of French on English place-names, and for his experiments into new methods of place-name interpretation.

Present-day research, of course, would not be possible without the pioneer work of earlier scholars, foremost of whom are W. W. Skeat and Henry Bradley, who may be said to have laid the foundations of the scientific study of English place-names. In the Bibliography are included those earlier county volumes which have not yet been superseded by more modern studies. Many include only the names of the more important places in the respective counties, but examples have been chosen from them so that the evidence presented in this book should be as representative as possible.

Names of Celtic and of pre-English origin present very special difficulties of interpretation, and final suggestions of etymology must be left to Celtic scholars. W. J. Watson made an important contribution to this subject, especially to the study of the Celtic place-names of Scotland. His successor in the University of Edinburgh, Professor K. H. Jackson, has continued this work and his *Language and History in Early Britain* is an impressive and scholarly book. Professor Jackson has here made a fundamental contribution to the whole subject, and it is inevitable that Chapter Three must owe greatly to it. But the interpretation of these place- and river-names is so specialized that I should not have felt able to discuss them at all, or to include examples of names of Cornish origin, had not Professor Jackson himself agreed to read my drafts and correct them. I owe him my deepest thanks for his detailed notes on both Chapters Three and Four. He has throughout shown me considerable kindness and generosity and it is a pleasure to acknowledge this publicly.

Many important papers have been written on the evidence provided by place-names on aspects of English history and culture, for which few documentary sources are available. Professor Dickins, Professor Ekwall, the late Sir Allen Mawer, Professor Hugh Smith and the late Professor James Tait have made important contributions, but one name above all others is outstanding, that of Sir Frank Stenton. Some of his important articles have been noted in the Bibliography, but to these should be added the Introductions to many of the Place-Name Society volumes, for which he, in collaboration with the late Sir Allen Mawer, was responsible. His is a pre-eminent position, as our most outstanding historian of the Anglo-Saxon period. Here, it is a pleasure to record his constant encouragement and help. To him and his wife, Lady Doris M. Stenton, I am further indebted for their respective suggestions of the extracts from Domesday Book (plate 1) and the Pipe Rolls (plate 2).

I also acknowledge my debt to the following works which have been of considerable help in the preparation of various chapters: Charles Henderson, *Essays in Cornish History*, Oxford, 1939, for Chapter III; G. J. Copley, *An Archaeology of South-East England*, Phoenix House, 1958, L. V. Grinsell, *The Ancient Burial-Mounds of England*, second edition, Methuen, 1953, and *The Archaeology of Wessex*, Methuen, 1958, Jacquetta and Christopher Hawkes,

Pre-historic Britain, Chatto and Windus, 1948, Jacquetta Hawkes, *A Guide to the Prehistoric and Roman Monuments of England and Wales*, Chatto and Windus, 1951, and J. F. S. Stone, *Wessex before the Celts*, Thames and Hudson, 1958, for Chapter X; D. Knowles and R. N. Hadcock, *Medieval Religious Houses, England and Wales*, Longmans, 1953, for Chapter XII; I. D. Margary, *Roman Roads in Britain*, two volumes, Phoenix House, 1955, for Chapter XV; and P. H. Reaney, *A Dictionary of British Surnames*, Routledge and Kegan Paul, 1958, and L. C. Hector, *The Handwriting of English Documents*, Arnold, 1958, generally.

Several friends have also been kind enough to read all or part of the drafts of this book. Professor R. M. Wilson of the University of Sheffield has read the whole of the original drafts and has made a contribution which only he will recognize. He has saved me from errors and has made numerous suggestions which have improved it in many ways. For his many kindnesses I owe him a debt I cannot repay. Professor Bruce Dickins has also read the whole of the drafts, and once again I stand deeply in his debt. His fatherly guidance, advice and help will always be remembered with affection. My colleague Professor J. S. Roskell, too, has shown his friendliness and generosity by reading much of the original draft, and I offer to him my thanks for the many valuable comments and suggestions which he made. Professor Lewis Thorpe has also earned my best thanks for the valuable notes he provided after reading the chapter on French place-names. My warm appreciation goes to Mr. and Mrs. J. J. E. Sharples, who have read many of the chapters, and, as new-comers to the study of place-names, saved me from pitfalls I had not personally recognized. Similarly, Miss Sheila Copping of the University of Nottingham deserves my especial thanks for her most accurate typing of the first draft of the manuscript. Finally, I offer formally my gratitude to my wife, who has been always my keenest critic, and whose support and encouragement have, as ever, been a great inspiration.

An attempt has been made to include in the main those place-names whose meanings are agreed upon by most scholars. Difficult, but well-known, names have often been deliberately omitted, and where the etymology is unknown or uncertain this has been clearly stated. When more than one meaning is possible, alternatives are sometimes given, but often a choice has been made, frequently frankly on the grounds of personal preference. For this I accept sole responsibility, as indeed for all the meanings suggested, though the vast majority appear in one or other of the works listed in the Bibliography. It should also be noted that where a name consists of more than one element, and of these one is under particular discussion, in most cases the meaning of the other element only is given. Although this method may not always be entirely satisfactory, it has avoided the constant repetition in translation of the same word, when numerous examples have been grouped together.

I have to thank all those readers who have been kind enough to send me notes on some of the names discussed in this book. Corrections have been made to the second edition, where necessary, as well as a few limited additions to the text and to the Bibliography. My warm and especial thanks are due to Mr. J. E. B. Gover who has kindly corrected several points, and has also provided a considerable number of parallels and several interesting names from his own unpublished collection of forms for Hampshire and Cornwall.

CONTENTS

CONTENTS

Chapter		Page

LIST OF ILLUSTRATIONS

COUNTY ABBREVIATIONS
(after The English Place-Name Society)

Bd	Bedfordshire
Bk	Buckinghamshire
Brk	Berkshire
C	Cambridgeshire
Ch	Cheshire
Co	Cornwall
Cu	Cumberland
D	Devon
Db	Derbyshire
Do	Dorset
Du	Durham
ERY	East Riding of Yorkshire
Ess	Essex
Gl	Gloucestershire
Ha	Hampshire
He	Herefordshire
Hrt	Hertfordshire
Hu	Huntingdonshire
K	Kent
L	Lincolnshire
La	Lancashire
Lei	Leicestershire
Ln	City of London
Mx	Middlesex
Nb	Northumberland
Nf	Norfolk
NRY	North Riding of Yorkshire
Nt	Nottinghamshire
Nth	Northamptonshire
O	Oxfordshire
R	Rutland
Sa	Shropshire
Sf	Suffolk
So	Somerset
Sr	Surrey
St	Staffordshire
Sx	Sussex
W	Wiltshire
Wa	Warwickshire
We	Westmorland
Wo	Worcestershire
WRY	West Riding of Yorkshire
Wt	Isle of Wight

PRONUNCIATION OF OLD ENGLISH
AND OLD NORSE SPELLINGS

The following equivalents, from Standard English except where stated, are purely approximate and in some cases of necessity simplified. They are intended as a guide to the pronunciation of the Old English and Old Norse (Scandinavian) words quoted in the text.

Vowels:

Old English. (It should be noted that the Old Norse letters probably had nearly the same value as those of Old English, but one or two letters used only in Old Norse are added below. The sign – indicates a long vowel in Old English and ′ a long vowel in Old Norse.

a	German M*a*nn	ī	*see*
ā	f*a*ther	o	h*o*t
æ (Æ)	h*a*t	ō	French b*eau*
ǣ	f*a*re	u	f*u*ll
e	s*e*t	ū	f*oo*l
ē	German S*ee*	y	French t*u*
i	s*i*t	ȳ	French p*u*r

Old Norse.

ę	s*e*t	ǫ	h*o*t

Diphthongs:

The Old English diphthong was pronounced as a single glide, but each of the vowels, from which it was formed, was heard. It will be sufficient for our purpose to assume that the pronunciation of each part was the same as that of the vowel itself. Three Old Norse diphthongs, found in words quoted in this book, can be represented as follows:

$$au \quad ǫ+u \qquad ei \quad e+i \qquad ey \quad e+y$$

Consonants:

All the Old English consonants were pronounced, so that ng = n+g, hl = h+l (compare Welsh ll), wr = w+r. They were pronounced like their modern equivalents in Standard English with these (simplified) exceptions:

c   before *e* and *i*, and after *i*, as in *c*hild; elsewhere, as in *c*old
cg   as in ju*dg*e
g   before *e* and *i*, and after *æ*, *e* and *i*, as in *y*et; elsewhere, as in *g*o
h   initially, as in *h*at; elsewhere, as in Scots lo*ch*
sc   as in *sh*all
f   usually, as in *f*ill; between vowels, as in o*v*en
s   usually, as in *s*it; between vowels, as in *z*est
þ, ð between vowels, as in fa*th*er; elsewhere as in *th*in.

These last two letters (called *thorn* and *eth* respectively) are written indiscriminately in Old English manuscripts to represent the two sounds noted above. In this book, and following recent English Place-Name Society practice, *þ* is used initially, *ð* medially and finally, though such a distinction is purely graphic.

The additional Old Norse symbols may be noted:

j   as in *y*oung
v   as in *w*ill

Chapter One

--------- ★ ---------

THE TECHNIQUE OF
PLACE-NAME STUDY

UNLESS early spellings of a place-name are available we can never be absolutely certain of its original meaning. Sometimes the early forms show that it had the obvious meaning suggested by the modern one: Ashwood is "ash-tree wood", Broadway "broad road or way" and Foxholes "foxes' earths". On the other hand, the early forms often make it clear that the modern spelling is quite misleading. Moreover, even when the modern name does represent accurately enough the original form, we may have to take into consideration the possibility of some change in the meaning of the word or words of which it is composed. Today *field* normally has the sense "enclosed piece of land" but originally, in Old English, it meant "open country", so that such names as Ashfield (Nt, Sa, Sf) and Broadfield (He, Hrt) had a different meaning from that which the modern form of this word might lead us to expect.

For the most part, however, the present spelling of a place-name either gives an entirely wrong idea of its original meaning or else is completely meaningless. Borstall (K) might suggest "boar's stall", a place in which boars were kept. The basic meaning is in fact "place of refuge", an ironic name when we remember that the first place of correction for young offenders was established here. Easter (Ess) has no connexion with the Christian festival, but means simply "sheep-fold", nor has Redmire (NRY) anything to do with red or a mire, for it was originally "mere or lake where reeds grow".

Such misleading names as these are not uncommon, and even more frequent are those which at first sight appear completely meaningless. Highlow (Db) is an apparent contradiction until we find that -low is derived from a word meaning "hill, mound or burial-mound". Nor is there anything in the present forms of Meaux (ERY) or Tring (Hrt) to tell us that the first was a "pool with sandy shores" and the latter a "slope on which trees grow".

Moreover, a study of the early spellings shows that place-names which are now identical in form are not necessarily identical in

17

origin. Aston is usually "eastern farmstead or village", but Cold Aston (Gl) and Aston on Clun (Sa) mean "ash-tree farmstead", and similarly most Bradleys are "broad wood or glade", but Bradley in the Moors (St) means "wood where boards are obtained". Nor is such a variation found only among the commoner names; it occurs also in such comparatively rare ones as Oulton. Places of this name in Cheshire, Staffordshire and the West Riding of Yorkshire mean "old farmstead", in Cumberland it is "Wulfa's farmstead", in Norfolk "Outhulf's farmstead" and the example in Suffolk represents "Āli's farmstead".

On the other hand, place-names of identical origin may appear with different spellings in Modern English. Northwich (Ch), Northwick (Gl) and Norwich (Nf) all mean "northern dwelling or dairy-farm", and Hadfield (Db), Hatfield, a common name, and Heathfield (So) "heather-covered open land".

It is clear from these examples that in many, if not the majority of cases, the modern form of the name gives no help at all in arriving at its earlier meaning. Even the most obvious name may originally have meant something quite different and the true etymology can be arrived at only by a consideration of the earliest ascertainable spellings of the name. Without these we can only guess, and any answer obtained by such means is almost certain to be wrong.

The vast majority of our old place-names, whether of cities, towns, villages, parishes or even farms, were in existence by the time of the Norman Conquest. Names of Celtic (and even of pre-Celtic) origin, some of which survive, were already in use before the coming of the Anglo-Saxons in the late 4th and 5th centuries. Others were given by the Anglo-Saxons between say the 5th century and the mid-11th century, while names of Scandinavian origin belong in the main to the late 9th, 10th and 11th centuries. Of course, names still continued to be given after the Norman Conquest and the process is still going on, as with the modern Peterlee. But it is precisely because our place-names in general are so old that it is necessary to trace the forms of them, as represented by their spellings, back to the earliest possible date.

Since many of our place-names date from the Anglo-Saxon period, the original forms of them would be in Old English. This is the name given to the language from the first beginning of the English settlements till about 1150. It is sometimes known as Anglo-Saxon, but it is more convenient to use this term as referring to the people and to use Old English for the language, and so help to emphasize its continuity with Middle and Modern English. From our point of view the most important characteristic of Old English is that it was an inflected language. In it, as in Latin or modern German, the relationship of one word to another was indicated by the endings of the words and the result was a considerable freedom of word-order in the sentence. As will be seen, some of the inflexions of Old English have left their traces in the forms of place-names.

The Anglo-Saxons took over some existing place- and river-names from the earlier British inhabitants of the country. Such names are usually referred to as British or Celtic, the two terms being used interchangeably, while the language in which these names are represented is now usually called Primitive Welsh. Once a name had been borrowed, however, it was assimilated as far as possible to Old English, its vowels and consonants being represented by the nearest English equivalents. It then developed linguistically like any other name of Anglo-Saxon origin, in fact as if it were a native English name.

During the 9th and 10th centuries settlements by the Vikings took place. Their language(s) differed from Old English, though there were similarities. Gradually these new settlers adopted English as their language but many words of Scandinavian origin, sometimes with Scandinavian vowels and consonants not found in English, became an integral part of the standard English vocabulary. The borrowings were, however, more extensive in the Northern and Midland dialects than elsewhere and this is reflected in the place-names of these areas.

The Scandinavian settlers in England included both Danes and Norwegians. The Danes settled principally in the East Midlands and in a large part of Yorkshire, while the Norwegians, who in the main had come to this country by way of Ireland and the Isle of Man, established themselves in the Lake District and in parts of Cheshire, Lancashire and North Yorkshire. As we shall see, there are a few place-name elements which allow us to distinguish between Danish and Norwegian settlers. Many names are completely of Scandinavian origin, but others are a mixture of Scandinavian and English words. The fusion of Scandinavian and native English was, however, complete, so that place-names of both types develop linguistically in the same way as those of Anglo-Saxon or of Celtic origin, the development depending, of course, on the dialectal characteristics of the areas in which they occur.

Though so many English place-names originated before 1066, comparatively few spellings of them from pre-Conquest times have survived, in the main because of the loss of many of the early documents. As a result of this most of the early forms come from the Middle English period, which linguistically extends from roughly 1150 to about 1500.

Names of French origin were given after the Norman Conquest and there are other names which can be shown to have originated in the Middle English period. But often when a name is not first recorded until the 13th or 14th century it is for the most part impossible to indicate in which period it was formed. It is usual in such cases, when the name is of English origin, to explain its etymology in terms of the Old English form of the word(s) from which it is derived. There are also some minor place-names, that is, the names of the less important physical features, small woods, copses, lanes and so on, which, although perhaps very old, were not sufficiently important to be recorded at an early date. Many in fact do not occur before the Modern English period, i.e. after 1500. Others are of fairly recent origin, a large number, for example, dating from the time of the enclosure of the open fields especially during the 18th century. Often they are first recorded in Enclosure Awards or Land Surveys of that period.

It may be as well at this point to give some indication of the more important sources from which the forms of place-names are obtained. The earliest for our knowledge of Romano-British names are the *Geography* of Ptolemy dated about A.D. 150, the *Antonine Itinerary* of about A.D. 300 and the *Cosmography* of the anonymous geographer of Ravenna about A.D. 670. These naturally are mainly concerned with Roman towns and forts and, since these names are often of Celtic origin, they are particularly useful in giving early forms of Celtic names. To these may be added place-names mentioned in inscriptions of all kinds, on tombs, altars, milestones and the like.

For the Anglo-Saxon period one of the most important sources is *The Anglo-Saxon Chronicle*, a history in annalistic form from the birth of Christ to 1154. The first sections appear to have been drawn up towards the end of the 9th century, but some of the earlier entries may well include data derived from a much older written and oral tradition. In addition, there is a long series of charters, wills and writs, many of which, even if written in Latin, contain early forms of place-names, and in some cases details of the boundaries of estates, in Old English. The charters are particularly important, though their geographical distribution is uneven. Some of the southern counties are well represented but comparatively few deal with places in the North or North Midlands. Moreover, many are preserved only in later copies, more particularly in collections of them (cartularies)

20

made during the 13th and 14th centuries. The forms found in such manuscripts are not always accurate copies of the spellings of the originals and some can be shown to have been modernized by the later scribes. Forms from such charters are, therefore, less reliable than those in originals or early copies, unless they can be shown to have been made by careful copyists.

Despite such sources, the vast majority of village and parish names, however old they may be, are not recorded from the Anglo-Saxon period. For most of them the earliest spelling is that found in Domesday Book (DB), compiled by 1086. It is as well to remember, however, that the scribes were Norman, to whom the names would appear barbarous, and that they would in any case tend to represent English sounds by the nearest equivalent in their own language. As a result the spellings of Domesday Book have often to be treated with considerable caution. Most of them can be satisfactorily explained, but in general, when the DB form is not supported by later spellings of the name, it is best to disregard it. This is the case with DB *Barcovere* for Birchover (Db) "birch-tree slope", where *a* is clearly a mistake for *i*.

The most important sources for the Middle English period are a number of official documents preserved in the Public Record Office. The earliest are the Pipe Rolls beginning in the 12th century and dealing with the payments due to the King from the sheriffs of the various shires as collectors of his Revenues, and also from various individuals, towns and cities. These are particularly important since they record annually many town, village and parish names. Others include Charter Rolls, dealing with royal grants and confirmation of grants of various kinds such as had been executed in the presence of witnesses; Close Rolls, concerning royal business addressed to individuals and so named because they were folded or closed up; and Patent Rolls, containing royal documents of a public nature written down and delivered on open sheets of parchment. In addition there are Assize Rolls, which record the causes heard by the travelling justices and Coroners' Rolls, dealing with judicial cases of interest to the Crown pending action by the King's Justices. These are important sources of minor names and river-names, as are Inquisitions *post mortem*, which deal with inquests held on the death of any of the King's tenants. Some of these have been printed, but most remain still unpublished. Whether printed or not, such sources must be carefully consulted if a representative series of spellings for any particular place-name is to be obtained. Most of this material was produced for a centralized bureaucracy for purposes of government

21

and was therefore written down by scribes of the Chancery or of some other administrative department at Westminster. As a result of this their spellings may indicate a pronunciation for some particular name which was not that current in the district itself.

There are also important sources of a more local character probably for the most part written down by local scribes and representing more accurately the actual pronunciation of the name. These include collections of land charters relating to ecclesiastical and private estates, manorial court-rolls, rentals and surveys of various lands. Again, much of this material is unpublished and is preserved in the Record Office and the British Museum. Some is to be found in other important national, local, university and college libraries, in the libraries of the great English houses, many of which, such as Belvoir and Chatsworth, have excellent collections, in the possession of the Deans and Chapters of Cathedrals, and also in private hands. More particularly the County Record Offices are becoming increasingly important in this field and, by collecting together materials previously widely dispersed, are making the task of the investigator much easier.

Some of the types of material already mentioned, such as rentals and surveys of lands, are found in increasing numbers during the modern period. Indeed, these, together with Terriers, which describe the site, boundaries and acreage of land in private or ecclesiastical possession, and Parish Perambulations, since they were usually written locally and in great detail, provide the best sources of minor names, which are often recorded there for the first time. Though some medieval maps and plans are extant, they do not appear in any number before the reign of Elizabeth I. Between Christopher Saxton's maps of 1574 and the first edition of the Ordnance Survey maps in the second quarter of the 19th century, hundreds of maps appear for all the English counties. Plans of estates, too, become plentiful in the first half of the 17th century and these again are a fruitful source for minor names and field-names. In the 18th century, Enclosure Awards begin to appear in large numbers and continue into the 19th, while in the 1830s and '40s there are Tithe Awards for most English parishes.

When, from such sources as these, a collection of forms has been made for any particular place-name, its development from the time of the earliest recorded spelling to the present day can be clearly seen. From this evidence, by using our knowledge of the changes undergone by the language during its development from Old to Modern English, we can deduce what is likely to have been the original form of the name, and from this its etymology. But in considering more particularly the Middle English forms it must be remembered that the same original sound may develop differently in the different dialects. Thus, Old English *manig* has given *many* in Standard English, but *mony* in some areas, and in Middle English such forms are usual in the Western dialects. The West Midlands dialectal form has in fact survived occasionally in modern place-name forms, and this is so in Monyash (Db) "many ash-trees". Again, Old English *hrycg* has regularly given *ridge* in Standard English, but it had varying developments in the different Middle English dialects. In the West and South-west it appears as *rugge*, in the South-east as *regge*, and in the North and East as *rigge*. Such variations are reflected in the Middle English forms of place-names, and may even survive today—hence Rudge, Redge and Ridge. It will be clear from this that without a good knowledge of the development of the English language, and of the different developments in the various dialects, a correct interpretation of the forms would be impossible.

Apart from dialectal developments, certain types of changes occur frequently in place-names, one of the commonest being the loss of a medial syllable. This is most often found in names which originally consisted of several syllables, especially in those which had a dissyllabic personal name as first element, such as Alstone (St) from Old English *Ælfrēdestūn* "Ælfrēd's farmstead", and Wolston (Wa) from Old English *Wulfricestūn* "Wulfric's farmstead". In others original medial -*ing*- has been lost, as in Ickleton (C) from Old English *Icelingtūn* "Icel's farmstead" and Wolverton (Wa) from Old English *Wulfweardingtūn* "Wulfweard's farmstead".

A further common change is the shortening of an original long vowel or diphthong in the first element of a place-name. Stanton (at least 20 counties) means literally "stone farmstead", referring to the material from which it was made, to some prominent stone, or in many cases to its situation on stony ground. The first element is Old English *stān*, modern *stone*, but in the original *Stāntūn* shortening of *ā* has taken place giving the modern Stanton. Moreover, this shortening must have taken place before the change of Old English *ā* to *ō* in the 13th century, otherwise we should have a modern form Stonton. Had shortening not taken place the present-day spelling would be Stoneton, as in Stoneton (Wa).

The weakening of the unstressed vowel in the *second* element of a place-name, seen in the modern Stanton from Old English *Stāntūn*, led not infrequently, especially between the 16th and 18th century, but sometimes earlier, to the confusion of two originally different words. For example, Old English *dūn* "hill" and *denu* "valley" normally appear in Modern English as *down* and *dene* and in the final element of place-names as *-don* and *-den*. But by the 16th century in place-names the vowels of both had lost their particular quality and, as endings, were pronounced alike. Hence, instead of Longdon "long hill" we have Longden (Sa) and instead of Grenden "green valley" the modern form is Grendon (He). Interchanges of this type occur between other pairs of words and the variant forms are noted in the list of place-name elements which serves as an appendix to this book.

These are only a few of the many variations which occur in the development of place-names, but a further variation may be mentioned. It has already been pointed out that the modern spelling of a name is often of no etymological value. On the other hand, the local pronunciation of it may be most significant, especially if this is different from the one suggested by the modern spelling of the name. The latter may have been affected by the spelling of Standard English, and a pronunciation based on the spelling may have arisen, whereas the local pronunciation may have developed regularly, uninfluenced by any change of spelling. In such cases the modern local pronunciation can serve as an excellent check against the suggested etymology. When this agrees with that expected from the original form of the name, taking into account the various sound-changes which it has undergone, we can be doubly sure that the etymology suggested is correct. Though our knowledge of the history of English sounds is fairly detailed, we know comparatively little about the everyday vocabulary of the Anglo-Saxons and consequently there are still place-names which cannot satisfactorily be explained, even though early forms may have survived. For example, Palterton (Db) appears as *Paltertune* in 1002. No such word as *palter-* is known in Old English, or in Celtic, or in any of the Scandinavian languages, so that in spite of the early spelling the meaning of the first element of this name remains a mystery.

The main difficulty is that most of our knowledge of the Old English vocabulary comes from the extant literature, of which in any case only a small part has survived. The subjects dealt with there cover a comparatively narrow range, and there are, therefore, many aspects of the vocabulary, such as topography, animal-names, and occupational names, of which we know little. On occasion, however, there is evidence to indicate that words unrecorded in the extant sources did actually exist in Old English. In some modern dialects the convolvulus or bindweed is called *bedwine* or *bedwind*, but no such word is known in Old English. Had it occurred there, it would have had some such form as *bedwinde*, and this would in fact provide an excellent etymology for the place-name Bedwyn (W), first recorded in 778 and again in about 880. It is, therefore, almost certain that *bedwinde* did exist in Old English, and the meaning of Bedwyn is likely to be "place where bindweed grows". In this way, as more and more work is done on the place-names of the country our knowledge of the vocabulary of the earlier periods of English constantly increases.

The importance of comparing names which have similar early spellings in order to deduce a satisfactory etymology for each is fully appreciated by place-name students. This can be well demonstrated by considering a group of names which seem to have as first element an Old English personal name, which is actually unrecorded in Old English sources. Just as our knowledge of the Old English vocabulary is limited, there must have been many personal names in use in Anglo-Saxon times which do not occur in the extant literature. The early forms of Codborough (Wa), Codnor (Db) and Cotheridge (Wo) suggest that the first part of each had the same etymology. Cotheridge, however, is recorded much earlier than the other two —as *Coddan hrycge* in 963. *Coddan* would seem to be the genitive singular of a personal name Codda and though this name is not recorded in Old English it would represent a perfectly regular Old English form, and could in fact be one of the sources of the surname Codd. Cotheridge would then mean "Codda's ridge" and by comparison Codborough would be "Codda's grove" and Codnor "Codda's ridge". The Old English spelling of Cotheridge thus suggests that there was an Old English personal name Codda and by comparing the early spellings of Codborough and Codnor with those of Cotheridge we are able to give a satisfactory explanation of these names too.

The study of place-names is based on an analysis of the early spellings of names in the light of the historical development of English sounds. Other evidence, of course, must also on occasion be used, especially a knowledge of the actual topography of the place being considered. The early forms of Stanmore (Mx) would suggest that it means "stony mere or pool" and this is supported by an examination of the topography. It has a clay soil with outcrops of gravel and there are several pools, one of which may well have been the "mere" which gave its name to the place. Without this supporting topographical evidence it is naturally unsafe to assume that the evidence of the early forms is alone a sufficient indication of the etymology, no matter how certain the linguistic evidence appears.

Equally important is a knowledge of local history. Without it, the correct explanation of Mandeville and Poges in Stoke Mandeville and Stoke Poges (Bk) could not be given. Local history shows that the former was held by the Mandeville family in the 13th century and the latter by the Poges (or Pugeis) family in the same century. The family names have been added to the existing place-name Stoke "place, meeting-place" to distinguish them from other places of the same name. There are hundreds of English place-names of this and similar types, for each of which some knowledge of local history is necessary in order to explain the origin of the distinguishing addition.

A further aspect of place-name study which calls for some attention is what is known as popular etymology. When the meaning of a name is no longer understood there is sometimes a tendency to assume that the elements in question are forms of other words still used in the current language. Similarly, when the form of one of the elements of a compound name has developed linguistically so as to be identical with, or similar to, the form of a common word in the language, there is a tendency to identify it with that word, and to alter the name, so as to make it intelligible. So, Old English *Strangwæsc* "strong flood or current" is now Strangeways (La). By the 14th century the second element *wæsc* had become *ways*, and this was mistakenly identified with *ways* "roads". The name must then have been popularly interpreted as "strange ways or roads", and the first part was changed accordingly, giving Strangeways as the modern form. The earlier form *Strang-*, however, is still reflected in the pronunciation of the surname of the Foxe-Strangeways family. It is not uncommon to find popular etymology at work in this way in place-names, but as a rule it does not give much difficulty, since it is usually recognizable, and can be easily explained.

Similar changes are sometimes found in names which have, or are thought to have, improper meanings. Shatterford (Wo) means "ford over the *Shitter*", *Shitter* being a river-name meaning "stream used as sewer or privy", the basis of which is the word *shite, shit* "dung". It is clear, therefore, that at some stage the association of the name with this word was considered improper, and the offending element was duly changed.

Chapter Two

---- ★ ----

TYPES OF PLACE-NAME FORMATIONS

PLACE-NAMES, whether of English, Scandinavian or Celtic origin, can be divided into two main types, habitative and topographical. The first from the beginning denoted inhabited places, homesteads, farms, enclosures, villages and the like. It includes such names as Higham (at least 12 counties) "high homestead", Norton (at least 24 counties) "north farmstead or village" and Wandsworth (Sr) "Wændel's enclosure". In names of this type, the second element describes the kind of habitation, while the first may be a descriptive word, a personal name, or the name of a tribe or of a group of people. These examples, like those which follow, are of English origin, but most of the place-name formations themselves occur also in Celtic or Scandinavian names, and those found only in the latter are discussed in the relevant chapters.

The second type consisted originally of a description of some topographical feature, whether natural or artificial. Here belong such names as Greenhill (in most counties) "green hill" and Blackburn (La, Nb) "dark stream". In this class too should be included such names as Coventry (Wa) "Cōfa's tree" and Taplow (Bk) "Tæppa's burial-mound", which were essentially topographical rather than habitative, although the first element is a personal name. It is clear, however, that many which were originally of this type became at an early date the names of inhabited places. The stages in the consequent extension of the meaning of such names have been excellently described by Professor Ekwall. When men made their homes near some distinctive feature of the landscape, they often adopted the existing name for the new settlement. Sherborne (Do, Gl, Ha, Wa) was originally a river-name meaning "clear stream", but when people came to live near the stream they adopted the name for their settlement. So, Sherborne came to mean "village on the *Sherborne*", and later "Sherborne village". Nevertheless, such river- and placenames were simply names given to physical features of various kinds. They were not originally settlements, and this distinguishes them from habitative place-names proper. But, of course, not all topographical

27

names have come to be used in this way. Many such old names still retain their original character, as for example Selwood Forest (So–W) "sallow wood", and Liddesdale (Cu) "valley of Liddel Water".

In addition to these two main classes, there is a small but important group of names of English origin indicating the settlement of a group or tribe, and distinguished from the first class by an ending in -*ing*(*s*) without the addition of a word meaning "homestead, farm, village". Hastings (Sx) was in origin the name of an Anglo-Saxon group, the *Hæstingas*, meaning "Hæsta's people", who settled in what is now a part of Sussex, and gave their name to the area in which they lived. The names of this type are of particular interest because of their origin and formation, and because they throw a good deal of light on the early history of the Anglo-Saxon invasions. They will, therefore, be dealt with in some detail later.

Reference has already been made to the fact that most place-names fall naturally into different parts, which are usually called "elements". Those which cannot be divided in this way are called *simplex*, that is, they consist of a single word, as with Stoke (found in most counties) which is derived from Old English *stoc* meaning "place, religious place, secondary settlement". In the same way Week (Co, Ha, So, Wt), Wick (Brk, Gl, So, Wo) and Wyke (Do, Sr) are from Old English *wīc* "dwelling, farm, dairy-farm" and Worth (Ch, Do, K, Sx) from Old English *worð* "enclosure, homestead".

Most place-names, however, are *compound*, that is they consist of two or more elements joined together. These are sometimes two nouns as in Marston (at least 20 counties) from Old English *mersc-tūn* "marsh farmstead" or Oakley (at least 12 counties) from Old English *āc-lēah* "oak-tree wood or glade". At other times it is an adjective and a noun as in Weston, a very common name, from Old English *west-tūn* "west farmstead" or Widnes (La) from Old English *wīd-ness* "wide headland".

In some compound place-names the first element was originally in the genitive case. This usually, though by no means always, signifies personal or group ownership of the type of place indicated by the second element. Old English was an inflected language, and the ending of the genitive varied according to the declension of the particular word. The genitive singular endings in -*es* and -*an* have left traces in the modern forms of place-names. The former appears as -*s* in Edgbaston (Wa) "Ecgbald's farmstead", Kingston (at least 20 counties) "king's farmstead" and Bickerston (Nf) "bee-keeper's farmstead". The latter remains as -*n* or -*en* when followed

28

by a vowel or *h*, as in Bardney (L) from Old English *Beardan-ēg* "Bearda's island", Itchenor (Sx) from Old English *Yccan-ōra* "Ycca's bank or shore" and Tottenham (Mx) from Old English *Tottan-hām* "Totta's homestead".

There are, however, numerous examples of names of this kind which never seem to have had genitive endings, as in Alkmonton (Db) "Alhmund's farmstead" instead of Alkmonston, and Kinwarton (Wa) "Cyneweard's farmstead" instead of Kinwarston. No certain reason is known for the absence of the genitive in such cases, but the distribution of the names of this type indicates that they occur most frequently in the North and North Midlands.

On the other hand, we sometimes find the genitive used in cases where we should not normally have expected it, a fact which, though it has long been recognized, has only recently been properly appreciated, largely as a result of the researches of Dr. E. Tengstrand. It is sometimes used when the first element is a river-name, as in Wyresdale (La) "valley of the River Wyre"; a tree, as in Alresford (Ha) "ford of the alder", presumably a ford marked by the presence of a particular alder; a plant name, as in Farnsfield (Nt) "open country of the fern", the most significant aspect of this open land being the growth of fern there; or an ordinary word, as in Beaconsfield (Bk) "open country of the beacon", this being presumably the most important feature of the district. The use of the genitive seems natural enough in such cases, but it is not entirely clear why it should have been used instead of a simple compound of the Marston and Oakley type.

There is also a small group of names consisting of two elements in which the order of these elements is reversed. This is the case with some names of Celtic origin, but the formation is also found in Cumbria, where men of Norwegian descent settled. Many of them had come to England from Ireland or the Isle of Man and, following Irish custom, they formed place-names by reversing the order of the elements. So, for example, we have Kirkoswald (Cu), literally "church Oswald", i.e. "St. Oswald's church", instead of Oswaldkirk, a name found in the North Riding.

A few place-names contain three elements and most of them follow a similar pattern. In several of them the medial element was originally *ford*, as in Wotherton (Sa), literally "wood ford farmstead or village". The most likely explanation of this name is that it was originally a topographical one, *Woodford* "ford by a wood", as in Woodford (Ch, Co, Ess, Nth, W). When a settlement was made near the ford, Old English *tūn* "farmstead, village" was added to the

29

existing name, itself a compound place-name, so that in fact Wother-ton really means "farmstead or village near *Woodford*". In such names the third element is a later addition to an already existing name, and there seem to be no proven examples of original place-names containing three elements. Here, however, the third element was added early, and this type is to be distinguished from a group of similar names in which the addition, usually called an affix, was made later, and whether prefixed or added often still remains as a separate word. The affix in East and West Drayton (Nt), Great and Little Wilbraham (C) and Lower and Upper Shuckburgh (Wa) has been added to distinguish adjacent places of the same name. Many such additions are the names of the holders of the manor in medieval times, as with Manningford Abbots and Manningford Bohun (W). The former was held by the abbey (hence Abbots) of Hyde, Win-chester, while a family called Bohun held the manor of Manningford Bohun in the 13th century. These descriptive words and names are not only used to distinguish neighbouring villages. Sometimes they differentiate places of the same name which, though in the same county, are many miles apart. This is the case with King's Norton and Bredons Norton (Wo); the former, which was held by the king in 1086, is near Birmingham, the latter near Bredon. In many cases, however, their use seems to be quite irregular.

One further aspect of the formation of English place-names should be mentioned. Place-names are normally used in adverbial contexts, chiefly indicated by the use of a preposition preceding the name itself. In Old English the usual preposition was *æt*, modern *at*, and this took the dative case. The result of this usage was that in the early Anglo-Saxon period *æt* seems to have been regarded almost as an integral part of the name. So, for example, in *The Anglo-Saxon Chronicle* reference is made to "a place which is called *æt Searobyrg* (Salisbury W)", in which it is clear that *æt* is considered as part of the name itself. It is difficult to decide when this formation became obsolete, but in the later part of the Old English period it is believed to have been used in documents simply as a written formula. The colloquial use of *æt* with the place-name in the dative case is clearly shown, however, by the large surviving number of dative forms in modern place-names. Barrow (Ch, Db, Gl, Lei, Sa, Sf, So) must represent the dative singular *bearwe* of Old English *bearu* with the meaning "at the grove or wood". Barrow upon Humber (L) is in fact recorded as *Adbaruae, id est Ad Nemus* in Bede's *Ecclesiastical History* written in 731, and as *Æt Bearwe* in the Old English trans-lation of this work. A comparison can be made between Barrow and

30

Bare (La), for the latter is derived from the nominative singular *bearu* "wood or grove". Thus we have Bare from the nominative singular and Barrow from the dative singular of the same word. Such pairs are by no means unusual.

The Old English dative singular ending most frequently found in place-names is *-e*. This has often been lost, but sometimes survives in simplex names like Sale (Ch) "at the sallow" and Cleve (He) and Cleeve (Gl, So, Wo) "at the cliff or slope". In the South-west of England, particularly in Devon, when preserved it is usually spelt *-a* as in Fludda "at the water-channel" and Wooda "at the wood" or occasionally *-er* as in Braunder "at the burnt place" and Forder "at the ford". In compound place-names traces of this dative singular ending have normally been lost.

The Old English ending of the dative plural was *-um*. Its use in place-names seems to have been far commoner in the North and Midlands than in the South. It occurs more frequently in simplex than in compound names and survives in modern spellings in a variety of forms. Many of these are found in names derived from Old English *Cotum* "at the cottages", e.g. Coatham (Du, NRY), Cotham (Nt), Coton (C, Db, L, Lei, Nth, O, Sa, St, Wa), Cotton (Ch, Nth, Sa) and Cottam (Db, ERY, La, Nt). Similarly there is Downham (La, Nb) "at the hills", Laneham (Nt) "at the lanes", Lytham (La) "at the slopes" and Skiplam (NRY) "at the shippons". Other modern spellings include *-holme* as in Hipperholme (WRY) "at the hippers or osiers" and *-om* as in Millom (Cu) "at the mills".

The great variety of modern spellings from the Old English dative plural *-um* shows clearly the importance of early spellings in place-name study. The modern spellings of the names mentioned above would have been completely misleading in the absence of early forms. This, indeed, is the most important fact to be grasped by all interested in the study of place-names. The original forms have often changed so greatly during their transition to the present day that in the absence of early forms it is difficult, if not impossible, to determine the original meaning.

The scientific study of place-names is a development of modern scholarship, but interest in the subject can be traced back at least to the 8th century in England. Bede adds explanations in Latin of some of the place-names he mentions in his *Ecclesiastical History*. He says of Chertsey (Sr) *Cerotaesei, id est Ceroti insula* "Chertsey, that is the island of Cerot", the latter a personal name of Celtic origin. Selsey (Sx) is described by Bede as *Selæseu, quod dicitur Latine insula uituli marini* "Selsey, which is called in Latin the island of the seal".

31

Place-name students can find little fault with many of Bede's suggestions, but he had, of course, an advantage over the modern student, for, though he wrote in Latin, his native tongue was Old English.

Similarly, Asser, who flourished in the late 9th and early 10th century, sometimes adds explanations in Latin of the place-names mentioned in his *Life of King Alfred*. For example, he describes Sheppey (K) as *Sceapieg, quod interpretatur insula ovium* "Sheppey, which is to be interpreted the island of the sheep". Of Berkshire he says *Berrocscire: quae paga taliter vocatur a Berroc silva, ubi buxus abundantissime nascitur* "Berkshire: which district is named from the forest of Berroc, where box grows most abundantly". Asser may well be correct, though Berroc is not itself a wood-name, and has nothing to do with box-trees as he seems to imply. It is derived from a Celtic word meaning "hilly".

Various 12th-century historians, such as Florence of Worcester, Henry of Huntingdon, Symeon of Durham, and William of Malmesbury, show a similar interest in the meanings of place-names. Henry of Huntingdon explains Huntingdon as *Huntendonia . . .* , *id est Mons venatorum* "Huntingdon . . . , that is Hill of the huntsmen". The first element is actually in the singular and the meaning is "huntsman's hill". Symeon of Durham, however, is correct when he explains Woodstock (O) as *Wdestoc, quod Latine dicitur silvarum locus* "Woodstock, which in Latin is called the place of the woods", though a better translation would be "place in the woods" Numerous examples in later writers show the continuing interest in the meaning of place-names, but many are merely excellent instances of popular etymology, and their interest is often chiefly antiquarian.

It should now be clear that the study of place-names is based on a patient collection of as many early spellings of the names as possible, on a careful analysis of this material in the light of the dialectal development of the sounds of the language, and a personal examination of the topography of the particular place, where this is necessary. Nor is place-name study dependent only on the work of scholars in the field of linguistics, although their studies are of paramount importance. It owes much also to scholars in the fields of social and economic history, historical geography and archaeology, whose contributions often provide the clue which enables the place-name student to explain a name more fully. The primary task of the place-name student is to offer a reasoned explanation of the meaning of place-names, but it is now clear that the results of his work will help to throw light on some of the dim corners of the past and so prove of the greatest value to the historian and the archaeologist.

Chapter Three

———— ★ ————

CELTIC PLACE-NAMES
AND RIVER-NAMES

THE earliest place- and river-names in England for which etymologies can be suggested are those of Celtic or British origin. There are, however, some names which, so far as present knowledge goes, appear to be neither Anglo-Saxon, nor Scandinavian, nor Celtic, and so may be earlier. Just as the Britons passed on some of their names to the Anglo-Saxons, so some of those given by even earlier inhabitants still persist. Some river-names have parallels on the continent, as with Tamar and Timbre (Spain), Soar and Saar (Germany), and these probably belong to a pre-Celtic stratum. So too does Wey (Ha-Sr), apparently identical with Wye (Db, Wales-He), the forms of which cannot be derived from any known or suspected Celtic or English root, as Professor Jackson has shown, though related words appear in languages akin to these. It now seems certain that a small group of pre-Celtic river-names is still in use today, whose history probably extends back to Neolithic times, and which one scholar has termed "Old European".

Just as these names would be taken over by Celtic settlers, so Celtic names were borrowed by the Anglo-Saxons. They were not, however, all adopted at the same time, since different parts of the country were occupied at different times, and these varied from the middle of the 5th century for Kent and the coastal areas of the East and South-east, to the 9th for Cornwall. The very fact that names were borrowed presupposes the survival of some remnants of the earlier British population in the district where the names occur. Exactly how the names passed from one language to the other it is difficult to say, but there is some evidence which suggests that many of the names were picked up by Anglo-Saxons who were completely ignorant of Celtic. This is particularly the case with the so-called tautological compounds, of which the first element is presumably the original Celtic name of the place and the second is an English word with the same meaning. So the first element of Penhill (NRY)

33

means "hill", while the second is the English *hill*. In fact, in Pendle Hill (La) *hill* has been added twice, for Pendle itself is from an earlier *Penhill*. By the time this had developed to Pendle the original meaning of the second element was forgotten, and a further explanatory *Hill* was added. Such names as these suggest that the meaning of the borrowed Celtic name was unknown to the Anglo-Saxons, who therefore added, by way of explanation, their own word for the particular topographical feature.

On the other hand, some names probably passed into English through men who spoke both languages. Some of the Anglo-Saxons may perhaps have learned Celtic, and no doubt some of the Britons picked up something of the language of their conquerors and later, in many areas, adopted it as their own. In addition, it is likely that there was at various times a certain amount of intermarriage between the two peoples, as is indicated by the use of *walh* "Briton" as the second part of some Old English personal names, while Cerdic, Cædmon and Cædwalla have names which are wholly Celtic; and it may be significant that Cædwalla's brother was called Mūl "mule", i.e. the half-breed. No doubt the children of such mixed marriages knew something of both languages. Certainly, the appearance of a small group of names in which a Celtic plural is represented by a plural in Old English would suggest some bilingualism. Otherwise it is difficult to believe that a plural in one language would have been represented by a plural in a very different language. For example, Dover (K) was originally a plural form in Celtic meaning "waters" and the Old English *Dofras* is similarly a plural. In the same way Wendover (Bk) "white waters"—the name of a chalky stream—is also represented by a plural form in Old English.

A further point to be considered is the fact that the sound-system of Celtic and Old English differed in some respects, and certain sounds or groups of sounds, which occurred in the former, were not found in the latter. If a Celtic name containing a sound that did not occur in an equivalent position in Old English was borrowed, then sound-substitution took place, and the unfamiliar sound was replaced by the nearest equivalent in Old English. Thus Eccles (Db, La, Nf) "church" is a borrowing of the Celtic *Eglēs*, but at that time Old English had no single medial *-g-*, and *-c-* was substituted for it, so giving the modern name. Eccles, which probably occurs also as the first part of other names such as Ecclesfield (WRY) and Eccleston (Ch, La), of which the second is English meaning "open land" and "farmstead" respectively, is an interesting name historically, since it indicates the former presence of a British population with an organized Christian worship.

The names of some of the important Roman towns and stations, as recorded in Latin sources such as the *Antonine Itinerary*, appear in forms in which the original Celtic name has been Latinized. This is the case with *Lindum Colonia*, the modern Lincoln, *Pennocrucium*, now Penkridge (St), and *Londinium*, London. It should be noted that the modern forms of such names are derived from the Celtic and not from the Latinized forms found in the documents, since these names would be passed on to the Anglo-Saxons by Celtic-speaking people.

Before considering the various groups of Celtic names, we may note Albion, an old name for Britain, which perhaps means "the world"—a very early example of British insularity, as Professor Kenneth Jackson points out.

The modern names of Roman towns and forts form an interesting and important group. The Celtic names from which they were derived may be either simplex or compound, and either type might later have an English or Scandinavian word added to it. In the following examples the Romano-British forms will be given where they are known.

Names wholly Celtic in origin include London, *Londinium*, "Londinos's town", Lympne (K), *Lemanis*, "place of elms" and Reculver (K), *Regulbium*, "great headland", while the Romano-British name of Carlisle (Cu), *Luguvalium*, means "Luguvalos's town". The Celtic form was borrowed into English, where in early sources it is spelt *Luel*. By the 9th century, Celtic *cair* "fortified place" had been prefixed to the Old English form, and this has given the modern Carlisle. Catterick (NRY), *Cataractonium*, seems to be derived ultimately from Latin *cataracta* "waterfall, rapids". It has been suggested that a Celtic river-name *Cataractona* was formed from this and was an earlier name of the Swale, perhaps so-named from the rapids at Richmond. Catterick would then have been named from the river and would mean "place on the *Cataractona*".

But in most of the names of Roman towns an Old English word has been added to the original Celtic name. The one most frequently found is *ceaster*, *cæster* "city, (Roman) town", itself borrowed from Latin *castra*. This has happened in the following examples, for which the meaning of only the Celtic part of the name is given. Several are named from the river on which they stand: *Corinium*, Cirencester (Gl), "town on the Churn", *Danum*, Doncaster (WRY), "fortress on the Don", and *Isca Dumnoniorum*, Exeter (D), a river-name used unchanged as a place-name. On the other hand, *Mamucium*,

Manchester (La), is perhaps "place on the breast-shaped hills"; *Viriconium*, Wroxeter (Sa), perhaps "Vriconos's town"; while the meaning of *Venta*, in *Venta Belgarum*, now *Win*chester (Ha), is quite unknown. *Durobrivae* "walled town at the bridges" was the Romano-British form of the modern Rochester (K), but when it was borrowed into Old English the first syllable of the Celtic name was lost, so that the first element of Rochester represents the second syllable of the earlier name, that is *-rob-*. Colchester (Ess) means "Roman fort on the Colne" and Colne is itself a pre-English name. But the earlier name of the place was *Camulodunum* "fortress of Camulos", the war-god of the Britons, and it is only by chance that, although the old British name has been lost, the modern Colchester is probably still partly Celtic in origin.

Other Old English words, such as *burh* "fortified place", were occasionally added to Celtic names in the same way. Thus the Romano-British form of Salisbury (W) was *Sorviodunum*. The earliest forms of Salisbury refer to Old Sarum but, when the move to the present town took place, the old name was retained. The meaning of the first element of the Celtic name is unknown, but the second means "fort". When the name was borrowed, this second element was replaced by Old English *burh*, a word having a similar sense, and it has early forms such as *Searobyrg* and *Searesbyrig*. The latter is, however, the one which has survived, but a change of the first *r* to *l* took place due to Anglo-Norman influence, hence the modern Salisbury. The present form of Old Sarum itself is due to a mistake. In medieval documents it normally appears in the Latinized form *Saresburiensis*, often abbreviated. The abbreviation used for *-resburiensis* was the same as that often used in Latin documents for *-rum* and it was consequently taken to represent that form. As a result it was expanded to *Sarum* instead of to the correct *Saresburiensis*, as has been pointed out by Dr. Hector.

Few other Old English words have been added to the names of Roman towns, but Lichfield (St) is worthy of note. This was formerly *Letocetum* "grey wood", and to the Celtic name has been added Old English *feld* "open land".

A Celtic etymology has been suggested for some of the present or former names of districts, especially of forests. Arden (Wa) is probably from a word which means "high, steep", topographically appropriate for the Forest of Arden; Leeds (WRY) may originally have been a folk-name "the dwellers on the violent river"; Maund (He) may have had an original sense of "the plain"; but the meaning of Cannock (St) and Chiltern (Bk-Hrt) is uncertain.

The Weald (K–Sx–Ha) was in Old English *Andredesweald*, literally "large tract of land of *Andred*", *Andred* representing the Romano-British *Anderita* "great fords", now Pevensey (Sx).

Comparatively few Celtic names were in origin the names of habitations. The vast majority are river-names and names of natural features, some of which were transferred to later settlements nearby. The fact that a modern village has a name of Celtic origin is *not* by itself evidence of continuous settlement from pre-English times, though of course it indicates that there was a British-speaking population in the neighbourhood from whom the name was borrowed. In most cases it is simply the name of some adjacent river, hill, wood or such like feature, which was subsequently given to the name of a habitation, sometimes without any change of form, as with Avon (Ha, W), from two different rivers of the same name. In addition, many such names appear as the first element of place-names to which an Old English (or Scandinavian) word has been added, as in the notable series Exeter, Exminster, Exmouth, Exmoor, Exwick in Devon, all named from the Exe. The connexion between the river-name and the place-name is usually obvious, but it may be obscured by later changes, as in Frome and *Framp*ton (Do, Gl), Avon and *Aune*mouth (D) and *Ave*ton Giffard (D).

In the past a British origin has been suggested for several river-names, as for example Amber (Db), Colne (Ess, Hrt-Bk), Clun (Sa), Hodder (WRY–La), Humber (ERY/L), Itchen (Ha, Wa), Kennet (Sf–C, W), Neen (Sa) and Nene (Nth–L), Ouse (Nth–Nf, NRY–ERY), Parret (Do–So), Soar (Wa–Nt), Tees (Du–ERY), Test (Ha), Till (Nb), Tweed (Scotland/Nb), Tyne (Cu–Nb), Ure (NRY), Wear (Du), Welland (Nth–L) and Witham (R–L). Recent research by Professor Jackson has, however, suggested that such derivations are at least doubtful, in some cases certainly wrong. No doubt they are all of pre-English origin, and may in fact belong to the group of pre-Celtic names mentioned above.

Sometimes, even when a name is certainly Celtic, no meaning can be suggested for it, because of the slightness of our knowledge of the early British languages. This is so with Aln (Nb) and Ellen (Cu), along with the place-name Alne (NRY), and Severn (Wales–Gl), mentioned already as *Sabrina* by Tacitus early in the second century A.D.

Tame (NRY, Wa–St, WRY–Ch), Team (Du) and Thame (Bk–O) are of identical etymology, while from the same root but with the addition of various endings come Tamar (Co–D), *Tamaris*, Teme (Wales–He), and Thames (Gl–Ess/K), *Tamesis*, *Tamesa*. The meaning

37

of the root is uncertain but may be something like "dark river" in *all* cases. It may be noted here that the *h* in Thames has never been pronounced, and was inserted by 17th-century antiquarians in an attempt to make the name more classical in appearance. Tarrant (Do) and Trent (St–L) are also identical and difficult names. Perhaps they mean "strongly flooding", which would certainly be appropriate enough for the Trent.

Often when a meaning can be suggested it is only a very general one, such as "river", as in Avon (D, W–Gl, W–Ha, Nth–Gl). "Water, stream" is the only meaning we can give to the root appearing in Dore (He), Dover (Beck) (Nt) and the place-names *Dover*-court (Ess) and *Dover*dale (Wo). This river-name occurs also in the second element of Calder (Cu, La, WRY) "rapid stream", and in place-names taken unchanged from the old names of the streams on which they stand, like Andover (Ha) perhaps "ash-tree stream", Candover (Ha) "pretty stream", and Toller (Do) perhaps "hollow stream".

"Water, river" may be the meaning of the root found in Esk(Cu, NRY) and Exe (So–D); Don (Du, WRY); and of the second element of Dalch (D), Dawlish (D), Divelish (Do), Douglas (La), Dulas (He), as well as the place-name Dowlish (So), all of which mean "black stream". The adjective "black", found as the first element in this last group, is also the source of Dove (Db/St, NRY, WRY), literally "black one".

Celtic adjectives form the base of several other river-names such as Cam (Gl) "crooked"; Carant (Gl) perhaps "pleasant"; Cray (K) "fresh, clean"; Frome (Do, Gl, He, So–W) perhaps "fair, brisk"; Laver (WRY) "babbling"; Taw (D) "silent, calm"; while that in Peover (Ch) and Perry (Sa) means "bright, beautiful", but in both cases an Old English *ēa* "river" was added later, though it has since been lost in the former. Here too may be noted Ivel (Bd–Hrt), identical with which is Yeo (So), "forked river".

Several Celtic river-names are derived from the names of trees and plants. It is possible that these may originally have been adjectives, with some such meaning as "abounding in", which later came to be used of rivers. So Warren (Burn) (Nb) may mean "abounding in alders", Cole (Wa–Wo) "abounding in hazels", Leam (Nth–Wa), Lemon (D) and Lymn (L) "abounding in elms", and Darwen (La), Dart (D), Derwent (Cu, Db, NRY–ERY, Nb–Du) "abounding in oaks".

A few are derived from nouns which occur also in British place-names. So, Cerne (Do), Char (Do) and Charn (Brk) come from a word meaning "rock, stone", hence perhaps "stony, rocky stream"; and a similar sense is likely for Crake (La), though derived from a different word.

The meanings of one or two river-names indicate that they were once objects of heathen worship, of which the best example, Dee (Wales–Ch), means literally "the goddess", i.e. "holy river".

A particularly interesting name is Hamps (St), which apparently means literally "summer-dry", appropriate enough for a stream which flows partly underground. Professor Ekwall has pointed out, that where it disappears it has also a bed on the surface which is often dry in summer, but fills in winter when the underground stream cannot take the flow of water.

Besides the river-names, there are a good many hill-names of Celtic origin, most of which are derived from words which mean simply "hill", as in the simplex Barr, now Great Barr (St). A derivative of this meaning "hilly" is found in Barrock (Fell) (Cu) and in the first part of Berkshire. Another British word meaning "hill" is that which appears in Welsh as *bre*. It occurs in the simplex form in Bray (D), while an English word meaning "hill" has been added to give Bredon (Wo), Breedon (Lei) and Brill (Bk), and "wood" to give Brewood (St). It is also found as the second element of a compound Celtic name in Clumber (Nt) "hill above the river Clun" (from which Clowne Db is named, and which is now called the R. Poulter), Kinver (St) of which the meaning of the first element is uncertain, and Mellor, earlier *Melver* (Ch, La) "bare hill". Similarly, the word now appearing in Welsh as *bryn* has given Bryn (Sa), and is the second element of Malvern (Wo) "bare hill".

A particularly common Celtic hill-name was that represented by modern Welsh *crug* "hill, ridge, barrow". It is found as a simplex name in various forms like Creech (Do, So), Crich (Db), Crook (D, Do) and Crutch (Wo); as the second element of compound Celtic names in Evercreech (So) perhaps "yew-tree hill" and Penkridge (St) "chief ridge"; and as the first part of various tautological compounds such as Churchdown (Gl), Church Hill (So), Crichel (Do), Crook Hill (Db), as well as Crookbarrow (Wo) and Crooksbury (Sr), where both elements apparently have the sense "barrow". An English word meaning "village" has been added in Christon (So) and Cruckton (Sa), one meaning "house" in Crewkerne (So), while *heath* and *field* are found in Crickheath (Sa) and Cruchfield (Brk).

The Celtic word now represented by Welsh *pen* seems to have had a variety of meanings—"head", "end", "hill". It is used in the sense "hill" in Penn (St) and the Somerset Pendomer and Pensel-wood, the endings of which are derived from a family name and Selwood Forest respectively. *Pen* is found occasionally in Celtic compounds such as Pentrich (Db) and Pentridge (Do) "boars' hill"; but the meaning is probably "end" in Pencoyd (He), Penge (Sr) and Penketh (La) "end of the wood", and Penrith (Cu) "end of the ford".

It may be noted that the name of the Pennines is not an authentic Celtic name at all. It appears first in the chronicle attributed to Richard of Cirencester by Charles Bertram (1723–65), which is certainly a forgery by the latter. Where he got the name from is unknown, nor do we know any name for the whole range before the 18th century.

Celtic wood-names are rarer, and, as has been seen, some of the names used later of forests, such as Arden, were not originally forest-names at all. Most of those which do occur come from the word which has given Welsh *coed* "wood", as in Chute Forest (W). This is the second element of a Celtic compound in Culcheth (La) and Culgaith (Cu) "narrow wood", and of Lytchett (Do) "grey wood" and Melchet Forest (W) "bare wood"; while a derivative of the same word has given Chideock (Do) "wooded". Tautological compounds include Cheetwood (La) and Chetwode (Bk), and an English word meaning "homestead" has been added in Chatham (Ess,K) and Cheetham (La).

Other Celtic words for topographical or natural features are found in King's Lynn (Nf) "pool", derived from a word occurring in *Lin*coln, and Ince (Ch, La) "island". Cark (La) means "stone, rock", as does the related name Carrock (Fell) (Cu). Crayke (NRY), Creake (Nf) and Crick (Nth) all mean "rock, cliff", and the same word appears in the hybrids Creaton (Nth) and Creighton (St), of which the second element is Old English *tūn* "farmstead, village". Another hybrid name is Charnwood (Forest) (Lei), a compound of *Charn*, derived from a Celtic word meaning "cairn, heap of stones" and English *wood*. Roos (ERY), Roose (La), and Ross (He, Nb) all have the same etymology, though the meaning may be either "moor, heath" or "hill, promontory". The same word is the second element of Moccas (He) "swine moor", with the loss of the medial *r* in the modern form.

The compound names mentioned so far are of the usual English type in which the defining element comes first, but there is also a type of compound, usually called an inversion compound, which is distinctively Celtic and perhaps comparatively late, in which the defining element follows. Hence, Cardew (Cu) is literally "fort black", i.e. "black fort", and Maisemore (Gl) has probably a literal meaning "field big", i.e. "big field". Names of this kind are common in Brittany, Cornwall, Ireland and Wales. In England they occur particularly in Cumberland and the neighbouring part of Northumberland, in Lancashire, Cheshire, Shropshire, Hereford-shire west of the Wye, in the border parts of Worcestershire and Gloucestershire, and in Cornwall. These were all areas of late English settlement. In Herefordshire and Shropshire there are also some purely Welsh names, e.g. Nant Mawr (Sa) "valley big", i.e. "big valley", and these are probably due to late Welsh migrations. Similar names in North Cumberland are probably due to the British reoccupation in the 10th and 11th century.

Professor Jackson has pointed out that the modern form of inver-sion compounds often has the stress on the second element, as in Glendúe (Nb) "valley dark" and Tretíre (He) "ford long". This is a characteristic of Celtic names, and is almost a sure sign of Celtic origin.

Examples of inversion compounds include Castle Carrock (Cu) "castle fortified", Landican (Ch) "church (of St.) Tecan" and Lancaut (Gl) "church (of St.) Cewydd", with which can be com-pared Llandudno "church (of St.) Tudno", Caradoc (He) "fort (of) Caradoc", Pensax (Wo) "hill (of the) Saxons", and Dunchi-deock (D) "fort wooded".

This type of compound is very common in Cornwall where local names are overwhelmingly Celtic and where the English did not settle till the 9th century. The native language remained in use till the end of the Middle Ages in most of the area, and in part of it till the 18th century. Only a small selection of Cornish names can be given, and in the main they are those of well-known places.

Many of the inversion compounds consist of Cornish *lan* "church" followed by the name of a Cornish saint, as in Lemellan "Mael-win", Lamorran "Moren", Landewednack "Winnoc", Lan-hydrock "Hydroc" and Lanivet "Nivet". Launceston may also belong here if the old Cornish name does in fact mean "church (of St.) Stephen", as is sometimes suggested; in any case, Old English *tūn* "village" was added later. We cannot, however, always be certain of the forms of the names of Cornish saints, for many are obscure, and this is so with the saint-name found in Landulph, Laneast, Lanlivery, Lansallos and Lewannick. Cornish *eglos* "church" occurs in Lanteglos, which may be "church of the valley" and in Egloshayle "church on the River *Hayle* (now the

41

Camel)". The name of the county town Bodmin also has religious associations, for its meaning is perhaps "house of the monastery". The early history of the monastery there is uncertain, but it is thought to have been founded by King Athelstan about 936, though there may have been a house of British monks at Bodmin at a much earlier date.

It is well-known that so far as surnames are concerned

> By Tre-, Pol- and Pen-
> Ye may know the Cornishmen

and, since most Cornish surnames are of local origin, these three elements are found in place-names. The first of them, Cornish *trev*, *tre* "homestead, hamlet", occurs in inversion compounds such as Tregair and Tregear "hamlet of the fort", Tremaine "hamlet at the stone", Trenowth "new hamlet", and Trerose "hamlet on the moor". Other habitative names are Gweek "village", Tywardreath "house on the sand", and Helston, a compound of a Cornish name meaning "old court" and Old English *tūn* "village". A particularly interesting name is that of Marazion, with its modern alternative Market Jew, though the two were originally separate names. It is situated opposite St. Michael's Mount, and among the early grants made to the monastery there was the right to hold a Thursday Market. This was held on the mainland, and gave its name to Marazion "little market", and also to Market Jew, which perhaps means "south market".

Pen- occurs in Penare, Penryn and Pentire, all "headland, promontory" as well as in Penzance "holy headland". Other coastal names include Towan "sand-dune", Treath "shore", Porth "harbour" and Porthallow "harbour on the R. Allow". In addition, we may note Ennis "island", Landrake "glade", Menna "hill" and Restormel perhaps "ford by the bare hill", from various natural or topographical features.

Two groups of place-names of English (or Scandinavian) origin are of special interest, since they may have as first element a word meaning "Briton" or "Welshman". The first contains Old English *walh* "foreigner, Welshman, serf". This may occur, in the nominative plural *Walas*, as a simplex name in Wales (WRY), but more often in the genitive plural *wala* as the first element of a compound. It is found with a word meaning "brook or stream" in Walbrook (Mx) and Walburn (NRY), "cottage" in the common Walcot, as well as Walcote (Lei) and Walcott (Nf), "valley" in Walden (Ess, Hrt, NRY), "island" in Wallasey (Ch), "farmstead, village" in Walling-

42

ton (Brk, Sr), Walton (Ch, Db, Ess, K, La, Sf, St, Sx, WRY), Walton on the Wolds (Lei) and Walton on Thames (Sr), "pool" in Walmer (K) and "enclosure" in Walworth (Du, Sr). The particular importance of this group lies in the fact that the existence of such names has often been used as evidence of the survival of considerable numbers of Britons in the districts settled by the Anglo-Saxons. Unfortunately, other common place-name elements would give forms with Wal- in modern English, e.g. *wall* "wall", *wald* "woodland" and even when Middle English spellings are available we cannot always be certain of the exact etymology. The numerous examples of Walton, other than those quoted above, however, seem to be derived from one or other of these words. Even when early spellings show conclusively that the first element is definitely *walh*, as in the group above, they cannot tell us that the meaning is, in fact, "Welshman" rather than "serf". In general, it may be suspected that the latter is the usual meaning, especially those with Old English *cot* "cottage" as second element. No doubt some of the names do show the survival of a British population in some districts, for example perhaps Walden, Wallasey, Walmer and Wales, but the evidence must clearly not be pressed too far.

Evidence on the same subject has been sought from the second group, that containing as first element *Bretta*, the genitive plural of Old English *Brettas* "Britons", which may occur in Bretton (Db, WRY) "farmstead, village of the Britons". A difficulty here is that in place-name forms it is very difficult to distinguish the Scandinavian word *Bretar*, genitive plural *Breta*, from the English word. When the second element of the name is Scandinavian the first very likely is too, as in Bretby (Db) and Birkby (Cu, La, NRY, WRY) "farmstead or village of the Britons", but we cannot be absolutely certain. When we are dealing with probable Scandinavian names of this type, it is most unlikely that they represent the settlements of Britons who have lived there continuously till the 9th or 10th century. More probably they represent later migrations of Britons from the North-west, perhaps accompanying the Vikings. In any case, even when we can be certain of the exact etymology, the very existence of such names would simply imply that the British population of the district was slight. Names such as Wales (WRY), Brettargh (La) "shieling of the Britons" and Briscoe (Cu) "wood of the Britons" (the last two probably Scandinavian compounds) could only have been given if Britons were a distinctive, and therefore probably an unusual, feature of the racial complex of the area.

In spite of reservations the distribution of Celtic names in England does provide significant evidence for the course of the Anglo-Saxon conquest of Britain. In a fundamental contribution to this subject Professor Kenneth Jackson has shown that, on the evidence of the survival of Celtic river-names, the country can be divided into four areas. Place-names fit so well into this distribution that it seems clear that even when all the English counties have been fully surveyed the final conclusions will not be very different. The four areas are marked on the map facing this page.

Celtic names in the first are rare. They consist mainly of the large and medium-sized rivers, with occasional examples of names of other types. This was the part of Britain settled first by the Anglo-Saxons down to about 550. Area II is an intermediate division; more Celtic names are found, including those of smaller rivers, particularly between the Tyne and Tees, while Celtic names of hills and woods also appear. This region shows the expansion of Anglo-Saxon settlement during the second half of the 6th century in the South, and the first half of the 7th in the North. The final stages of the Anglo-Saxon conquest of Britain between the mid-7th and the early 8th century are represented by Area III. Here, in addition to the type of names already mentioned, are found Celtic names of streams, villages and homesteads. Finally, Wales, Monmouthshire, South-west Hereford-shire and Cornwall form Area IV. In this area both place- and river-names are overwhelmingly Celtic, and no rivers are shown on the map since it is unnecessary.

Few historians would now hold to the earlier view that the Anglo-Saxon conquest resulted in the almost complete extermination or displacement of the Britons. They must certainly have survived the Anglo-Saxon conquest to a greater or lesser degree in different parts of the country. Town life had declined, and some of the Romano-British towns may already have been deserted. There is little or no support, however, for the view that the invaders sacked most of them, though this may well be true of isolated examples like the sacking of Pevensey, as described in *The Anglo-Saxon Chronicle* in the annal for 491. The evidence of archaeology supports the view outlined here.

The evidence of place-names shows that the Britons were nowhere completely exterminated, though more of them survived in some areas than in others, but the degree of survival in Area I may have been greater than is often allowed. Many, no doubt, were driven out or killed, but it is likely that most of those who survived were reduced to slavery or otherwise depressed in status. The comparative absence of Celtic names in Eastern England does indeed suggest that the Britons who remained there were quickly absorbed into the life of

BRITISH RIVER NAMES

——— Certainly or probably Celtic
·············· Possibly Celtic

AREA
III

AREA
II

AREA
IV

AREA
III

AREA
I

AREA
III

AREA
IV

AREA
I

the new settlers. In the gradual westward extension of the Anglo-Saxon settlement a similar situation is found, but the increased number of Celtic names here suggests that the Britons were not expelled to the same extent. At the same time the English settlers were probably not so numerous as in more easterly districts. In the West of England, however, the relatively high proportion of Celtic names is probably due partly to the late date of English settlement and partly to the comparative strengths of Britons and English. Here, the Britons must have been fairly numerous, and they therefore retained their language and their way of life much longer than was the case elsewhere. This was certainly so in Cornwall, where Celtic names are most numerous.

In this connexion the contrast between the place-names of Cornwall and Devon is most striking, for there are few Celtic names in Devon as compared with Cornwall. We know that large numbers of Britons had crossed to Brittany from Devon in the late 5th and again in the late 6th century; and the place-name evidence—the comparatively few Celtic names, the overwhelmingly English ones—certainly suggests that Devon was sparsely occupied by Britons at the time of the English settlements there. In Cornwall, on the other hand, the British population remained, and Celtic place-names are common.

Chapter Four

———— ★ ————

THE ANGLO-SAXON KINGDOMS,
THE ENGLISH SHIRES,
HUNDREDS AND WAPENTAKES

THE Germanic tribes who invaded and settled in Britain during the late 4th and the 5th century are traditionally divided into the Angles, Saxons and Jutes. In fact, we owe this classification to Bede, who tells us of the invaders: "They came from three very powerful nations of the Germans, namely the Saxons, the Angles and the Jutes. From the stock of the Jutes are the people of Kent and the people of Wight, that is the race which holds the Isle of Wight, and that which in the province of the West Saxons is to this day called the nation of the Jutes, situated opposite the Isle of Wight. From the Saxons, that is, from the region which is now called that of the Old Saxons, came the East Saxons, the South Saxons and the West Saxons. Further, from the Angles, that is from the country which is called *Angulus*, and which from that time until today is said to have remained deserted between the provinces of the Jutes and the Saxons, are sprung the East Angles, the Middle Angles, the Mercians, the whole race of the Northumbrians, that is of those people who dwell north of the River Humber, and the other peoples of the Angles."

It seems likely that here Bede is drawing on genuine tradition. No doubt he could have deduced the Saxons from the names of Wessex, Sussex and Essex, but the names alone would not have told him that Kent was occupied by the Jutes, or that the Mercians and Northumbrians were Angles. There is, too, other evidence to support his classification. The kings of Mercia claimed descent from kings known to have reigned in Angel (*Angulus*), while the memory of the Jutes in Hampshire survived long enough for a late 11th-century chronicler to tell us that the New Forest was called by the English *Ytene* "of the Jutes", i.e. belonging to the Jutes. Nevertheless the documents of the period make it apparent that Bede's distinction was not much observed and, already in his time, it seems clear that the original tribal differences had little significance. Furthermore, Bede makes no mention of the Frisians who according to the 6th-century historian Procopius also took part in the settlement of Britain; nor does Bede mention any of the smaller tribal groups of whom we know from other sources.

At the time when Bede was writing, early in the 8th century, there were seven Anglo-Saxon kingdoms in existence, the so-called Heptarchy. In the South-east was Kent "the land of the Cantii", apparently derived from a British tribe of that name, known already to Julius Caesar, and whose original meaning is uncertain, but may be "the Hosts". The other Jutish settlement was in the Isle of Wight, Romano-British *Vecta* or *Vectis*, and in the Meon Valley (Ha). This is a Latinization of a British name of uncertain origin, of which the Old English form was *Wiht*, and from this the modern form is derived.

To the west of Kent was the kingdom of Sussex, corresponding more or less with the modern county; further west was Wessex, a name revived by 18th-century antiquarians; across the estuary of the Thames was Essex. These three were originally folk-names, "the South Saxons", "West Saxons" and "East Saxons" respectively, the new names coming to be used of the districts in which the tribes had settled. What "Saxon" itself meant is uncertain, but it may be a derivative of *seax* "knife, sharp single-edged sword or dagger", the tribe taking its name from its characteristic weapon.

East Anglia is merely a convenient Latinized form of Old English *East Engle* "East Angles", originally a folk-name which was later applied to the district they occupied. The Angles seem to have derived their name from *Angel*, the district from which, according to Bede, they migrated to Britain. In all probability, it included part of the modern Jutland and the adjoining islands. The name is connected with *angle* "fish-hook", itself from Old English *angel*, a word with the same meaning, here probably used in some such topographical sense as "bend of a river, land in the bend of a river". Little is known of the Middle Angles mentioned by Bede. Their kingdom has left no trace in modern place-names, and by the mid-7th century the district they occupied formed part of the West Midlands kingdom of Mercia. Mercia itself, represents Old English *Merce* "boundary people", a word better known with reference to the later *marches* of Wales and Scotland. Mercia, of course, bordered on all the Old English kingdoms except Kent and Sussex. Which particular boundary is meant is not really certain, but either the western boundary with the Welsh or the northern one with Deira is most likely.

To the south of the Humber is Lindsey, now one of the divisions

The Anglo-Saxon Kingdoms and Peoples

of Lincolnshire. The first element here is a district name *Lindis*, derived from a Celtic word meaning "pool", which appears also in Lincoln. The second element is Old English *ēg* "island", and no doubt before the drainage of the fens the name was apt enough.

Northumbria, Old English *Norðhymbre* "the people living north of the Humber", at the height of its power included the North of England, east of the Pennines, and also much of the Lowlands of Scotland. The district was called *Norðymbraland* "land of the Northumbrians", a name which still survives in the modern county of Northumberland. Northumbria itself was formed by the amalgamation of the kingdoms of Deira and Bernicia, derived from the tribal names *Dere* and *Bernice*, which have left no trace on the modern map. Both were ultimately British district names, the original meaning of which is uncertain. Deira may be from a Celtic word meaning "waters" and, if so, would perhaps suggest that the centre of the original kingdom was along the rivers flowing into the Humber. *Bernice* may mean "people of the land of mountain passes", a suitable description for those who lived in and around the Pennines.

The Anglo-Saxon kingdoms were, however, only the final result of a gradual amalgamation of small tribes into larger units. The process may perhaps be seen at work among the West Saxons, since during the early period they are sometimes referred to as *Gewisse*, a name which seems to mean something like "confederates". The names of some of the smaller tribes are known, partly by the trace they have left in the place-names of the area, and partly from the *Tribal Hidage*, an 11th-century copy of an earlier document, which gives what appear to be the contributions due by the various districts and peoples to the 7th-century Mercian kings.

Middlesex, for example, was originally a tribal name "the Middle Saxons", used later also of the land in which they lived. As the name suggests, these people must have occupied a central position between the East Saxons of Essex and the West Saxons of Wessex, and their territory probably included both modern Middlesex and Surrey. Little is known of the Middle Saxons historically, though "Middlesex" was later a province of the East Saxon Kingdom. However, they must once have been sufficiently important for a district to be named after them. At least part of that district, the modern county of Middlesex, still bears their name.

England, as we know it today, was only slowly conquered by the Anglo-Saxons, and in many parts of it British kingdoms survived for some considerable time. The Anglian settlement of Cumbria was comparatively late, but Carlisle was firmly in English hands by 685.

Devon was not altogether overcome before the 9th century, and the occupation of Cornwall was even later, and never fully carried out, while the British kingdom of Elmet in South-west Yorkshire survived until the 7th century. Of these regions Cumbria is a convenient modern geographical term, the base of which is found as the first element of Cumberland "land of the Cymry"; *Cymry* itself is ultimately a Celtic name and means "men of the same country, the (joint-)countrymen". Cumbria in the early 7th century comprised not only England west of the Pennines and north of the Ribble, but also Scotland south of the Antonine Wall and west of the Southern Uplands. By the end of the century only the northern part remained independent, and this was called Strathclyde "valley of the Clyde", Clyde itself meaning "the washer".

Devon and Cornwall both retained their British names—Old English *Defnas* being the Anglo-Saxon version of Celtic *Dumnonii* "the deep ones", perhaps referring to the mines there, while the first element of Old English *Cornwalas* is the Celtic *Cornovii* "the promontory folk", the second element being the plural of Old English *walh* "foreigner, Welshman". The original meaning of Elmet is unknown, but reminiscences of it still remain in Barwick in Elmet and Sherburn in Elmet (WRY).

The division of the country into administrative units called shires took place in the main during the 9th and 10th century. Originally Old English *scīr* meant "division of the people", but at a comparatively early date it seems to have come to refer to the district inhabited by this division, and from this to a "division of the kingdom for administrative purposes". Today, the word not only appears as part of the name of some, though not all, of the counties, but is still used of smaller districts that were formerly administrative units, as in Hallamshire (WRY), Hexhamshire (Nb) and Richmondshire (NRY), formerly "land within the jurisdiction of the manor of Hallam", "of Hexham" and "of Richmond".

Some of the Anglo-Saxon and British kingdoms, such as Devon, Cornwall, Kent, Sussex and Essex, became shires, but for the most part, the Anglo-Saxon shires did not correspond to the old tribal divisions. Some of the West Midland ones were purely artificial divisions created for defence. Shropshire, for example, was formed, probably in the 10th century, by a union of two tribal districts, that of the *Magonsǣtan* "settlers around Maund (He)" and that of the *Wreocensǣtan* "settlers around The Wrekin (Sa)". The shire was named from Shrewsbury, and was responsible for the defence of the fortification there.

The earliest shires, formed by the end of the 8th century, were in Wessex. Each district took its name from some town or royal estate, which became the centre of local administration, as with Wilton for Wiltshire, Southampton for Hampshire and Somerton for Somerset. The West Midland shires, as also Oxfordshire, Buckinghamshire and Hertfordshire, seem to have been formed on the West Saxon pattern. These areas were then under the control of Wessex, and the shires were probably created in the reign of Edward the Elder, 899–925, to assist in defence against the Danes. Each represents an administrative district responsible for the maintenance of a defensive centre, as was the case with Shropshire and Shrewsbury, and similarly for example with Herefordshire and Hereford and Staffordshire and Stafford.

The East Midlands shires of the Danelaw also came into existence during the 10th century. These, too, took their names from the most important town of the area which thus became the centre of local government. Earlier, however, the town had been the headquarters of one of the Danish armies. Thus Derbyshire, Nottinghamshire, Leicestershire, Northamptonshire, Huntingdonshire, Bedfordshire and Cambridgeshire represent the district occupied by divisions of the Danish army with their headquarters at Derby, Nottingham, Leicester, Northampton, Huntingdon, Bedford and Cambridge respectively. Lincolnshire was formed in a similar way, but in this case was a union of two such areas. The district of the army of Lincoln was joined with that of the army at Stamford to form the shire which took its name from Lincoln.

South of the Humber Rutland is the only modern county which had not come into existence before the Norman Conquest. The southern part of it formed part of Northamptonshire; the northern, from 1002, was regularly assigned as dower to the queen, and no doubt the fact that such a small district ever became a county is due to its royal associations. It is first so named in 1204, when "the county" of Rutland was granted as dower by King John to Queen Isabella.

North of the Humber the only pre-Conquest shire was Yorkshire. Considerable Scandinavian settlement took place here and, no doubt, like the East Midland shires, it represents the district (perhaps the old kingdom of Deira) occupied by the Danish army whose headquarters were at York.

Before the Norman Conquest modern Lancashire, south of the Ribble, formed part of Cheshire; the remainder, together with South Westmorland and South-west Cumberland, belonged to Yorkshire.

52

After 1066 most of what is now Lancashire was held by Roger of Poitou. Such a group of manors under a single lord was known as an Honour, and the county developed out of the Honour of Lancaster, probably in 1194.

In the reign of William the Conqueror the greater part of modern Cumberland and Westmorland probably formed a border province held by the king of Scotland. It was recovered by William Rufus in 1092 and granted to Ranulf le Meschin, who surrendered it to the crown when he became Earl of Chester in 1120. Most of those parts of the modern counties which had previously been assessed with Yorkshire were then added, and the whole area was divided into the sheriffdoms of Carlisle and Westmorland. The "county of Cumberland" is first recorded in the sheriff's accounts in 1177.

Northumberland is derived ultimately from the Anglo-Saxon kingdom of Northumbria, which was gradually reduced to the status of an earldom with its centre at Bamburgh. The name Northumberland appears first in its contracted modern sense in 1065. During the 11th century it is used with increasing definiteness of this district, except for certain areas which formed part of the lands of the bishops of Durham.

The land between the Wear and the Tyne was given to the Church of St. Cuthbert by the Danish king Guthred in 883 and was consequently known as "the land of St. Cuthbert". The seat of the bishop was moved from Chester-le-Street to Durham in 955 and to the new cathedral there went the relics of the saint. Already before the Norman Conquest this had become the centre of a great lordship, and during the 11th and 12th century additional areas came into the hands of the bishops. The Bishop of Durham exercised regal rights over his lands, and by the end of the 13th century they were known as a palatinate, that is, a district, the lord of which held jurisdictions which elsewhere belonged only to the sovereign. Though the palatinate was abolished in 1646, it was revived after the Restoration and survived until 1836, when jurisdiction was finally vested in the Crown.

Although the shires came into existence in various ways, their names fall into three separate groups—those originally tribal or folk-names, those originally district names and those derived from the names of towns. Essex, Middlesex, Sussex, Kent, Devon and Cornwall, as already noted, were tribal-names, whether Anglo-Saxon or British. Norfolk "the north folk" and Suffolk "the south folk" were the peoples who lived respectively in the northern and southern parts of East Anglia. In all these cases the original names came to be used as those of the districts, without the further addition of a word meaning "land or district".

The same is true of Dorset and Somerset, which were also earlier folk-names, though in these cases they are derived from place-names, to which Old English *sǣte* "settlers, dwellers" has been added. Hence Dorset, Old English *Dornsǣte*, means "settlers around *Dorn*", a shortened form of Dorchester, of which the first element is derived from Romano-British *Durnovaria*, which has not yet been properly explained. To the Celtic name of the town the Anglo-Saxons added Old English *ceaster* "Roman fort", so that their name was *Dornwaraceaster*, now Dorchester. The Old English form for Somerset was *Sumortūnsǣte* "dwellers around Somerton", and Somerton means "summer farmstead". Either the *sǣte* was added to the first part only of the name, or *tūn* was lost at an early date, the resulting *Sumorsǣte* giving modern Somerset.

In Cumberland, Northumberland and Westmorland, a final element meaning "large tract of land" has been added to the genitive plural of tribal- or folk-names. Westmorland means "land of the *Westmōringas* (people of the western moor)", who lived around the upper valley of the Eden.

Four of the shire names were from the beginning the names of districts. Kent and the first element of Berkshire are of Celtic origin, while Surrey and Rutland are English names. Surrey dates from the settlements of the Middle Saxons on both sides of the Thames in modern Middlesex and Surrey. The latter is the southern part of this district and was appropriately called "the southern region". Rutland is, of course, a good deal smaller than the other shires with the same ending, and the name probably means "Rōta's estate".

The remaining counties, with the exception of Durham, have the word -shire added to the name of an important town in the district. The county of Durham came into existence at a comparatively late date, and here the same form is used indifferently of county and town. The name itself is probably an Anglo-Scandinavian compound, appearing in early sources in some such form as *Dunholm* "hill island", appropriate topographically for a place situated on the hill in the prominent bend of the Wear. The change of *n* to *r* in the modern form is due to Norman influence.

The names of the other shires can be classified according to the language from which they are derived—Celtic, hybrid Celtic and Old English, Old English, or Scandinavian. The first element of Lincoln, the Romano-British *Lindum Colonia* of the Ravenna geographer, is from the Celtic word which gives Welsh *llyn* "lake", and no doubt it refers to the widening of the Witham, a notable feature of the river here, and still in part remaining as Brayford Pool, below the hill on which the cathedral stands.

The hybrid Celtic–Old English names include Cambridge, Gloucester, Lancaster, Leicester, Wilton and Worcester. Of these, Cambridge was in Old English *Grantanbrycg* "bridge over the Grante", the modern form of the name being in the main due to Norman influence. Grante, now called Cam in Cambridge, is quite probably a pre-Celtic name. Gloucester, Romano-British *Glevum*, comes from a Celtic name meaning "bright spot or place", and to it has been added Old English *ceaster* "Roman fort". The modern Lancashire is a shortening of an earlier Lancastershire. Lancaster itself is "Roman fort on the Lune", Lune being a Celtic river-name (found also in NRY) of uncertain meaning. The exact etymology of Leicester is more difficult, though the second element is certainly the same word as occurs in Lancaster. The first has been explained as a folk-name ultimately derived from a Celtic river-name. The river in question cannot have been the Soar, on the banks of which Leicester stands, since this name is recorded early, and always in forms such as *Sore*. It must refer to one of its tributaries which was formerly called *Leire*, and which gave its name to Leire (Lei). Consequently, the first element would mean something like "dwellers on the banks of the *Leire*", but the meaning of this river-name is unknown. Wiltshire, earlier Wiltonshire, takes its name from Wilton "farmstead on the Wiley", and Wiley is also a river-name, of pre-English origin but of uncertain meaning. Worcester means "Roman fort of the Wigoran", an Anglo-Saxon tribal name, which appears also in Wyre Forest (Wo). This tribal name is perhaps ultimately the pre-English name of a stream or river, near which the people lived, though it is not now possible to identify it.

Most of the names of the county towns, however, are of English origin, and five of them have a second element *-ford*, an indication of the importance of river-crossings for the early settlers. The first element of Bedford is a personal name Bēda; Hertford and Oxford are named from "hart" and "oxen" respectively; Stafford means "ford by the landing-place", and Hereford (identical with Harford D) "army ford", probably referring to a ford sufficiently wide to be used by an army on the march.

The modern forms of Buckingham and Nottingham would suggest that the endings are of identical origin. Early spellings show, however, that in Buckingham it is Old English *hamm* "enclosure, plot of ground by a river", but in Nottingham Old English *hām* "homestead". So, Buckingham was "enclosure of Bucc's people" and Nottingham "homestead of Snot's people". The earliest recorded spelling of Nottingham is *Snotengaham*, but the initial *S* had been lost by the early 12th century due to Norman influence, and hence the modern form.

Sou*thampton*, from which Hampshire took its name, and Nort*hampton* similarly appear to have the same etymology; but Northampton represents an original *Hāmtūn* "home farm", and Southampton is from *Hammtūn* "farmstead on flat land by a river". The two names, however, would later need to be differentiated because of the similarity in their forms. By 962, Southampton had already been given its distinctive prefix, but the North- in Northampton does not appear before 1065, after which the county name also has the longer form. In Hampshire, on the other hand, the shorter form has survived with the loss of the medial -*ton*-, although for a time *Hamtonshire* and *Southamtonshire* are found side by side. A still further shortened form *Hantescire* occurs in Domesday Book and Hants, the usual abbreviation of the county name, has developed from this. The abbreviation Northants for Northamptonshire is not, however, found in early spellings, and must have been formed later by analogy with Hants.

Huntingdon has been already discussed in an earlier chapter; but Warwick is a difficult name, which may mean "dwellings by the weir". Early spellings show that Shropshire is named from Shrewsbury, Old English *Scrobbesbyrig* probably "Scrobb's fortified place". The difference between the present name of the town and that of the county is due to various changes having taken place in both forms, including the loss of the medial -*bury*- in the latter. The usual abbreviation for Shropshire, Salop earlier *Salopescire*, is derived from a Normanized form of the English name. Cheshire is a shortened form of Chestershire and is named from Chester. The Romano-British name of Chester was *Deva*, as noted previously. Throughout most of the Roman period Deva was the headquarters of the Twentieth Legion and this is reflected in the earliest English forms of Chester, *Legaceaster*, etc., "camp of the legion(s)". The first part of the name was, however, lost in the Old English period, and the resulting simplex form *Ceaster* has given the modern Chester.

The only county name of definitely Scandinavian origin is that of Derbyshire, though in addition the present form of Yorkshire owes much to Scandinavian influence. Early sources make it clear that Derby "farmstead or village where deer are found" has replaced the former English name of the place which was *Northworthy* "north enclosure". The *Chronicle of Ethelwerd*, written about 1000, tells how the body of the English alderman Athelwulf, killed in battle against the Danes at Reading in 871, was brought for burial "into the place which is called Northworthy, according to the Danish language, however, Derby". The earliest recorded spellings of York, found in Greek and Latin sources, are *Eborakon, Eburacum* and *Eboracum*. This is a Celtic name, probably "Eburos' estate". By the time of the earliest Anglo-Saxon settlement there, it had probably become *Evorōg*, and the invaders seem to have taken the first element of the name as being identical with Old English *eofor* "wild boar", and so substituted their own word for the Celtic one. To it they added a common place-name ending *wīc* "dwelling, farm, camp", so giving the Old English *Eoforwīc*. Further changes occurred during the Scandinavian occupation of York. The Old English name was similarly adapted by them to *Eórvík*, later becoming *Jórvík*, of which York is the modern form. Latin *Eboracum* is, however, the usual spelling in official documents of the 12th and 13th century and this still continues in ecclesiastical use, when the Archbishop of York signs himself . . . *Ebor.*

Yorkshire is divided into three parts, the East, North and West Ridings. These divisions, like the term Riding itself, are of Danish origin. Riding is the Scandinavian *þriðjungr* "third part", which was borrowed into English as *þriðing*. This would give an early form like *Norththriding* which would regularly become *Northriding* and so North Riding. The other divisions had forms such as *Eastthriding* and *Westthriding* and the combination of the consonants *t* and *th* would become *tt* and so *t*, hence *Easttriding, Westtriding—Eastriding, Westriding*, and finally East Riding and West Riding.

Lindsey, the most northerly of the Parts of Lincolnshire, similarly has North, South and West Ridings, but the term is not found in any other county. Of the two other parts of Lincolnshire, Kesteven is a hybrid Celtic and Scandinavian name. The first part is a Celtic word meaning "wood"; the second is Scandinavian *stefna* "meeting", later "district with a meeting-place". Holland (identical with Holland Ess, La, Hoyland WRY and Hulland Db "land by a hillspur" is of English origin, the place-name later becoming the name of the district.

Two other counties, Kent and Sussex, had similar major subdivisions in Anglo-Saxon times. The *Lathes* of Kent probably represent the provinces of the old kingdom, and the *Rapes* of Sussex perhaps have a similar origin. Both are Old English words, the first meaning "division of land" while the second is derived from the same word as modern *rope*. Its use in this sense is apparently due to the Germanic custom of enclosing the precincts of a court with ropes.

Most of the English shires were divided into smaller administrative districts called *hundreds*. These were probably formed in the 10th century, though an earlier date is possible for those in the West Saxon shires. In theory the hundred represents a district assessed for purposes of taxation at one hundred hides, but in practice they were rated at a higher and a lower figure. The hide was originally the amount of land which would support a household; this naturally varied according to the fertility of the soil, but on an average it seems to have been about 120 acres. The hundred enjoyed particular financial and jurisdictional functions and had its own court and meeting-place. The number of such divisions within the counties inevitably varied—Huntingdonshire had four, while Sussex had sixty-seven.

In the Danelaw the equivalent of the hundred was called the *wapentake*. This is the modern form of Old English *wæpengetæc*, itself a borrowing of Scandinavian *vápnatak*. Originally the word seems to have denoted the symbolical brandishing of weapons by which decisions at public meetings were confirmed. It then came to be used of the meeting itself and, at a later date though apparently only in England, of the district from which the members of the assembly were drawn. In all probability wapentake was the regular word for this administrative area throughout most of the Danelaw, but, in those parts of it which were early reconquered or less completely Scandinavianized, the term was replaced by the hundred of the other counties. Today, the division into wapentakes is found only in the three Yorkshire Ridings, Nottinghamshire, Leicestershire and the northern parts of Lincolnshire. However, in other counties some of the divisions now called hundreds are referred to as wapentakes in early sources, as for example in Northamptonshire and parts of Derbyshire.

In the four northern counties, as in some of the southern counties of Scotland, the division is into *wards*. This apparently meant "district to which certain defensive duties were assigned", and its use in this sense seems to belong to the period after the Norman Conquest. Many of them are named from river-valleys, as in Glendale (Nb), Eskdale (Cu) and Lonsdale (We) from the Glen, Esk and Lune; others from medieval castles or manors such as Bamburgh (Nb) "fortified place of Bebbe (a late 6th-century queen of Bernicia)", Morpeth (Nb) "murder path" and Easington (Du, as in Bk, ERY, NRY) "farmstead associated with Ésa"; while two of the Westmorland wards are simply East Ward and West Ward.

The names of the hundreds and wapentakes fall into three main groups according to their origin, and they have been analysed in detail by the Swedish scholar Professor O. S. Arngart (formerly Anderson). A few have district names, usually no longer in use as such; some take their name from the meeting-place of the hundred; while the greatest number is that named from a village or manor in the area. Only the second of these groups will be discussed here, the district names having already been dealt with, while the last group is more conveniently considered as place-names rather than as hundred-names.

The second group consists of topographical names referring to hills, burial-mounds, clearings, trees, stones and the like. These presumably became the names of hundreds and wapentakes because they were the meeting-places of the district assemblies. This is certainly the case with Barrow Hundred (Do), formerly *Hundredsbarrow Hundred* "hundred burial-mound", i.e. "burial-mound where the hundred meets". The site of the meeting-place is still known, since Hundred Barrow survives as the name of a Bronze Age round barrow near Bere Regis.

A few names describe what happened at the meeting. Spelhoe (Nth) and Spelthorne (Mx) are "speech hill" and "speech thornbush" respectively. Modbury (Do) means "moot hill", and the first element of this name appears in a large group of widely-distributed minor names such as Moot Hill, Moatlow, Mootlow and Mutlow, this last surviving as the name of a place in Cheshire. These were hills or mounds on which the assembly of the shire, hundred or village was held. A comparable Scandinavian name is Thingoe (Sf) "assembly mound". Two similar names are the Scandinavianised Skyrack (WRY) "oak where the shire meets" and the English Shirley (Ha) "glade where the shire meets", which became the names of a wapentake and a hundred respectively. Wittery (Sa) is probably also a name of this type. It means "wisemen's tree", i.e. "tree where the wisemen meet", and the "wisemen" in this case may well have been the members of the hundred court.

The site of the hundred assembly would be chosen for various reasons, the most usual being the ease of access from the different parts of the district. A hill or a mound was a not uncommon place for it—some of these, particularly the burial-mounds, must already have possessed names. Unfortunately Old English *beorg* and *hlāw* could mean either "hill" or "barrow" and it is not always easy to say which is the correct interpretation. However, in some cases the barrow still survives and can be identified, and in general where the first element is a personal name "burial-mound" is perhaps the most likely meaning, the name presumably being that of the person buried there. So the hundred-names Brightwellsbarrow (Gl) and Bountisborough (Ha) are "Brihtwald's barrow" and "Bunt's tumulus", while Offlow (St) is "Offa's burial-mound" and Huxloe (Nth) "Hōc's burial-mound". When the first element is not a personal name "hill" is often the sense, as in Stanborough (D) "stony hill" and Radlow (He) "red hill".

Old English *clif* had a variety of meanings ranging from the modern sense of "steep face of rock" to "slope". The wapentake of Rushcliffe (Nt) met on the "brushwood hill-side", that of Staincliff (WRY) at the "stony rock" or "crag".

A few hundred-names are derived from Old English words such as *stoc* and *stōw*, commonly used in place-names with a meaning "place, site". In the case of *stōw* it is certain that the word had also developed the sense "meeting-place", as in Broxtow (Nt) "Brōcwulf's meeting-place" and Northstow (C) "north meeting-place". It seems probable that a similar extension of meaning had taken place with *stoc*, as in Stoke (Bk, Nth).

A further group of hundred-names have as second element Old English *lēah* "wood, glade in a wood". As a rule, the meaning here is probably "glade", as in Bisley (Gl), Budleigh (D) and Godley (Sr), from the personal names Bise, Budda and Godda; in Bradley (Gl, L) "broad, spacious glade", and Wetherley (C) "glade for wethers".

Many of the names are descriptive of some such feature as a tree or a stone. Appletree (Db) is self-explanatory; but most of the hundred-names in *-tree* have a personal name as first element, Beohha in Becontree (Ess), Ēadwine in Edwinstree (Hrt) and Wīhstān in Wixamtree (Bd). The particular trees occurring most frequently are the oak, ash and thorn, as in Tipnoak (Sx) "Tippa's oak-tree", Catsash (So) "Catt's " or "wild cat's ash-tree", and Elthorne (Mx) "Ella's thorn-bush".

Usually, *-stone* is combined with a personal name, as in Tibaldstone (Gl) "Þeodbald's stone" and Kinwardstone (W) "Cyneweard's stone", but the first element of Hurstingstone (Hu) is a folkname meaning "dwellers in the wood". Staine (C) and Stone (Bk, So) are, however, simplex names, the hundred meeting-place being marked by a conspicuous stone. A similar name, Staple (Sx, W) "pillar, post", suggests that the meeting-place was marked by a post, while in Whitstable (K) the post was "white".

Most of the Scandinavian names in this group refer to wapentakes, and can be classified in a similar way; but three words occur particularly frequently as the second element in these names.

Old Norse *haugr* could mean either "mound" or "hill". The first element in Grimshoe (Nf), Haverstoe (L) and Wraggoe (L) are the Scandinavian personal names Grímr, Hawarth and Wragge respectively, and presumably they refer to the burial-mounds of the men so-named. On the other hand, in Greenoe (Nf) and Langoe (L), where the first elements are the adjectives "green" and "long" respectively, and where there does not seem to be evidence to the contrary, the meaning is probably "hill". There can, however, be no doubt that the meaning is "tumulus" in Threo (L) "three barrows" and Forehoe (Nf) "four barrows".

Similarly, Old Norse *lundr* could mean either "wood" or "grove", particularly "sacred grove", and the last meaning may explain why such a site was often chosen for the assembly-place of the wapentake. In modern names *lundr* sometimes appears as -land, as in Aveland (L) and Framland (Lei) from the personal names Ave and Fráni.

The third of these words is the modern *cross*, ultimately Latin *crux*, *crucem*. The Latin word was borrowed into Old Irish where it appears as *cros*, and this in turn entered the vocabulary of the Norwegian invaders of Ireland, who passed it on to their later settlements in the north-west of England. From there, by means of the Scandinavian settlers in the North and Midlands, it gradually spread southwards, eventually making its way into the everyday vocabulary. In place-names it is common in the North and in the East Midlands, but elsewhere is usually found only in late forms, from the 16th century onwards. In the hundred-names it occurs as far south as Norfolk and Huntingdon, counties which once formed part of the Danelaw. Almost all examples have a Scandinavian personal name as first element, which perhaps suggests that the cross was a memorial to the man after whom it was named, Osgot (Ásgautr) in Osgoldcross (WRY), Bróðir in Brothercross (Nf) and Gildi in Guiltcross (Nf). Normancross (Hu) "Northman's or Norwegian's cross", however, is a significant name historically. It indicates the presence of a man of Norwegian origin in the southern part of the Danelaw, where the settlers were predominantly Danes. Such a name could have arisen only in a district where it was unusual to find Norwegians among the settlers.

Perhaps the most interesting of all the wapentake-names is that of

Lawress (L) "Lag-Ulfr's coppice". The modern equivalent of the personal name would be Law-Wolf. The lawman was one of the chief men in the wapentake, and in Norway and Iceland a famous lawman was sometimes distinguished by having *Lag-* or *Laga-* prefixed to his name. Law-Wolf was, therefore, sufficiently famous to be so distinguished. The name Lawress suggests that the wapentake held its meetings at a coppice owned by its own headman.

Chapter Five

———— ★ ————

THE EARLIEST
ENGLISH SETTLEMENT-NAMES

THE earliest substantial settlements by the Anglo-Saxon invaders took place during the latter part of the 5th century, and were by way of the coast or the banks of the navigable rivers of the south-east and of East Anglia. Traditionally, these settlements are associated with the names of Hengest and Horsa, two Germanic chieftains who had been engaged as auxiliaries by the British king Vortigern in his struggles against the Picts and Scots. They had been allowed to settle in Kent, but soon revolted and within a few years had occupied the whole of the county.

On the whole, however, documentary evidence for the early history of the conquest is vague and unsatisfactory. For a fuller knowledge of the progress of the invasions we must turn to the evidence of archaeology and place-names. With the first of these we are not really concerned, but from the place-names we can get some indication of the areas of early settlement, and of the main routes followed by the invaders in their penetration inland, though such evidence must be used with care.

Most of the common elements, like Old English *tūn* "farmstead, village", remained in constant use throughout the Old English period, and place-names containing them could have been given at almost any time, even though they do not happen to have been recorded until much later. The only type of place-name which can be shown to have been confined to the earliest period of the settlement is that with the Old English ending *-ingas*, surviving today as -ings (Hastings) or more frequently as -ing (Reading). Even here, the question of whether a name with this ending is early depends on the form of the first element, as Professor Hugh Smith has pointed out in his recent and scholarly discussion of this problem.

The form *-ingas* is simply the plural of Old English *-ing* which, in genealogies and similar contexts, is added to a personal name to give the meaning "son of, descendant of", so that Alfred the Great occasionally appears as *Ælfred Æpelwulfing* "Alfred, son of Athel-wulf". In the plural it is regularly added to a personal name, and used to denote a dynasty, as in the case of the Wuffingas "the descendants of Wuffa", the latter being apparently the first of the East Anglian kings. But this plural form seems at a very early date to have developed the sense "dependants of, people of", as in Hastings, from Old English *Hæstingas* "the people of Hæsta". Folk-names of this type are found also in other Germanic areas, and apparently represent a group of people associated together under a single leader. Such groups seem to have been typical of the migration period, and did not consist only of the blood relatives of the leader. Each would include also a number of dependants (along with their wives and children), unrelated by blood to the lord, but bound to him by a personal oath of loyalty.

The Old English place-names in which a personal name was followed by -*ingas* were not originally place-names at all, but rather folk-names which became place-names when the folk concerned settled in some particular place. So, Reading (Brk) was originally a folk-name *Rēadingas* "the people of Rēada", but when these people settled in their permanent home in Berkshire *Rēadingas* became a place-name, which must have meant originally something like "place or district of the Rēadingas".

The plural form, however, rarely survives into Modern English, though, in addition to Hastings, we have Cannings (W) "the people of Cana", Barlings (L, and identical with Barling Ess, and Birling K, Nb, Sx) "of Bærla", and Filkins (O) "of Filica". Usually the final -s has been lost, and the frequent spelling today is with -ing as in Reading, or even -in as in Kiplin (NRY) "the people of Cyppel", or -en as in Kitchen End (Bd) "of Cycca".

It has long been recognized that such names as these belong to the earliest periods of English settlement in Britain, since they reflect a social organization which must precede the establishment of the Anglo-Saxon kingdoms. Consequently, their geographical distribution is particularly significant, since it will define the areas first settled, and indicate the routes by which the settlers penetrated the country.

Unfortunately, this ending was also used to denote the settlers in some particular district, in which case it was compounded with a first element denoting a natural feature, and this usage continued later in the Old English period. For example, Avening (Gl) means "dwellers by the Avon", Epping (Ess) "on the upland", and Nazeing (Ess) "on the spur of land". Another name of this type is Spalding (L) "dwellers near the ditch", a not-unexpected feature of the fens. The *Spaldingas* were apparently a large tribe, for offshoots gave the name also to Spaldington (ERY) "farmstead or village of the Spaldingas". Some of these names may well date from the invasion period but, because of the continued use of the type in the Old English period, it cannot be used as safe evidence of the early date of the settlements so-called. Only those place-names which have -*ingas* added to a first element consisting of a personal name will provide certain evidence of an early date.

It cannot, however, be over-emphasized that the Old English place-names in -*ingas* present very considerable etymological problems. It is often difficult with an individual name to decide whether it is derived from a personal name or from a word for a topographical feature, and alternative etymologies have to be given for some names. The pioneer in the interpretation of these important place-names was Professor Ekwall, and his suggestions of etymology are the ones most widely accepted today.

Because an original Old English -*ingas* so often appears today as -*ing*, we should not know that a particular name was in fact derived from this form *without the evidence of early spellings*. Even when this is certainly the case, we cannot always be sure of the exact etymology. No topographical word is known which would explain the early forms of Kettering (Nth), and the first element looks like a personal name. But again, none is known which gives an entirely satisfactory solution. In other cases the particular personal name is not recorded in Old English, but can be presumed to have existed there, because of its presence in other Germanic languages.

Group-names, in the genitive plural, are also found compounded with other elements, the commonest of which is *hām* "homestead village". So, we have Birmingham (Wa) *Beormingahām* "homestead of the Beormingas (Beorma's people)" and Gillingham (Do, K, Nf) *Gyllingahām* "homestead of the Gyllingas (Gylla's people)". Occasionally the medial syllable has been lost, hence Atcham, sometimes called Attingham (Sa) "homestead of Eata's people", Goodmanham (ERY) "of Gōdmund's people", Langham (Ess) "of Lahha's people", and Longham (Nf) "of Lāwa's people". There are also a few examples of this type in which the first element is a topographical folk-name, as in Hoveringham (Nt) "homestead of the Hoferingas (dwellers on the hump of ground)" and Uppingham (R) "of the Yppingas (dwellers on the higher ground)". These last, however, like the topographical group-names formed from Old English -*ingas* cannot be used as evidence of primary Anglo-Saxon settlement, though many are likely to be very old.

The relationship between names like Birmingham and those like Hastings is so close as to suggest that both were in use at about the same time. The former type may have continued to be given as place-names for a generation or so after the latter type had become obsolete, merely because they are original place-names and not group-names which have later become place-names. But there can be little significant difference in the dates, and both belong to the period of primary Anglo-Saxon settlement in various parts of this country.

The genitive plural of a group-name is sometimes followed by different elements. In all the names which follow only the personal name from which the group-name is derived will be given. So, from Old English *burh* "fortified place" we have Wellingborough (Nth) "Wendel"; from *burna* "stream", Bassingbourn (C) "Bassa"; from *feld* "open country", Haslingfield (C) "Hæsela"; from *ford* "ford", Manningford (W) "Manna"; from *lēah* "wood, glade", Headingley (WRY) "Headda"; from *tūn* "farmstead, village", Knedlington (ERY) "Cneddel or Cnytel"; and from *worð* "enclosure, homestead", Bobbingworth (Ess) "Bubba". These names form a small but important class, belonging no doubt to a similar period to those in *-ingahām*; but they are by no means so numerous as the latter, while some are not in fact the names of settlements, so they will not be considered in the following survey.

The various parts of the country were, of course, settled at various times, and the names of this type may well have been used in some areas long after they had become obsolete in others. Settlement in the North-west was much later than in the East or South, but a group of pioneers moving westwards might still retain an earlier form of social organization, and so give a name like Manningham (WRY), Melling (La) or Addingham (Cu, WRY) at a time when such an organization, and the names resulting from it, had become obsolete in the South or East. The dates at which names in *-ingas* and *-ingahām* were still being formed must have varied considerably in various parts of the country, partly due to the nature and type of the settlements themselves, and partly to the varying stages which had been reached.

Only a selection of the place-names in *-ingas* and *-ingahām* can be mentioned here, but examples will be noted from each of the counties in which they occur, together with the number of each found there. The figures must not be taken too seriously, since in some cases an alternative etymology is perhaps possible, and additional examples of the type may turn up, especially in those counties not yet surveyed by the Place-Name Society. But it is unlikely that any changes to be made in the light of later evidence will have much effect on the conclusions already drawn from the distribution of these types of names.

In the examples below only the personal name from which the group-name is derived will be given. "People of, dependents of" is to be understood for each name from -ingas, and "homestead of the people or dependents of" for those from -ingahām.

Kent has 15 -ings and 8 -inghams, including Birling, Cooling "Cūla", Detling "Dyttel", Halling "Heall", Malling (also Sx) "Mealla", Postling "Possel", Yalding "Ealda", as well as Bellingham "Bera" and Wingham "Wiga".

The largest number of -ings, 45, is found in Sussex, and these include Angmering "Angenmær", Cocking "Cocca", Didling "Dyddel", Ferring (identical with Feering Ess) "Fēra", Iping "Ipa", Oving (also Bk) "Ufa", Tarring "Teorra", Wittering "Wihthere" and Worthing "Worð". The names in -ingahām present more difficulty, since in early spellings it is not easy to distinguish hām from hamm "enclosure, water-meadow", an element particularly common in this county, but for some of them, for example Sessingham "Seassa" and Tillingham (also Ess) "Tilli", derivation from -ingahām seems reasonably certain.

To the north in Surrey the 8 -ings include Godalming "Gōdhelm", Tooting "Tōta" and Woking "Wocc", and the 3 -inghams are Effingham "Effa", Warlingham "Wærla" and Woldingham "Wealda". Further to the west along the coast such names decrease in number. There are only 5 -ings in Hampshire: Basing "Basa", Eling "Ēdla", Hayling (identical with Healing L) "Hægel", Worting "Wyrt" and Wymering "Wīgmær", and a single -ingham, Ellingham (also "Ēdla"). In the Isle of Wight no -ings have been found and only 3 -inghams: Billingham (also Du) "Billa", Whippingham "Wippa" and Wilmingham "Wilhelm".

Berkshire has 4 -ings, Reading, Eling "Ēli", Sonning "Sunna" and Wasing, of which the first part has not yet been satisfactorily explained; but there is only a single -ingham, Wokingham "Wocca". Wiltshire has only Cannings, Dorset only Gillingham and Somerset only Locking "Locc".

In the coastal counties north of the Thames the numbers are again high. Essex has 24 -ings, as for example Barking (also Sf) "Berica", Havering "Hæfer", Matching "Mæcca", Patching (also Sx)

"Pæcci", Wakering "Wacer" and a group of five place-names derived from the one folk, the *Gigingas* "Giga's people", a name surviving today as Ing. In each of these a distinguishing epithet has been added. In Fryern*ing*, the Fryern- means "of the brothers (i.e. Knights Hospitallers)"; *Ing*atestone is "Ing at the stone", from some prominent stone there; *Ing*rave has its -rave from Ralf, the Domesday Book holder of the manor; Margarett*ing* is from the dedication of its church to St. Margaret, while Mountness*ing* contains the family name Mounteney. In contrast to these, there are only 6 -inghams which include Bockingham "Bōta" and Corringham "Curra".

A similar concentration, of 11 -ings, appears in Suffolk, e.g. Beckling "Beccel", Byng "Bǣga", Gipping "Gyppa" and Swefling "Swiftel", and there are also 15 -inghams including Aldringham "Aldhere", Badingham "Bēada", Framlingham "Framela", Gislingham "Gysela", Helmingham (also Nf) "Helm", Letheringham "Lēodhere" and Mettingham "Matta".

Even more (19) are found in Norfolk, including Blickling "Blicla", Dalling (2) "Dalla", Gissing "Gyssa", Harling "Herela", Kelling "Cylla", Palling "Pælli", Rising (2) "Risa" and Wendling "Wendel", together with 42 -inghams, the largest number found in any one county. These include Antingham "Anta", Banningham "Banna", Dersingham "Dēorsige", Erpingham "Eorp", Framingham "Fram", Hevingham "Hefa", Kenningham "Cyna", Raveningham "Hræfn", Saxlingham (2) "Seaxel", Walsingham "Wæls", Wreningham "Wrenna" and Sandringham. This last was originally identical with Dersingham, but the distinguishing prefix Sand- was added later.

To the north in Lincolnshire the numbers decrease to 7 and perhaps 23 respectively. These include Minting "Mynta" and Horbling. The latter is an unusual name in that Old English *horu* "dirt, mud" has been prefixed to the original *Billingas*, identical with Billing (Nth) "Billa's people", so that the name means "muddy *Billing*". Of the possible 23 -inghams we may note Alvingham "Ælfa", Bassingham (identical with Bessingham Nf) "Basa", Folkingham "Folca", Helpringham "Helprīc", Immingham "Imma", Leasingham (identical with Lessingham Nf) "Lēofsige", Messingham (identical with Massingham Nf) "Mæssa" and Waddingham "Wada".

Westwards from the coastal counties there is again a striking decrease in the number of these names. North of the Thames in Middlesex are Ealing "Gilla", Yeading "Geddi" and perhaps Wapping "Wæppa", but no -inghams. In Buckinghamshire there is only Oving; in Oxfordshire, Filkins, Goring (also Sx) "Gāra" and Kingham (identical with Keyingham ERY) "Cǣga"; and in Gloucestershire perhaps a single -ingham, Arlingham "Eorl".

In Hertfordshire there is only Braughing "Breahha"; in Bedfordshire Kitchen End, Knotting "Cnotta" and perhaps Wootton Pillinge "Peol", where Wootton is the name of the parish in which Pillinge is situated. Huntingdonshire has Gidding (identical with Gedding Sf) "Gydda", Yelling "Giella" and Wintringham (also ERY, and identical with Winteringham L) "Winter".

There are no names in -ings in Cambridgeshire, though two in Suffolk and one in Huntingdonshire are close to the county boundary, but there are four -inghams, Badlingham "Bæddel", Dullingham "Dulla" and two Willinghams, each of which has a different personal name as the source of the folk-name. The parish-name Willingham is identical with North Willingham and Willingham by Stow (L) and means "homestead of Wifel's people", while Willingham, near Carlton, "homestead of Willa's people" is identical with Cherry Willingham and South Willingham (L) and Willingham (Sf).

In Northamptonshire, there are Billing, the difficult Kettering, and Wittering "Wiðer", together with Cottingham (also ERY) "Cotta" and Rockingham "Hrōca"; in Rutland only Empingham "Empa"; in Leicestershire only Peatling "Pēotla"; and in Nottinghamshire, Gedling "Gēdla", Hickling (also Nf) "Hicela" and 4 -inghams, Nottingham, Beckingham (also L) "Becca", Collingham (also WRY) "Cola" and Walkeringham "Walhhere".

In the West Midlands there are no examples of the plural -ings combined with a personal name, and place-names in -ingham are also very rare. Birmingham and Hunningham (identical with Honingham Nf) "Hūna" are the only examples in Warwickshire. None has survived in Worcestershire, but there are perhaps four lost -inghams in that county, while further west Ballingham "Badela" is the only example in Herefordshire. To the north, in Shropshire, there is Atcham, and in Staffordshire, Pattingham "Peatta". In Cheshire there are Altrincham "Aldhere" and Kermincham, Tushingham and Warmingham, perhaps derived from Cēnfrið, Tūnsige and Wǣrmund respectively.

North of the Humber, a number of place-names containing Old English -ingas are found, particularly in the East and North Ridings of Yorkshire. In the former there are 5, Fitling "Fitela", Gembling "Gemela", Skeffling perhaps "Sceftel", the difficult Leavening, and Nunkeeling. This last was originally identical with Kelling (Nf), and

69

the distinctive prefix refers to the medieval Benedictine nunnery there. These are supported by perhaps 12 examples of *-ingahām*, which include Brantingham "Brant", Everingham "Eofor", two Frodinghams (also L) "Frōda" and Yedingham "Ēada".

In the North Riding there are 6 -ings—Kiplin, Gilling (2) "Gētla", Lilling "Lilla", Pickering perhaps "Pīcer" and Fylingdales "Fygla". In this last -dales is from its situation, at a point where several small valleys run into Robin Hood's Bay. Here, however, there are only 3 -inghams, as against the 12 possible examples in the East Riding, Barningham (also Nf, Sf) "Beorn", Hovingham "Hofa" and Lastingham "Lǣsta".

Further north a single example of *-ingas* has been noted. Birling in Northumberland, and the same county has 8 -inghams, amongst them Chillingham "Cēofel", Ellingham (also Nf)"Ella or Eli", Eltringham "Ælfhere" and Ovingham "Ofa". Durham, however, has only two certain examples, Billingham, and Wolsingham "Wulfsige". Similarly the West Riding has only 4, Collingham, Addingham (also Cu) "Adda", Manningham "Mægen" and Walkingham "Walca".

Across the Pennines, Lancashire surprisingly has a few more such names than might have been expected; there are three widely separated names in -ings and three in -ingham. Two of the former are identical—Melling perhaps "Malla"—and the other is Staining (identical with Steyning Sx) perhaps "Stān". The -ingham names are Aldingham "Alda", Padiham "Padda" and Whittingham (also Nb, and identical with Whicham Cu) "Hwīta". Further north, Westmorland has no such names, and Cumberland has 3 -inghams only, Addingham, Whicham and Hensingham perhaps "Hȳnsige".

The geographical distribution of these names suggests that the earliest settlement was heaviest in Sussex, Kent, Essex and East Anglia, in all of which large concentrations of -ings are found. Only in Norfolk and Suffolk, however, are these accompanied by even greater numbers of -inghams.

In the South-east the names seem to occur in clusters, particularly along the Medway and Darent, and in North Kent by the Thames. They are clearly to be connected with similar groups in Surrey, and suggest that the settlers there came by way of the Thames. There are similar clusters along the Sussex coast, but these decrease most strikingly as we enter Hampshire. A few examples occur along the Thames and its tributaries, in Berkshire and north Hampshire, but further west they are rare.

In Essex and East Anglia concentrations of both -ings and -ing-

70

hams are found along most of the important rivers. They are rare in the fenland district of Cambridgeshire, but to the south and west occur over a wide area, especially along the rivers which flow into the Wash. In Lincolnshire there are several groups along the Witham, the Trent, and their tributaries, and along the Trent in Nottinghamshire.

In the West Midlands no examples occur north of Watling Street, and three of the -inghams, Atcham (Sa), Birmingham and Hunningham (Wa) are situated on Roman roads. Settlement here was clearly later than in the areas to the East, and no doubt represents colonization into the expansive central woodlands, from the South by way of the Severn and Avon, from the North down the Trent, and along the Roman roads.

The settlers entered Yorkshire along the estuary of the Humber, and up the Derwent and Ouse. There are, in fact, concentrations of early settlements represented by -ings and -inghams in the tongue of land between the Humber and the sea, near the Humber further upstream close to the Roman road from Brough to York, and in the North Riding along the Derwent and its tributaries. Further to the north, other examples are to be found beside the Tees and Wear, Till and Aln, and some of these are also close to Roman roads. Across the Pennines, the Cheshire names are probably to be associated with the larger, but more scattered group, in Lancashire. They were the result of later colonization, from the original settlements in Northumbria. The three Cumberland -inghams presumably have a similar origin.

Archaeological evidence in the main supports that of place-names, though there are some unresolved problems. Those in the East and South-east seem to represent settlements made in the latter part of the 5th and in the early 6th century. Further, objects which can be dated to the 5th century have been found in graves, for example in Lincolnshire, Nottinghamshire, Northamptonshire, and in east and central Yorkshire, as well as in the eastern and south-eastern counties. The Anglo-Saxon cemetery at York is, in fact, one of the earliest in the whole country. In all these areas numerous early names of the folk-name type occur. No objects which can be dated earlier than the mid-6th century, on the other hand, have been discovered in Derbyshire, a county in which there are no early names of this type. Similarly little archaeological evidence pointing to early settlement comes from Warwickshire or Worcestershire, and in both counties there are only occasional examples of place-names in -ingham, and none at all from Old English -ingas.

It is impossible to date closely the period during which these place-names were being given. But the general history of England, south of the Humber, suggests that they can hardly have continued in use much later than the first half of the 6th century. They are found quite profusely where settlement is known to have taken place before that date, but do not occur to any marked degree where it is thought to have commenced after the middle of that century. The agreement between the evidence of place-names and that of archaeology is significant, and in parts of the North-east Midlands it is even closer, for both place-names and archaeology suggest that Anglo-Saxon settlement took place in the late 5th and early 6th century in Nottinghamshire, but not till the mid-6th century in Derbyshire.

North of the Humber, the early names in east Yorkshire cannot be much later than those to the south, while the north Yorkshire names may be dated a little later, but hardly more than a generation or two. Elsewhere in the north, however, historical evidence suggests that the Anglo-Saxon settlements were certainly later—in Durham and Northumberland not much before the middle of the 6th century, and in Lancashire perhaps not much earlier than the middle of the 7th.

In addition to the early place-names derived from Old English -ingas and -ingahām, there is a small but interesting group, of which the first element is the name of a Continental Germanic or English tribe. There is no evidence to show that these necessarily indicate primary settlement, but some of them belong to a very early period. The meaning of many of these names has been long appreciated, but they have been recently reconsidered in detail by Professor Ekwall, who has also indicated their historical importance. One that is likely to belong to the earliest periods of the Anglo-Saxon settlements is Swaffham (C, Nf) "homestead or village of the Swabians", a tribe in West Slesvig closely associated with the Angles in their continental home, as is indicated, for example, in the Old English poem *Widsith*, and it may be significant that both places are in areas settled by the Angles.

The Anglo-Saxons are known to have had very early relations with the Frisians. Professor Ekwall has suggested that the early forms of Friston (Sf) and Frieston (L) "farmstead or village of the Frisians" indicate that these names belong to an early period, and would therefore support the evidence of the 6th-century historian Procopius, who says that some Frisians took part in the Anglo-Saxon occupation of Britain.

When the names of the English tribes are found in place-names outside the areas primarily settled by them they are probably due to

72

later migrations of small groups. So Englebourne (D) "stream of the Angles" and Englefield (Brk) "open land of the Angles" are in Wessex. Similarly, Saxham (Sf) "homestead of the Saxons" is in East Anglia; Saxton (C) and Saxondale (Nt) "farmstead" and "valley of the Saxons" respectively are in the territory of the Middle Angles and Saxton (WRY), identical with Saxton (C), in Mercia. Exton (Ha) "farmstead of the East Saxons" is an isolated settlement of these people in Wessex, and the presence of Mercians in the land of the Middle Angles is indicated by Markfield (Lei) "open land of the Mercians", and in Northumbria by Markingfield (WRY), originally identical with Markfield. Old English *Cantware* "people of Kent" is the first element of Canterton (Ha) in Wessex, and of Conderton (Wo) in Mercia, both meaning "farmstead or village of the Kentishmen".

None of these names certainly indicates primary settlement, but this may be the case with Saxham (Sf) and Saxton (C). Both are situated in an area through which the Saxons may have passed on their way to Wessex, and they may represent groups which settled in Anglian territory instead of continuing inland with the rest of their tribe.

Note: Over the past twelve years a complete reassessment of the significance of place-names derived from *-ingas, -ingahām* etc. has taken place. The etymology and meaning of these formations are not in question, and they remain as set out in this chapter. What has, however, emerged clearly from the studies is that the *close correlation* between these names and early Anglo-Saxon burial sites is illusory, and that the two groups, the place-names and the burial-sites cannot belong to the same period. It has been shown that while the burial-sites are to be associated for the most part with the *immigration* phase of Anglo-Saxon settlement in Britain, the place-names represent rather a slightly later and *colonising* phase. This suggests a 6th-century date for the latter in south-eastern England.

Furthermore, research into place-names derived from Old English *hām* (pp. 146–7), particularly *wīchām*, has shown that *hām* must have been used in the very earliest period of Anglo-Saxon penetration here. The Wickhams and Wykehams (p. 147) seem to have denoted small settlements in the neighbourhood of, or associated with, a Roman *vicus*, and so indicate some direct communication between the Romano-British and English peoples and confirm in a very striking way the early use of *hām* in our place-names.

A comparison between the distribution patterns of the names derived from *-ingas*, and *-ingahām* and *hām*, together with a detailed examination of the sites of each in terms of land-utilisation, comparing these in terms

73

of drift geology, has suggested an entirely different pattern of stratification of the groups—that the *hāms*, as a group, predate the *-ingahāms*, which in turn predate the names derived from *-ingas*. This is entirely at varience with views consistently held up to 1966. It must, of course, be emphasised that the three groups cannot be regarded as clear-cut for there must have been some overlapping between them. What is clear, nonetheless, is that the stratification pattern suggested above is the most likely one with our present state of knowledge.

It is impossible to suggest precise dates for these groups of place-names, but those suggested at pp. 71–2 must be revised. Perhaps it is safest at present simply to say that the formation of place-names in *-hām*, *-ingahām* and *-ingas* probably extended from the first federate settlements of the late 4th century down to the end of the 7th century. It would be imprudent to attempt anything more precise.

For the detailed evidence on which these hypotheses are based, see J. McN. Dodgson, "The Significance of the Distribution of English Place-Names in *-ingas*, *-inga-* in South-east England", Margaret Gelling, "English Place-Names derived from the Compound *wichām*", and B. Cox, "The Significance of the Distribution of English Place-Names in *hām* in the Midlands and East Anglia", collected together and reprinted in *Place-Name Evidence for the Anglo-Saxon Invasion and Scandinavian Settlement*, E. P. N. S., 1975, and J. Kuurman, "An Examination of the *-ingas*, *-inga-* Place-Names in the East Midlands", in *Journal of the English Place-Name Society*, vol. 7, 1975. For a convenient discussion of this evidence see Kenneth Cameron, *The Significance of English Place-Names*, British Academy, 1976.

Chapter Six

———————— ★ ————————

SCANDINAVIAN PLACE-NAMES

THE earliest permanent settlement of the Viking invaders in this country is recorded in *The Anglo-Saxon Chronicle* in the annal for 876 when a Danish army settled in Northumbria. The settlement there, however, was apparently restricted to Yorkshire, and in particular to the Vale of York. In the following year part of Mercia was occupied, presumably the district of the five boroughs of Derby, Nottingham, Leicester, Stamford and Lincoln, and some three years later East Anglia was occupied. These three areas of England were settled by Viking armies, mostly composed of Danes, and later known as the Danelaw, i.e. the area subject to Danish law.

The boundary of the Danelaw is given in a treaty of 886 between King Alfred and Guthrum, the leader of the East Anglian Danes. It follows the Essex side of the estuary of the Thames to the confluence of the River Lea, then up the Lea to its source. From there it runs to Bedford, along the River Ouse to Watling Street, with the line of Watling Street forming the probable western boundary. Few places of any importance to the south of this line have names of Scandinavian origin, and they are uncommon immediately to the north or east of it. There are certainly more in Northamptonshire, but the greatest concentrations of such names in the East Midlands lie to the north of the River Welland, and in the west as far as the River Derwent in Derbyshire. In Norfolk and part of Suffolk they are well-represented, but are not as frequent there as in Leicestershire or Lincolnshire where the thickest concentration is in the Wreak valley (Lei) and south-west of Grimsby (L). In all three Ridings of Yorkshire and in South Durham they are found in considerable numbers, but further north they are relatively scarce.

The great majority of the habitative place-names of Scandinavian origin must have been given in the late 9th, 10th or 11th century, but we have no means of determining whether a particular name belongs to the earlier or later stages of settlement. In some cases, however, the meaning indicates a secondary settlement away from an established centre, and so suggests a comparatively late date. It

75

is also necessary to distinguish between those names which are entirely Scandinavian and those which are composed of a Scandinavian and an English word, the so-called hybrid names. Both types are found in the names of habitations and in those of topographical features. The latter have been included in the relevant chapters elsewhere, and here we shall for the most part be concerned with habitative place-names.

The settlers in eastern England are usually referred to as Danes and, indeed, the general history of the Danelaw shows this to be true. At the same time, however, place-names indicate that Frisians and Norwegians were also present. Later, some of the Danes moved westwards from their kingdom with its centre at York into parts of Cumbria, as well as into parts of Lancashire and Cheshire. But in all these districts settlements were made by men of Norwegian origin, who had formerly lived in Ireland or the Isle of Man. In 901 such a settlement was made in the Wirral, and there were others in Cumberland and in parts of Lancashire during the first half of the 10th century. From Cumbria they moved eastwards to establish a Norwegian kingdom at York, but such place-name evidence as there is for this is found particularly in the North Riding, much less so in the East and West Ridings.

The place-names of these districts show some distinctive characteristics, the most important of which is the inversion compound, in which the usual order of the elements as found in English place-names is reversed, and this follows Celtic practice. So, there is Aspatria, literally "ash-tree Patric", i.e. "Patric's ash-tree", Bewaldeth "homestead Aldgȳð", a feminine personal name, and Seatoller "shieling alder", in Cumberland; Brigsteer "bridge Styr" i.e. "Styr's bridge", and Rigmaiden, apparently "ridge maiden", in Westmorland. A second characteristic is the occurrence of Irish (often called Goidelic) personal names in place-names in the northwest and in parts of Yorkshire. Examples of these include Bueth in Boothby, Corc in Corby, Glassan in Glassonby and Melmor (Maelmuire) in Melmerby (also NRY), in Cumberland; Maelchon in Melkinthorpe, in Westmorland; Cairpre in Carperby, Gaithan in Gatenby, Maelsuithan in Melsonby, in the North Riding; Dufgall (Dubhghall) in Duggleby, in the East Riding and Eogan in Yockenthwaite, in the West Riding. In addition, Old Norse *erg* "shieling, hill pasture", a loan-word from Irish, is found only in areas of Norwegian-Irish settlement. Hence, there is Arrowe (Ch) from the dative singular, Arras (ERY) from the nominative plural, and Airyholme (NRY), Argam (ERY) and Arkholme (La) from the dative plural. This word occurs also in such compounds as Birker (Cu) "birch-tree", Docker (La, We) "valley", Mosser (Cu) and Mozergh (We) "moss", Salter (Cu) "salt", and Winder (Cu, La, We) "wind, i.e., windy", as well as others with a personal name as first element— Golcar (WRY) "Guðleikr", Grimsargh (La) "Grímr", Mansergh (We) "Man" and Sizergh (We) "Sigríðr (feminine)".

In the north-west too several distinctively Norwegian words are found, which occur only rarely elsewhere. *Brekka, fell, gil* and *slakki* have been noted in other chapters, but here we can add *búð* "booth, temporary shelter". This is normally represented by such early spellings as *bouthe* and *buthe*, whereas the corresponding Old Danish *bōth* has usually given Middle English *both(e)*. The first is the source of Bewcastle (Cu), Bowerdale (Cu), Bouth (La) and Bootham in York, this last from the dative plural. The Danish word on the other hand is the source of Booth (Db, La), Hay Booth (La) "enclosure with a booth", and Dunnishbooth (La), and Thurlowbooth (Db) from the personal names Dunning and Thurlak.

A similar word is *sætr* "mountain pasture, shieling", as in Ambleside (We) "river sandbank", Appersett (NRY) "apple-tree", Selside (We) "willow" and Summerseat (La) and Wintersett (WRY), denoting shielings used only in summer and winter respectively, as well as Arkleside (NRY) and Hawkshead (La), of which the first elements are the Scandinavian personal names Arnkell and Haukr, and Oughterside (Cu) from the Old English Ūhtrēd.

Old Norwegian *skáli*, dialectal *scale*, "temporary hut or shed" has given Scales (Cu, La) and Scholes (WRY) but occurs occasionally as far south as Scole (Nf). In addition, there is Bowscale (Cu) "hut on the curved hill", Portinscale, with a first element meaning "prostitute", Seascale "sea" and Winscales "wind(y)", in Cumberland; Brinscall "burnt", Feniscowles "muddy" and Loudscales "on the River Loud", in Lancashire; Holmescales "belonging to Holme", in Westmorland; Gammersgill "Gamall's hut", in the North Riding; and Summerscales (identical with Summersgill La) and Winterscales, huts used in summer and winter respectively, in the West Riding.

A further feature of the Scandinavian place-names of the north-west and of parts of Yorkshire is the survival of the genitive singular *-ar-* as *-er-*, as in Beckermet, Bowderdale and Harter Fell in Cumberland; Winderwath "Vinand's ford" and Witherslack "valley of the wood" in Westmorland; Amounderness "Agmundr's headland", Litherland "land of the slope" and Harterbeck "stream of the hart", in Lancashire; Amotherby and Bellerby in the North Riding; Holderness in the East Riding; and Aismunderby and Beckermonds in the West Riding. Elsewhere, the formation is by no means so common, but occurs occasionally in Lincolnshire, as in Dalderby "farmstead of the valley".

There are, however, one or two distinctively Danish words, the most important of which is *þorp*. Its meaning in Danish place-names is "secondary settlement, outlying farm", and this, no doubt, is the sense it has in England, since the places so-named are usually small villages or farms. Moreover, some of the names themselves indicate that the particular place was dependent on a neighbouring village, as in the case of Ashwellthorpe (Nf) which belonged to Ashwell, and Staveley Netherthorpe and Staveley Woodthorpe (Db), belonging to Staveley. In addition, some of those which have the simplex form, Thorpe (Cu, Db, ERY, L, La, Lei, Nf, NRY, Nt, R, St, WRY), have been distinguished by an affix which is the name of a near-by village, as for example Thorpe Langton (Lei), Kilton Thorpe (NRY), Mattersey Thorpe (Nt), Sneaton Thorpe (NRY), and Whitley Thorpe (WRY).

The first element of many names derived from this word is a personal name and a selection of these will be found at the end of the chapter. Several of the numerous other compounds are self-explanatory, as with Easthorpe (ERY), identical in meaning with Aisthorpe (L) and Owsthorpe (ERY), Kingthorpe (L), Newthorpe (Nt, WRY), Northorpe (L, WRY), Southorpe (L), Woodthorpe (Db, WRY), as well as Millthorpe (L) and Milnthorpe (Nt, We, WRY). Birthorpe (L) means "outlying farm by the birch-trees" and Londonthorpe (L) "outlying farm of (i.e. by) the grove", the first element being the genitive singular of Old Norse *lundr*, while Biscathorpe (L) was named from the bishop (of Durham), Copmanthorpe (WRY) from "chapmen", and Danthorpe (ERY) from "Danes".

There was, however, an Old English *þrop, þorp* "hamlet, outlying farm", of which the early forms may be confused with those of Old Danish *þorp*, though as a rule the geographical distribution will indicate clearly enough which is the source in any particular case. In addition, if we find spellings in -*throp* we can be fairly certain that the name is English, since Old Danish *þorp* does not seem to occur at all in this form. Thorpe (Du, Ess, Sr), Throop (Do, Ha), Throope (W), Thrup (O, W), Thrupp (Brk, Gl, Nth) and Drupe (D) are almost certainly all derived from Old English *þrop*. The same is true also of the self-explanatory Castle Thorpe (Bk), Eathorpe (Wa) and Eythrope (Bk) "by a river", Souldrop (Bd) "in a gulley", Upthorpe (Hu, Wo) "upper", as well as Tythrop (O), which means "double hamlet or outlying farm", Swanthorpe (Ha) "of the swineherds", and Abthorpe (Nth), Bigstrup (Bk) and Princethorpe (Wa) from the Old English personal names Abba, Bicel and Prǣn respectively.

Another element which seems in English place-names to be a specifically Danish word is *toft* "site of a house, homestead". It is common, especially in minor names, in the East Midlands and Yorkshire, but extremely rare in the north-west, if indeed it occurs there at all. As a simplex name it survives as Toft (Bd, C, Ch, L, Nf, Wa) and Tofts (Nf), while Fishtoft (L) has had the obscure Fish- prefixed later. The first element in a number of names is a personal name, some of which are noted at the end of the chapter, but there are others in which it is an adjective or noun. So, in Altofts (WRY) it means "old", in Bratoft (L) "broad" and in Nortoft (Nth) "north". The Lincolnshire Huttoft, Sandtoft and Wigtoft were situated on a "hill-spur", on "sandy soil" and perhaps near a "creek or inlet" respectively, and Eastoft (WRY), Thrintoft (NRY) and Willitoft (ERY) near an "ash-grove", a "thorn-bush" and "willows".

A few names containing Old Scandinavian *holmr, holmi* "island, water-meadow, dry land in a fen" survive as Hulme (Ch, La, St) and, as second element, Kettleshulme (Ch) and Levenshulme (La), with the personal names Ketil and Lēofwine. These forms in *hulme* were till recently thought to represent the distinctively Danish spelling of the word, *hulm*; and *hulm(e)* is in fact found in the early spellings of many more names which are today spelt *holme*. It has now been demonstrated, however, that the -*u*- spellings either reflect a traditional medieval scribal tradition or represent a Middle English dialect form, and so they can no longer be used as evidence for Danish as distinct from Norwegian settlement.

There are, of course, many place-name elements which could equally well be either Danish or Norwegian, as for example *bȳ*, the commonest Scandinavian element in English place-names, and found in all parts of the Danelaw as well as in the north-west, where it was certainly a living word in the early Middle English period. Its meaning is "farmstead or village" and as a rule it is impossible to decide which is the exact sense in any particular name. In Cumberland, Westmorland and the North Riding, however, it still often denotes individual farms, and Professor Hugh Smith has suggested that this usage is rather Norwegian than Danish. But in general the nationality of the settlers can only be determined when the first element is an Old Irish personal name, and therefore to be associated with Norwegian settlement, or one used only by the Danes, not by the Norwegians, and denoting Danish settlement.

Scandinavian *bȳ* is particularly common as the final element, but is rare as a first element, and is not found at all in the simplex form By. It is, however, sometimes difficult to distinguish between a Scandinavian compound and one consisting of an English and the Scandinavian word. For example, the first element of Fenby (L) "fen", Moorby (L) "moor" and Smisby (Db) "smith" could be derived from either a Scandinavian or an English word, and in these cases the former is perhaps more likely. On the other hand, there are some names of which the first element is definitely Old English—Brooksby (Lei) "of the brook", Riby (L) "rye", Walby (Cu) "by the (Roman) wall", Wauldby (ERY) "on the wold" and Welby (L) "by a spring or stream". It has been suggested that in some of these names Old Scandinavian *bȳ* has replaced an earlier English word, such as *tūn*. Certainly it is remarkable that there are at least nine examples of the hybrid Willoughby (L, Lei, Nt, Wa), as well as Wilby (Nf) "willow farmstead", and this name may well originally have been identical with Willoughton (L), Willington (Bd, Db) and Wilton (C, ERY, He, Nf, NRY). This is perhaps also the case with Appleby (L, Lei, We) "apple-tree farmstead", originally identical with the common Appleton.

There is, however, documentary evidence to show that *bȳ* has replaced an Old English *byrig*, the dative singular of *burh* "fortified place", later "manor". In these cases the similarity of the forms may be partly responsible, but at any rate it has taken place in Greasby (Ch) "fort by a grove", Thornby (Nth) "by a thorn-bush", as well as Badby (Nth), Naseby (Nth) and Rugby (Wa) from the personal names Badda, Hnæf and Hrōca respectively, and Quenby (Lei) probably originally "queen's manor". In one or two examples, moreover, we know that a Scandinavian name has completely replaced an earlier English one, as with Derby (Db) and *Northworthy*, and also with Whitby (NRY) "Hvíti's farmstead" or "white farmstead", the site of which has long been identified with *Streoneshalh* "Strēon's nook of land".

In most cases, however, the place-names derived from *bȳ* are Scandinavian compounds and some of them can be compared with similar names in Scandinavia itself. A large proportion have a Scandinavian personal name as first element, and a selection is given at the end of the chapter, while others are named in relation to a neighbouring place, as with Asterby (L) "eastern", Swinderby (L), "southern", Westby (La, WRY) and Westerby (Lei) "western", Itterby (L) "outer", Yearby (NRY) "upper" and the Cumberland Netherby "lower" and Overby "higher". Some are from a natural or artificial feature, as in Aby (L) and Burnby (ERY) "stream", Barby (Nth), Barrowby (L, WRY) and Huby (NRY) "hill", Dalby (L, Lei, NRY) "valley", Keelby (L) and Ribby (La) "ridge", as well as Raby (Ch, Cu, Du), Robey (Du) and Roby (La) "boundary mark". The Lincolnshire Grasby means "farmstead in a stony district" and Grebby "on stony ground", while the common Sowerby denotes a farmstead or village on muddy or swampy ground. The first element is only occasionally the name of a tree, but "lime" occurs in Linby (Nt), "willow" in Selby (WRY), and more frequently "ash" in Asby (Cu, We) and the common Ashby. Animal names are only rarely found, as in Grisby (L) "young pig" and Wetherby (WRY) "wether", and note also Beeby (Lei) "bee farm".

A few are named from groups of people, as with Flotmanby (ERY) "sailors", Hunmanby (ERY) and Hunsonby (Cu) "dog-keepers", and Sutterby (L) "shoe-makers", as well as a group of which the first element is a national name. These, together with a few others, are particularly valuable in that they indicate that the settlers in the various districts were not homogeneous groups, and, further, that even in some areas of the Danelaw the settlements of Danes themselves must have been thinly spread. For example, Danby (NRY), Denaby (WRY) and Denby (Db) "village of the Danes" could only have been given where Danes were an unusual feature in the district. On the other hand, Ingleby (Db) "village of the English" must have been in an area where Danes were settled in considerable numbers. The presence, however, of other nationalities among the Danish settlers is testified by a number of place-names— Norwegians by Normanby (L, NRY), as well as Normanton (Db, L, Lei, Nt, R, WRY), Frisians by the Lincolnshire Friesthorpe and Firsby, and by Frisby (Lei), Faroese by Ferrensby (WRY), and Irishmen or Norwegians from Ireland by Irby (Ch, L, NRY) and Ireton (Db), this last comparable with Normanton. In the place-names of the Danelaw, outside Yorkshire, personal names of Irish origin are unknown, except perhaps only in Mammerton (Db), a hybrid name, where the first element may be Melmor, as in Melmerby (Cu, NRY). If this is so, Mammerton would be associated with Ireton, a name occurring twice in the same district, and would indicate settlement by men from the north-west of England in Derbyshire, for which there is no evidence from place-names elsewhere in the East Midlands.

One group of hybrids deserves special mention. This consists of a Scandinavian personal name and Old English *tūn* "farmstead, village", examples of which have for convenience been put at the end of the chapter. Comparatively few are found in the North-west, or in Yorkshire. They are, however, fairly common in Derbyshire, Leicestershire and Nottinghamshire, but less so in Lincolnshire where Scandinavian compounds are especially numerous. A few occur in Northamptonshire, one or two in Cambridgeshire, as well as Bedfordshire and Staffordshire. Most recent research has dealt with this aspect of the place-names of Nottinghamshire, Leicestershire and Derbyshire where such hybrid names occur in groups in areas where Scandinavian compounds are uncommon, and where considerable English settlement had taken place before the arrival of the Danes. It is suggested, therefore, that here these names represent expansion of Danish settlement away from established centres, that they are older English villages taken over by the Danes, and that the name of the new Danish owner has simply replaced that of the original English settler.

In addition to place-names wholly or partly of Scandinavian origin, there are numerous English names, whose forms have been modified in various ways as a result of Scandinavian influence. When Old English *c* occurred initially before *e* or *i*, as in *cēse* or *cild*, it was pronounced as in the modern forms of these words, *ch*eese and *ch*ild. In the Scandinavian languages, however, the sound in this position is *k*. Hence, the initial consonant in Keswick (Cu, Nf, WRY) and Kildwick (WRY) is due to the influence of the Scandinavian sound, for these names were originally identical with Chiswick (Ess, Mx) and Childwick (Hrt) respectively. In the same way Kepwick (NRY) would otherwise have given Cheapwick or Chipwick, and Kettlewell (WRY), apparently "stream in a narrow valley", is in place of Chettlewell. Similarly, Old English *sc* was pronounced *sh*, as in *scelf*, modern *shelf*, or *æsc*, modern *ash*. This sound was also unknown in the Scandinavian languages where its place is taken by *sk*. Hence Skelton (Cu, ERY, NRY, WRY) can be compared with Shelton (Bd, Nf, Nt, Sa, St), Skipton (NRY, WRY) with Shipton (Do, Gl, Ha, O, Sa), and Skipwith (ERY) and Scopwick (L) with Shopwyke (Sx), as well as the river-names Skerne (Du) and Skidbrook (L). Medially, the same substitution has taken place in Minskip (WRY), derived from Old English (*ge*)*mænscipe* "community", i.e. "place communally held", and finally, in Matlask (Nf), where, however, Old English *æsc* "ash-tree" may have been replaced by Old Norse *askr*, as was probably the case in Askham (Nt, WRY) "ash-tree homestead". Similarly Old Norse *steinn* "stone" has replaced Old English *stān* in several names such as Stainburn (Cu), Stainforth (WRY), Stainland

(WRY), Stainley (WRY), Stainmore (NRY–We) and the common Stainton instead of Stanburn, Stanford, Stanland, Stanley, Stanmore and Stanton respectively. Old Norse *rauðr* "red" has taken the place of the English word in Rawcliffe (La, NRY, WRY), which otherwise would have given Radcliffe; and it is at least possible that Old Norse *austr* "east" has replaced Old English *ēast* in Owston (L, WRY), and Austwick (WRY) and Owstwick (ERY), which would then have been identical in etymology with the common Aston and Astwick (Bd, Nth).

Finally, a group of names which belong to the period after the Norman Conquest contain Middle English *bigging* "building, house", a word derived from the verb *big*, itself from Old Norse *byggja* "build". This element is common in the East Midlands, but has been noted as far south as Surrey. It frequently survives as Biggin, and in the self-explanatory compound Newbegin (NRY) and the common Newbiggin. Indeed, many of the names which survive today in the simplex form are first recorded as *Newbigging*.

The following are examples of names containing a personal name compounded with the elements discussed above:

Cheshire:

bȳ   Frankby "Franki".
hybrid *tūn*   Croxton (also C, L, Lei, Nf, St) "Krókr", Thurstaston (identical with Thurston Sf) "Þorsteinn".

Cumberland:

bȳ   Arkleby "Arnkell", Hornsby (identical with Ormesby Nf, NRY, and Ormsby L) "Ormr", Motherby "Mōthir (Old Danish)", Thursby (identical with Thoresby L, NRY, Nt) "Þórir or Þúrir".
hybrid *tūn*   Askerton "Ásgeirr", Orton "Orri".

Derbyshire:

bȳ   Stainsby "Steinn".
þorp   Boythorpe (also ERY) "Boie", Hackenthorpe "Hákun", Oakerthorpe "Ulkel" (Old Danish).
toft   Hardstoft "Hjǫrt".
hybrid *tūn*   Foston (also ERY, NRY) "Fótr", Kedleston "Ketill", Roston "Hrosskell", Scropton "Skropi", Swarkeston "Swerkir" (Old Danish), Thurvaston (also Thoroton Nt) "Þurferð".

Durham:

bȳ   Aislaby (also NRY, and identical with Aslackby L) "Áslákr", Killerby (also NRY, and identical with Kilwardby Lei) "Kilvert" (exact form uncertain).

hybrid *tūn* Blakeston "Bleikr", Claxton (also Nf, NRY, and identical with Clawson Lei) "Klak" (Old Danish), Ouston (also Nb) "Ulkel" (Old Danish).

Lancashire:

bȳ Formby "Forni", Hornby (also NRY, We) "Horni".
hybrid *tūn* Flixton (also ERY, Sf) "Flic" (Old Danish), Urmston "Urm" (Old Danish).

Leicestershire:

bȳ Barsby "Barn", Blaby "Blá", Gaddesby "Gaddr", Ingarsby "Ingvarr", Kettleby (also L, and identical with Ketsby L) "Ketill", Saxby (also L) "Saxi", Saxelby (identical with Saxilby L) "Saxulf" (Old Danish), Sysonby "Sigsteinn".
þorp Boothorpe "Bo" (Old Danish), Bromkinsthorpe "Brúnskinn", Oakthorpe and Othorpe "Āki" (Old Danish), Osgathorpe "Ásgautr", Ullesthorpe "Ulfr".
toft Knaptoft "Knapi", Scraptoft "Skrápi".
hybrid *tūn* Barkestone (identical with Barkston L, WRY) "Bǫrkr", Bilstone (identical with Bildeston Sf) "Bildr", Grimston (also ERY, Nf, NRY, Nt, Sf, WRY) "Grímr", Odstone "Oddr", Slawston "Slagr", Snibston "Snípr", Sproxton (also NRY) "Sprok", Thringstone "Þraéingr", Thrussington "Þorsteinn", Thurcaston "Þorketill", Thurlaston (also Wa) "Þorleifr", Thurmaston "Þormóðr".

Lincolnshire:

bȳ Aunby and Aunsby "Auðun", Barnetby "Beornnōð" (Old English), Bleasby "Blesi", Bransby (identical with Brandsby NRY) "Brandr", Grimsby "Grímr", Gunby "Gunni", Haconby "Hákun", Hemingby "Hemingr", Keadby "Keti", Manby "Manni" (Old Danish), Osgodby (also ERY, NRY) "Ásgautr", Raithby "Hreiðarr", Spilsby "Spillir", Stainsby "Stafn", Wragby (also WRY) and Wrawby "Wraghi" (Old Danish).
þorp Addlethorpe (also WRY) "Eardwulf" (Old English), Caythorpe (also Nt) "Káti", Gainsthorpe "Gamall", Ganthorpe "Germund" (Old Danish), Grimsthorpe "Grímr", Hasthorpe "Haraldr", Scunthorpe "Skúma", Upperthorpe "Hūnbald" (Old English), Wilsthorpe (also Db, ERY) "Vífill", Yawthorpe apparently "Ioli" (Old Danish).
toft Habertoft perhaps "Hagbarðr".
hybrid *tūn* Baston "Bakr", Gelston perhaps "Giǫfull".

Norfolk:

bȳ Alby (identical with Ailby L) "Áli", Clippesby (identical with Clixby L) "Klyppr", Hemsby perhaps "Heimir", Herringby "Hæringr", Mautby (identical with Maltby L, NRY, WRY)

84

"Malti" (Old Danish), Oby (identical with Oadby Lei) "Auði", Rollesby "Hróðulfr", Scratby "Skrauti", Tyby (identical with Tythby Nt) "Tidhe".

þorp Alethorpe "Áli", Bagthorpe "Bakki" (Old Danish), Broomsthorpe "Brúnn", Calthorpe "Kali", Freethorpe "Frethi" (Old Danish), Gasthorpe "Gaddr", Ingoldisthorpe "Ingiáldr", Saxthorpe "Saxi", Sculthorpe "Skúli", Swainsthorpe (identical with Swinethorpe L) "Sveinn".

hybrid *tūn* Aslacton "Áslákr", Cawston "Kálfr", Garveston "Geirulfr", Helhoughton "Helgi", Kettlestone "Ketill", Scoulton "Skúli", Skeyton "Skeggi", Starston and Sturston (also Db) "Styrr", Thelveton "Þialfi", Thurgarton (also Nt) "Þorgeirr".

Northamptonshire:

bȳ Catesby (identical with Cadeby L, Lei, WRY) "Káti", Corby (also L) "Kori".

þorp Apethorpe "Api" (Old Danish), Gunthorpe (also L, Nf, R) "Gunni", Wigsthorpe (identical with Wiganthorpe NRY) "Víkingr".

toft Sibbertoft "Sigbiǫrn".

hybrid *tūn* Knuston "Knūt" (Old Danish), Strixton "Stríkr".

Nottinghamshire:

bȳ Budby "Butti", Granby "Grani", Ranby "Hrani", Skegby "Skeggi", Walesby (also L) "Valr".

þorp Gunthorpe "Gunnhildr (feminine)", Owthorpe "Úfi", Staythorpe "Stari", Winthorpe "Vígmundr".

hybrid *tūn* Clipston (also Nth) and Clipstone (also Bd, Nf) "Klyppr", Colston "Kolr", Gamston "Gamall", Gonalston "Gunnúlfr", Osberton (identical with Osbaston Lei) "Ásbiǫrn", Rolleston "Hróaldr", Thrumpton "Þormóðr", Toton "Tófi".

Rutland:

þorp Belmesthorpe "Beornhelm" (Old English), Kelthorpe "Ketill", Tolethorpe "Tóli".

hybrid *tūn* Glaston perhaps "Glaðr" (or "Glæd", Old English).

Suffolk:

bȳ Barnby (also NRY, Nt, WRY, and identical with Barmby ERY) "Biarni".

toft Lowestoft "Hloðvér".

hybrid *tūn* Flowton (identical with Flockton WRY) "Flóki", Gunton (also Nf) "Gunni", Kettlebaston "Ketilbiǫrn", Somerleyton "Sumarliði", Ubbeston "Ubbi".

Westmorland:

bȳ Colby (also Nf, and identical with Coleby L) "Koli", Nateby (also La) "Nate", Soulby (also Cu, and identical with Sulby Nth) "Sūle" (Old Danish).

þorp Crackenthorpe "Krakande", Hackthorpe "Haki".

East Riding:

bȳ Gunby "Gunnhildr (feminine)", Scalby "Skalli", Thirkleby "Þorgils", Uncleby "Húnkell".

þorp Hilderthorpe "Hildiger" (Old Danish), Kettlethorpe (also L) "Ketill", Raisthorpe "Hreiðarr".

hybrid *tūn* Barmston (also Du) "Bjǫrn", Rolston "Hrólfr", Scampston "Skammr".

North Riding:

bȳ Ainderby "Eindriði", Amotherby "Eymundr", Bagby "Baggi", Battersby "Bǫðvarr", Bellerby "Belgr", Cleasby "Kleppr", Helperby "Hjalp (feminine)", Romanby "Hrómundr", Slingsby "Slengr", Thormanby and Thornaby "Þormóðr", Ugglebarnby "Uglubarði".

þorp Agglethorpe "Ācwulf" (Old English), Carthorpe "Kári", Ganthorpe "Gamall", Towthorpe (also ERY) "Tófi".

toft Antofts "Aldwine" (Old English).

hybrid *tūn* Oulston "Ulfr", Scruton "Skurfa", Sigston "Sigge".

West Riding:

bȳ Balby "Balli" (Old Danish), Flasby and Flaxby "Flatr", Fockerby "Folkvarðr", Hellaby "Helgi", Thorlby "Þóraldr".

þorp Armthorpe "Earnwulf" (Old English), Gawthorpe (identical with Gowthorpe ERY) "Gaukr", Goldthorpe "Golda" (Old English), Hexthorpe "Heggr", Oglethorpe "Oddkell", Streetthorpe "Styrr", Wrenthorpe "Wīfrūn" (Old English feminine).

hybrid *tūn* Brotherton "Bróðir", Flockton "Flóki", Thurlston (also Sf) "Thurulf" (Old Danish).

See addendum p. 233.

Chapter Seven

———————— ★ ————————

THE INFLUENCE OF FRENCH
ON ENGLISH PLACE-NAMES

ALTHOUGH the number of place-names of French origin is comparatively small, it should be remembered that the group does not include names derived from, or containing, French words which had become an integral part of the Middle English vocabulary. Distinctively French names are often those of monasteries and castles, and some may well have been transferred directly from France. It is, of course, impossible always to be sure whether this is the case, but Blanchland (Nb) "white glade", Freemantle (Ha) "cold cloak", a descriptive name given to a forest, Grosmont (NRY) "big hill", Kirmond le Mire (L) "goat hill", identical with the French Chèvremont, Montacute (So) "pointed hill", with the modern name in a Latinized form, Richmond (NRY, WRY), in this case "strong hill", and Beamond End (Bk), Beaumont (Cu, Ess, Hrt, La, Lei) "beautiful hill" all have their parallels in France. In fact, we know that the priory of Grosmont was named from its mother house near Limoges and that Marmont (C) took its name from Marmande (Lot et Garonne). In some cases the name was no doubt equally appropriate to the English place, as with some of the Beaumonts, and similarly with Richmond (NRY), a name given to the castle, built shortly after the Norman Conquest, on a site above the River Swale. Richmond (Sr), however, was named by Henry VII from his earldom of Richmond, when he rebuilt the palace at the place formerly called *Sheen*, which had been burned down in 1501, though the meaning would accurately describe Richmond Hill. Ridgmont (Bd, ERY) "red hill" may have been named from Rougemont in France, but the name of the Bedfordshire place at any rate was appropriate enough, for the sandstone there has a reddish colour. Mountsorrel (Lei) "sorrel-coloured hill" is presumably identical with Mont-sorel, but was no doubt named from the pinkish granite there, which is still being quarried today. Similarly, Egremont (Cu) is certainly identical with the French Aigremont, but "sharp-pointed hill" is as topographically appropriate for the Cumberland castle as it is for the French places.

On the other hand, Cause (Sa) may well be named from Caux in Normandy, said to have been the home of the Norman family which held the English place after the Conquest.

Many French place-names in England contain the word *bel* or *beau* "beautiful, fine", presumably with reference to the place or to the scenery around. Examples include Beachy Head (Sx), with Head added later, and Beauchief Abbey (WRY) "fine headland"; Beadlow (Bd), Beaulieu (Ha), Bewdley (Wo) and Bewley (Du, We) "beautiful, fine place"; Beamish (Du) "fine mansion"; Bear Park (Du), Beaurepaire (Ha) and Belper (Db) "beautiful, fine retreat"; Beaufront Castle (Nb) "fine brow"; Beauvale (Nt) "beautiful valley"; Belasis (Du), Bellasis (Du, Nb), Bellasize (ERY) and Belsize (Hrt, Mx, Nth) "beautiful, fine seat"; Belvoir (Lei) "beautiful view"; and Butterby (Du) "beautiful find". An especially interesting name, which may be included here, is Belgrave (Lei), recorded as *Merdegrave* "martens' grove or pit" in Domesday Book. The first element appears to have been associated with Old French *merde* "filth", and by about 1135 had been replaced by *bel*, presumably for reasons of euphony.

Occasionally, the French name given to a monastery has a religious significance, as in Dieulacres (St) "may God increase it" and Gracedieu (Lei) "grace of God". Comparable also are Mount Grace (NRY), and St. Michael's Mount (Co), no doubt named from the mother house of Mont-St.-Michel in France, as well as Haltemprice (ERY) "great enterprise", the name given to the priory which moved there in 1325–26. Similarly, there is Landieu (Du) "glade of God" and Vaudey (L) "valley of God". Rewley Abbey (O) "royal place", however, commemorates its foundation on land which had belonged to Richard, brother of Henry III.

As with place-names from other sources, the French names occasionally refer to some natural or artificial feature. So, Boulge (Sf) means "uncultivated land covered with heather", Bruera (Ch), Temple Bruer (L) and Bruern (O) "heath", Cowdray Park (Sx) "hazel copse", Kearsney (K) "place where cress grows", Salcey Forest (Nth–Bk) "place abounding in willows", as well as Caidge (Ess) "enclosed piece of land" and Malpas (Ch) "bad, i.e. difficult passage". The Prae (Hrt) means "the meadow" and the same word, with French *de la* "of the" prefixed, is found in Delapre Abbey (Nth).

Devizes (W) represents the plural of Old French *devise* "boundary" and the 12th-century castle there was on the boundary between two hundreds. Pleshey (Ess), identical with Plessey (Nb), from Old French *plessis* "enclosure made with interlaced fencing", is also found in France in Plessis-les-Tours. The Essex name dates from about 1100 and was given to the castle built by Geoffrey de Mandeville.

The French diminutive suffix -*et* was occasionally added to an older name, as in Claret Hall (Ess) "little Clare" from the near-by Clare (Sf), of which the meaning is uncertain, Cricket (So) "little *Cruc*", a Celtic name identical with Crich (Db) "hill", and Hampnett (Gl, Sx) "little *Hampton*", the older name meaning "at the high farm".

But if comparatively few place-names are of French origin, on the other hand a good many of the earlier Old English or Scandinavian ones have been influenced in one way or another by that language. In a few cases a part of the earlier name has apparently been replaced by a French word, usually one related, whether in sound or meaning, to the element which it replaces. French *eau*, Old French *ewe*, "water" has replaced Old English *ēa* "river, stream", in the name Eau found several times in Cambridgeshire and Lincolnshire, as in Old South Eau, but the replacement here is late and does not seem to be recorded before the 19th century. The change, however, took place early in Caldew (Cu) "cold river", recorded as *Caldeu* in 1189. Similarly, *mond* "hill" has replaced various Old English and Old Norse words: Old English *mūða* in Jesmond (Nb), formerly *Gesemuthe* "mouth of Ouse Burn", with forms in -mond from at least 1414; Old Norse *mót* in Beckermonds (WRY) "confluence of the streams" and Old English *mōt* in Eamont (Cu) also "junction of the streams". The commonest alternation is that of French *ville* with Old English *feld* "open land", especially in the south and west. No doubt this is in part due to the dialectal development of *f* to *v*, which results in Middle English spellings in -*velde*. Occasionally the -*d* is also lost, and popular etymology would help to account for confusion between -*ville* and -*vele*. Surviving examples include Clanville (Ha, So) "clean open land", Enville (St) "level open land", Longville (Sa) "long open land" and Turville (Bk) "dry open land" as contrasted with Tovil (K) "sticky open land". In addition, a late substitution of *ville* for Old English *welle* "spring, stream" has taken place in Wyville (L).

A much more important type of French influence on place-names, however, comes from the changes in the spelling and pronunciation of pre-Conquest names introduced by scribes, accustomed to copying Anglo-Norman and Latin, using a language and sound system which was unfamiliar and difficult. When these scribes came across sounds or combinations of sounds which were absent from French or Latin, they would tend to substitute for them the nearest sounds in those languages. At the same time, it is not always easy to distinguish sound substitutions due to this cause from those which are the result of some dialectal development in English itself. Often enough the early forms of a place-name as recorded in official documents will show differences from those which were written locally. Some of these may reflect the differences between London English and the local dialect, others may be the result of Anglo-Norman scribal influence. Many of the changes in spelling or pronunciation found in the early forms of place-names occur only sporadically and have not survived. But the modern forms of other names still reflect the influence of Anglo-Norman scribes. Often it is the name of an important town, or that of a place situated near or belonging to a castle or monastery, as was pointed out by the late Professor R. E. Zachrisson who was the first scholar to work in detail on this aspect of place-names.

In general, the influence of Norman scribes is very strong in Domesday Book and in official records of the 12th century, while certain particular changes are commonly found in 13th-century sources. After this, however, the influence gradually decreases in the numerous names in which it has not survived. In the following examples the meaning of a place-name will not be given if that name is discussed in another chapter.

One of the commonest examples of Anglo-Norman influence in place-names is in the representation of Old English *c* before *e* or *i*. In such a word as Old English *ceaster* the initial *c* had the sound represented in modern English by *ch*, but this sound did not occur initially in Norman-French where, in such cases, the *c* was pronounced as *ts*, later becoming *s*, though still represented by *c* in writing. Both the Anglo-Norman spelling and, sometimes, the sound have survived in a number of names containing *ceaster*, such as Cirencester, Gloucester, Leicester and Worcester, as well as Alcester (Wa), Frocester (Gl), Towcester (Nth) and Wroxeter (Sa), in the last of which *x* is for an earlier *ks*. The same change has occurred in Cerne (Do), for Cherne, and in Cippenham (Bk) identical with Chippenham (C), both pronounced with initial *s*. In early forms *s* sometimes occurs as an alternative spelling, and has survived in Seighford (St), with the same etymology as Chesterford (Ess). Medially *s* for an original Old English *c* (ch) appears in Messing (Ess), identical in origin with Matching in the same county, in Whissonsett (Nf), Old English *Wicingaset* "fold of the Wicingas", and in Linslade (Bk), Old English *Hlinclād* "hill path". A similar sound-substitution has occasionally taken place in names containing Old English -ic, as in Diss (Nf), from Old English dīc "ditch", and Dishforth (NRY) "ford by a ditch", as compared with Ditchford (Nth). Here too belongs Chatteris (C) in which Old English rīc "stream" was perhaps added to an older Celtic name meaning "wood".

Another common instance of Norman sound-substitution is that of initial T- for English Th-, a sound which did not occur in Anglo-Norman. So we have Tingrith (Bd), Turville (Bk) identical with Therfield (Hrt), Tusmore (O), Turnworth (Do) "thorn-bush enclosure", as well as Tarleton (La), Turton (La) and Turweston (Bk) in which Old English tūn "farmstead, village" has been compounded with the Scandinavian personal names Þaraldr, Þori and Þurfastr respectively. Other examples include Torworth (Nt) "Þorðr's enclosure" and Torrisholme (La) "Þóraldr's island". Spellings with T- and Th- occur in the early forms of all these names, and it is interesting to note the as yet unexplained fact that the first element of five of these is a Scandinavian personal name in Þ- (Th-).

Similarly, Anglo-Norman initial J-, pronounced as in modern judge, is sometimes substituted for Old English G- before e or i, where the latter was pronounced like y in modern yet. This J- has survived in Jarrow (Du), Jesmond (Nb) and Jevington (Sx), the last representing Old English Geofingatūn "farmstead or village of Geofa's people".

Anglo-Norman influence is also responsible for the occasional loss of s before a following consonant, and in an initial position this has affected the modern form of at least two place-names, Nottingham, discussed elsewhere, and Trafford (La), originally identical with Stretford (La). In Trafford the a for e and ff for tf are probably also due to Norman influence. Medially s has similarly been lost in some of the names derived from Old English ceaster already noted, e.g. Exeter and Wroxeter.

There seems also to have been confusion in Anglo-Norman between initial G- and C-. This is particularly noticeable in the early spellings of names beginning with Cl- or Cr-, for which Gl- and Gr- are sometimes found. But although G- for C- is frequent in the 13th and 14th century, it rarely survives in the modern forms. Examples, however, are Glendon (Nth), with G- first occurring in 1205, and identical with Clandon (Sr), and Glenfield (Lei), G- first recorded in the mid-13th century, as compared with Clanfield (Ha) "clean open land".

An interchange of the consonants l, n and r due to Anglo-Norman influence is common in the early forms of place-names. For example, Salisbury has early forms such as *Saresbury*, but the first *r* has been replaced by *l*, and *Sales-* is in fact found in late 11th-century spellings. Similarly an *l* has interchanged with *r* in Bulphan (Ess), Old English *Burgefen* "fen with or near a fortification", while in Durham, Old English *Dunholm*, original *n* has been replaced by *r*.

In the 13th century, names containing Middle English *an* followed by another consonant sometimes appear as *aun* due to a sound change which took place in Anglo-Norman. Such spellings still remain in some modern place-names, as for example Saunton (D) identical in origin with Santon (Cu, L, Nf), Staunton (Gl, He, Lei, Nt, So, Wo) with the common Stanton, and Staunton on Wye (He) with Standon (Hrt). Similarly there is Raunds (Nth) "at the edges or borders" instead of Rands, Saundby (Nt) "Sandi's farm", Taunton (So) earlier *Tantūn* "farmstead or village on the River Tone", as well as Braunston (Nth, R) and Braunstone (Lei), identical in origin with Brandeston (Sf), Brandiston (Nf) and Branston (Lei, St) "Brant's farmstead".

The development of Old English personal names beginning with *Æðel-* to *Ail-*, as in Aylburton (Gl) and Aylmerton (Nf), from Aðelbeorht and Æðelmǣr and Old English *tūn* "farmstead", was thought to be distinctively Norman. It has, however, recently been shown to be an Old English and not a Norman change at all.

The vocalization of *l* to *u*, especially when it followed *a*, is a sound-development which took place early in Anglo-Norman, though rarely recorded in place-names before the 12th and 13th century. Often forms in *al* and *au* occur side by side, but the latter survives only occasionally, usually spelt *aw*, as in Fawkham (K) "Fealcna's home-stead", Hawnby (NRY) "Halmi's farm", and Sawtry (Hu) "salters' stream". Similarly, forms in *au* occur in the 13th century for Faulkbourn (Ess) "falcon stream" and Maulden (Bd), identical in origin with Malden (Sr). In both cases the forms with *aul* are late and apparently represent a compromise between *au* and *al*. On the other hand, Sawley (Db) "hill or mound where sallows grow" and Sawley (WRY) "sallow wood or glade" represent a change which took place in English in the 16th and 17th century.

No doubt some of the villages which exist today did not come into existence until after the Norman Conquest. But if these new villages made use of Old English elements to form their names we can rarely distinguish them from earlier settlements. Only if they include a word or personal name, whether French or continental German, which was not in use in this country until after the Conquest, can we be certain that such names were not formed in the Anglo-Saxon period. After the Norman Conquest radical changes took place in the types of personal names used in England. Though Old English names continued in use for some time, indeed one or two have had a continuous history to the present day, for the most part they gradually fell into disuse. The Normans introduced their own personal names, chiefly French or continental German in origin, and a little later biblical names, which are hardly ever found in Anglo-Saxon England. Few of the place-names which have such a post-Conquest personal name as first element are those of places of any importance, but their geographical distribution seems significant. The largest single group is that compounded with Old English *tūn* "farmstead, village" and later also "manor". These are rare in the North and Midlands, but we may note Williamston (Nb) from William, Howton (He) from Hue, i.e. Hugh, Rowlstone (He, identical with Rolleston W) from Rolf, Walterstone (He) from Walter, and Botcheston (Lei) from Bochard. They also occur occasionally in the central South, e.g. Marlston (Brk) from Martel, and Mainstone (Ha) from Mayhew, i.e. Mathew; more so in Wiltshire where they include Faulston from Fallard, Flamston from Flambard, and Richardson from Richard, while Dorset has Bryanston from Brian (a Norman name of Breton origin), Ranston from Randulf, and Waterston from Walter. In Devon and Dorset there are also some places with a family-name as first element, while the former contains the largest concentration of place-names with a post-Conquest personal name. These include Drewston (in Drewsteignton) from Drew, Johnstone from John, Jurston from Jordan, Penson and Penstone from Pain, and Stevenstone from Stephen. Post-Conquest personal names are only rarely compounded with other English elements for habitations, but we may note Painswick (Gl) "Pain's farm". Few of the names dealt with here are recorded before the 13th century.

Personal names introduced into England during the Middle English period are also found compounded with Scandinavian *bȳ* "farm, village". This type of compound does not occur in the Midlands, and is rare in Yorkshire where, however, there is Jolby (NRY) from Johel, i.e. Joel. It is not found in Cheshire, Lancashire or Westmorland, but is particularly common in Cumberland especially around Carlisle. Here, there are Aglionby from Agyllun, Allonby and Ellonby from Alein, Etterby from Etard, Lamonby from Lambin, Ponsonby from Puncun, Rickerby from Ricard (Richard), and Wigonby from Wigan. Some of these personal names, such as Alein and Wigan, are French names of Breton origin, others, like Lambin, are Flemish, and this may perhaps indicate the presence of Bretons and Flemings among the 12th-century settlers in Cumberland. That Flemings did in fact settle there is indicated by the name Flimby "village of the Flemings". In addition, there are a few names of this type which have a Scandinavian *þorp* "outlying farmstead" as second element, e.g. Buslingthorpe (L), Mablethorpe (L), Painsthorpe (ERY), Painthorpe (WRY) and Waterthorpe (Db), from the personal names Buselin, Malbert, Pain and Walter respectively, while with Old Norse *þveit* "clearing, meadow" there is Bassenthwaite (Cu) from the Anglo-Norman Bastun.

Chapter Eight

———————— ★ ————————

PREPOSITIONS AND ADVERBS
IN PLACE-NAMES

W E have already seen that in Old English the preposition *æt* "at", which took the dative case, might be regarded as an integral part of a place-name, and that its former use is shown today, chiefly, by traces of the old dative ending in the modern forms of such names as Barrow, Cotton, Sale, etc.

Middle English *atte* "at the" is commonly used in personal names from the 12th to the 14th century to indicate an original place of residence, which might later be adopted as a surname. Such forms as John *atte Broke* "John who lived near the brook", Robert *atte Cliffe* "Robert who lived near the cliff", and Richard *atte Halle* "Richard who lived near the hall" occur frequently in medieval documents and often contain the earliest recorded reference to a place-name, which may survive as Brook, Cliff or Hall Farm.

Moreover, Middle English *atte* is merely a weakened form of the Old English masculine or neuter *æt þæm* or feminine *æt þære*, which would give *atten* and *atter* before being reduced to *atte*, a form which actually survives in Havering atte Bower (Ess) "at the (king's) residence". Occasionally, traces of the earlier forms may survive in modern place-names. When the name originally began with a vowel it sometimes happened that the final -*n* and -*r* of *atten* and *atter* were taken as belonging to the following word, with the result that Middle English *atten Ashe* "at the ash-tree" sometimes appears as Nash (Bk, He, Sa). Similarly Noke (O) means "at the oak-tree", Nechells (St, Wa) "at the land added to a village", Nempnett (So) "at the plain", and Nayland (Sf) "at the island". A compound name of this type is Knockholt (K) "at the oak wood". In each of these names the form of the preposition and definite article was *atten*.

The final -*r* of *atter* has survived in Ray (Bk, W) and Rea (C, Sa-Wo, Wa) "at the river", as also in Rye (Sx) "at the island", Rivar

(W) and River (Sx) "at the edge of the hill", and Rock (Wo) "at the oak". Thurleigh (Bd) must have come from *at ther Leye* "at the glade", since the definite article has become part of the name.

Other prepositions used in the formation of place-names include Old English *bī* or *be*, as in Byfleet (Sr) "by the stream". In such names as this *bī* is used elliptically, and it is clear that some word like "place" or "village" is to be understood. So a better translation of Byfleet would be "(place, village) by the stream". Similar names with *bī* include Biddick (Du) "by the ditch", Biddulph (St) perhaps "by the mine", Bygrave (Hrt) "by the ditch" and Bythorn (Hu) "by the thorn-bush".

The same preposition appears also as the first part of *begeondan* "beyond", *beneoðan* "beneath" and *betwēonan* "between", which seem to be particularly frequent in Devonshire place-names. In many of the modern forms, however, initial *be-* has disappeared, as in Indicombe "on the other side of the valley", Indio "on the far side of the river", Yendamore "beyond the mire", Yondercott "beyond the cottage", and also Naithwood "beneath the wood", Neadon "beneath the down" and Nethercleave "beneath the steep slope". Tweenaways is "between the ways", while Tinhay, Tinney and Twinyeo all mean "between the waters". These are all in Devon, but elsewhere we have Twineham (Sx) "between the streams" and Yarnbook (W) "beyond the brook".

Old English *binnan* (from *be innan*) "within, inside" is the first element of Benwell (Nb) "within the wall", with reference to Hadrian's Wall. Bembridge (Wt) "inside the bridge" is apparently so-named because of its position at the end of a peninsula, which in early times could only be reached by sea or by the bridge at Brading. The same preposition occurs also in Bindon (Do) "on the inside of the down", and in the affix in Barton Bendish (Nf) "Barton inside the ditch", the village being situated to the west of Devil's Ditch. Old English *bufan* (from *be ufan*) "above, over" is used elliptically in Boveney (Bk) "above the island", Boveridge (Do) "above the ridge", Bovingdon (Hrt), Bovingdon Green (Bk) and Bowden Park (W) "above, i.e. on top of, the hill" and Bowcombe (Wt) "above the valley".

Other prepositions similarly used include *fore, under* and *uppan*. The first, meaning "in front of", is found in Fordon (ERY) and Forhill (Wo) both "in front of the hill". *Fore* was also used in the formation of nouns like *foreburg* "outwork", the source of Forrabury (Co), and *foreland* "headland, promontory", found in North Foreland (K). Old English *under* "under, below" is fairly common in place-names, such as Underbarrow (We) "at the foot of the hill", Underley (We) "below the wood or glade", Underley (Sx) and Underly (He) "at the foot of the slope", and Underwood and Weston Underwood (Db) "below the wood". It is prefixed to older names in Undermillbeck (We) "below Millbeck", where Millbeck means "mill stream", and Underskiddaw (Cu) "at the foot of Skiddaw", the latter probably being "craggy hill". The preposition in Uphill (So) is Old English *uppan* "upon, above", and the name seems to mean "(place) above the creek".

Old English *in*, when used in place-names, is commonly preceded by an adverb of direction—north, south, east or west. So we have Norrington (W), literally "north in the village", elliptically for "(land) north in the village", and similarly there are Siddington (Gl), Sinton (Wo) and Sodington (Wo), Eastington (D, Do, Gl, Wo), and Wessington (W). A similar formation with the Old English adverb *upp* is found in Upton Park (Ess) "(land) higher up in the village", where the earlier medial -in- has been lost.

The only Scandinavian preposition to occur in place-names is *í, in*. This is used medially between two nouns in Loskay (NRY) and perhaps Loscoe (Db, WRY) "house with a loft in the wood".

Some of the prepositions discussed above are also used in the distinguishing additions (affixes) to older names, as in Barton under Needwood (St), Stanton by Bridge (Db) and Morton upon Swale (NRY). Since, however, most medieval documents are in Latin, prepositions used in this way will normally appear in such sources in their Latin equivalents, and sometimes the Latin preposition has survived in the modern form of the name, most of which have been collected by Professor Bruce Dickins. Thus Latin *juxta* "near" occurs in Bradwell juxta Coggeshall (Ess) and Langton juxta Partney (L), where the second name is that of a neighbouring village; but that this is not invariably the case is shown by Bradwell juxta Mare (Ess) i.e. "by the sea". Similarly, *sub* "below, underneath" is found in Stratford sub Castle (W) "below the castle", with reference to Old Sarum, and Thorpe sub Montem (WRY) "at the foot of the hill", this last with the full Latin form of the affix. *Super* "on" remains in Weston super Mare (So) "on sea", which can be compared with the English form in St. Annes on the Sea (La) and Sutton on Sea (L). Latin *in* "in", followed by the ablative case, is frequent in the early forms of place-names. Since it has the same form as the corresponding English word, it is impossible to be sure which of them is represented in the modern form of Shotton in Glendale (Nb) and Henley in Arden (Wa). It is certainly the Latin word, however, in Easton in Gordano and Weston in Gordano (So), for Gordano is the ablative singular of the Latinized form of English *Gorden* "muddy valley". Latin *cum* "with" occurs in the names of joint parishes, as in Chorlton cum Hardy (La), Langar cum Barnstone (Nt), Poulton cum Seacombe (Ch), and compare Woodford cum Membris (Nth) i.e. "with its dependencies". The English form is found in Tiddington with Albury (O). This usage is common in the North Midlands, but is rare south of the Thames and not found at all in the extreme North or North-west of England.

The French preposition *en* "in", followed by the definite article *le*, is used in the same way as the corresponding English word, in Alsop en le Dale (Db) "in the valley" and Stretton en le Field (Lei) "in the open country", but the preposition has been lost in Barnoldby le Beck (L) "on the stream" and Hamble le Rice (Ha) "in the brushwood". Indeed, this formation is common and other cases will be found elsewhere.

Examples have already been given of the adverbial use in place-names of *north*, *south*, *east* and *west*. These could be either adjectives or adverbs in Old English, but their derivatives *norðan*, *sūðan*, *ēastan* and *westan* were adverbs only. In the early forms of place-names they are sometimes preceded by *bī* and used elliptically in the sense " (place lying) north, south, east or west of", as in Norney (Sr) " (place lying) north of the marshy land" and Nornay (Nt) " (place lying) north of the river", as well as in the affix in Barningham Norwood (Nf) "Barningham (lying) north of the wood". From the other adverbs are derived Siddington (Ch) "south of the hill", Southover (Sx) "south of the bank", Eastney (Ha) "east of the island", Eastnor (He) "east of the ridge", Westbourne Park (Mx) "west of the stream" and Westwood (K) "west of the wood". Occasionally traces of the preceding preposition *bī* survive, as in Bestwall (Do) " (place lying) east of the wall", i.e. the town-wall of Wareham. Other adverbs used in this way include Old English *dūne* "down, below" in Dunthorp (O) " (place lying) below the hamlet", and *ufan* "above, over" in Oveny Green (K) "above the marshy land".

A special use of Old English *wiðinnan* "within" and *wiðūtan* "outside" is found in London and elsewhere. In the former case, the adverbs were used when there were two wards of the same name, one of which was inside the walls, the other outside. Hence Cripplegate Within, Cripplegate Without and Farringdon Within, Farringdon Without. Similarly, Carlisle has St. Cuthbert Without, the part of the parish outside the city, while elsewhere there is Hensington Within and Hensington Without (O). In medieval Latin sources the

English words will normally be translated as *intra* and *extra*, and these are still sometimes used to describe parishes inside or outside a town boundary, as in Romsey Intra and Romsey Extra (Ha).

Old English *sundor* "asunder, apart" has two elliptical meanings in place-names. Its basic sense is "something detached or separated from somewhere else", and so "remote", as in Sundorne (Sa) "remote house" and Sundridge (K) "remote pasture". It was also used in the sense of "privileged or private", the meaning in Old English *sundorland* "privileged or private land", which has given Sunderland (Cu, Du, La).

Similarly Old English *upp* "up, higher up" was used in two senses in place-names. With words for habitations it means "higher" in contrast to another settlement on lower ground, as in Upham (Ha) "higher homestead or village", Upton, a common name, "higher farmstead or village" and Upwick (Hrt) "higher farm". A similar sense is also likely in Offord (Hu) "higher ford" and Upwood (Hu) "higher wood". The corresponding Scandinavian form, however, is probably found in Upleatham (NRY) "at the higher slopes" and Upsall (NRY) "higher homestead".

Where the second part of the name is a river-name *upp* is no doubt used elliptically of a "(place) higher up the river", as with Uplowman (D) further up the Loman than Tiverton, Uplyme (D) as compared with Lyme Regis (Do) on the Lim or Lyme, and Upway (Do) which is upstream from Broadway on the Wey.

As was the case with prepositions, the adverbs may be prefixed to a village name, as in Down Ampney (Gl), Up (now Upper) Lambourn (Brk) and Up Waltham (Sx). Occasionally a pair of such names is found like Downholland and Upholland (La) "lower"and "higher Holland" and Down Hatherley and Up Hatherley (Gl) "lower" and "higher Hatherley".

Chapter Nine

———— ★ ————

AFFIXES IN PLACE-NAMES

MANY of the older village names, especially common ones such as Norton and Sutton, have a word either prefixed or added to them. This may be a descriptive word, or a family or personal name, and is often used to distinguish two places with the same name, though in some cases the use appears to be quite arbitrary. Some of the affixes are very old and others, which have not survived, occur also in medieval documents. Indeed, some villages have had different affixes at various times, and which, if any, has survived is largely a matter of chance. Those no longer current, however, are of the same type as those still used and will not, therefore, be considered here. The most important contribution to this aspect of place-names was made in 1924 by James Tait in the first volume published by the English Place-Name Society, and his general conclusions still in the main hold good.

These distinguishing affixes usually appear today as separate words, and are of two main types: those descriptive of the village, whether of its situation, shape, size, or its proximity to some hill, valley or the like, or to some more important place; and those containing the name of a former holder or owner of the manor, whether lay or ecclesiastic.

Affixes of the first type are often adjectives, particularly common being those describing the cardinal points of the compass. In these cases the names usually occur in pairs, as in North and South Weston (O) and East and West Anstey (D), but occasionally all four are used as in North, South, East and West Brunton (Nb). Also common are *Middle, Nether* "lower" and *Over* "higher", as in Middle Claydon (Bk), Nether and Over Haddon (Db), but in modern names Nether has sometimes been replaced by *Lower*, and Over by *Upper*, as in Lower Caldecote (Bd) and Upper Heyford (Nth). In medieval documents, however, the Latin equivalents are often used, and these survive unchanged in Walton Inferior and Superior (Ch). *High* is also common, hence High Barnet (Hrt) and High Wycombe (Bk), and is sometimes contrasted with *Low* as in High and Low Worsall

(NRY). *Haut*, the corresponding form in medieval French records, has survived only in Ault Hucknall (Db). Another common adjective of situation is *Hanging* "situated on sloping ground", as in Hanging Grimston (ERY) and Hanging Langford (W). Hutton Hang (NRY), however, with a suffix ultimately from the same root, has adopted it from the near-by Hang Bank "wooded slope", which is also responsible for the name of Hang Wapentake.

Other affixes refer to the size or shape of the place, as with Great and Little Rissington (Gl). Again, these will appear as *Magna* and *Parva* in medieval documents, and the Latin words have survived in Ash Magna and Parva (Sa) and are particularly common in Leicestershire, where there is Appleby Magna and Parva, Glen Magna and Parva, and Wigston Magna and Parva. With these we may compare the Cornish St. Columb (i.e. St. Columba) Major and Minor. Old English *micel*, *mycel* "big" has been prefixed in Mitcheldean (Gl), and the shortened form, *Much*, occurs in Much Wenlock (Sa) and Much Woolton (La) and as far East as Much Hadham (Hrt). The *mickle* in Mickleover (Db) and Mickle Trafford (Ch) has either been influenced by or is derived from the corresponding Old Norse *mikill*. *Long* is commonly used of a straggling village as in Long Buckby (Nth); and *Broad*, perhaps in the sense of spacious, appears in Broad Chalke (W) and Broadwindsor (Do); while *Round* is apparently found in a single name Acton Round (Sa).

Old appears occasionally as in Old Sodbury (Gl) and has survived as *All* in All Cannings (W). *New*, on the other hand, is rare and where it occurs, as in New Hutton (Wc), it may refer to a comparatively modern building estate.

Sometimes the affix refers to colour, as in Black Notley and White Notley (Ess), where a contrast between different types of soil is probably intended. The reference is also likely to be to the colour of the soil in Black Callerton (Nb) and Black Heddon (Nb), but at Black Torrington (D) it is the river which is said to have a blackish colour. In some names, such as White Roding (Ess) and White Staunton (So), *White* probably describes the church or some other prominent building. French *blanc* occurs once in Aston Blank (Gl), which perhaps means "bare Aston", from a lack of vegetation. Old English *gylden* "golden" is also found occasionally as in Guilden Morden (C) and Guilden Sutton (Ch). The exact sense of this affix is uncertain, but it may indicate particularly fertile land.

The soil at Clayhidon (D) is clayey, as it is also around Holton le Clay (L). Here the French definite article is presumably short for *en le*, i.e. "in the Clay", as in Mareham le Fen (L) and Thornton le Fen (L). The adjective *Fenny* is also found, in Fenny Bentley (Db) and in Sutton Veny (W), which has dialectal *v* for *f*. The neighbourhood is stony at Middleton Stoney (O), Stony Middleton (Db) and Stoney Stoke (So), and sandy at Sand Hutton (NRY). In Chislehampton (O) the affix means "gravel, shingle", and that in Barton Turf (Nf) presumably indicates a district where good turf was found.

Dry may refer either to a near-by dried-up stream or to dry higher ground in marshland, as in Dry Doddington (L) and Dry Drayton (C), the last contrasting with Fen Drayton. Latin *sicca* "dry" has survived in Marston Sicca (Gl), an alternative name to Long Marston. The suffixes in Thornton Watless (NRY) and Willoughby Waterless (Lei) both have the same meaning, "waterless", but that in the first, originally the name of a separate place, is from a Scandinavian word corresponding with the English word in the second. Westley Waterless (C), however, is misleading, since there is no lack of water here, and Waterless is for *Waterlees* "water clearings or meadows".

Cold, usually referring to a village in an exposed situation, occurs frequently as in Cold Brayfield (Bk) and Coldmeece (St), as well as Coal Aston (Db), with *Coal* representing a dialectal development of *cold*. Another name with perhaps a similar meaning is Blo Norton (Nf), of which the affix may mean "bleak, cold".

Stocking Pelham (Hrt) has *Stocking* from Old English *stoccen* "made of logs", presumably an allusion to buildings so-constructed, while Leaden Roding (Ess) is said to owe its distinctive addition to its lead-roofed church. In the same way, a group of names has a distinguishing *Steeple*, including Steeple Barton (O) and Sturton le Steeple (Nt). The presence of a castle is also indicated by such names as Castle Ashby (Nth) and Castle Rising (Nf).

The affix in Brant Broughton (L) and Brent Pelham (Hrt) means "burnt" and may commemorate the destruction of the place by fire, or perhaps the fact that the land around was cleared by burning. The corresponding Latin form has also survived, in Bradfield Combust (Sf).

A few miscellaneous names with various affixes may be noted. English Bicknor (Gl) and Welsh Bicknor (He) are on opposite sides of the River Wye. *Port* in Milborne Port (So) means "market town", and the *Harness* in Berkeley Harness (Gl) means "jurisdiction, district". A group of comparable names, including Eaton Socon (Bd) and Walton-le-Soken (Ess), has as its affix Old English *socn*, modern *soke*, "district under a particular jurisdiction". The *Bierlow* in Brightside Bierlow and Ecclesall Bierlow in the West Riding is

102

from a Scandinavian word used in England of a small administrative district. Latin *ambo* "both" has been added in Barughs Ambo (NRY), Fulfords Ambo (ERY) and Wendens Ambo (Ess), usually at a late date, to indicate two villages of the same name forming a single parish, and compare also the West Riding Bradleys Both and Marstons Both. Two other Latin affixes are *forinseca* "lying outside the bounds" and *intrinseca* "lying inside the bounds", the second of which survives in Ryme Intrinseca (Do), as contrasted with the lost *Ryme Extrinseca*. An earlier *Forinseca* appears as *Foreign* in Rye Foreign (Sx), the name of the larger area which included the corporate liberty of Rye.

One or two affixes may be contemptuous, for example Full Sutton (ERY) "dirty Sutton", Stratton Strawless (Nf) "without straw" and Thorpe Thewles (Du) "immoral". Other affixes indicate some former pursuit for which the place was noted, and often there is only a single example of each. Iron Acton (Gl) must have been famed for its iron-mines, Cole Orton (Lei) for coal, Glass Houghton (WRY) for glass-making, and Kirkby Overblow (WRY) for smelting, since *Overblow* means "of the smelters". The affix of a group of names, including Potter Hanworth (L), Potters Marston (Lei) and Potter Somersal (Db), indicates the former existence of potteries. To these can be added Husbands Bosworth (Lei), apparently "husbandmen's Bosworth", in a farming area, distinguishing it from Market Bosworth (Lei) "Bosworth with a market". This last is commonly found, for example in Market Lavington (W) and Market Rasen (L), while Old English *cēping* also "market", the source of the simplex Chipping (La), has frequently been added to a village name, as in Chipping Warden (Nth) and Chipping Wycombe (Bk). The Latin word is *forum* and this has survived in Blandford Forum (Do), which is also called *Chipping* Blandford in early forms.

A few places are distinguished by a term for the produce for which they were well-known—beans in Barton in the Beans (Lei) and Barton in Fabis (Nt), cress in Carshalton (Sr), flax in Flax Bourton (So), saffron (introduced into England in the 14th century) in Saffron Walden (Ess), cows in Cow Honeybourne (Gl) and pigs in Toller Porcorum (Do), from the Latin genitive plural "of the pigs". Here, too, can be noted Wickham Skeith (Sf) "Wickham with a racecourse".

The affix in a good many village names refers to some nearby natural or artificial feature. It is usually a noun, and may be preceded by the definite article, by a preposition, or by both, whether English or French. In Borrowash (Db) and Stoke Ash (Sf) it must

103

have been a prominent ash-tree, while Cherry Willingham (L), Hatfield Broad Oak (Ess), Barnby in the Willows (Nt) and Newton le Willows (NRY) are similarly self-explanatory. On the other hand, it is a "building" in Botolph Claydon (Bk), a "dwelling" in Bower Hinton (So), a "mill" in Millmeece (St) and Corfe Mullen (Do), this last from French *mulin*, and a "bridge" in Bridge Trafford (Ch), Bridge Walton (Sa) and Longbridge Deverill (W) "Deverill near the long bridge".

In other names the affix denotes a "stream", as in Fleet Marston (Bk), and "water", i.e. a river, in Water Newton (Hu) and Waterperry (O), as well as Allerton Bywater (WRY), from their situation beside the Nene, Thame and Aire respectively. One place, St. Nicholas at Wade (K), has Old English *wæd* "ford", and Ferry Fryston (WRY) is so-named from a nearby ferry over the Aire.

Watton at Stone (Hrt) must owe its name to some prominent stone, and the same is true of Sutton at Hone (K), from Old English *hān*, modern *hone*, "stone". The wall of Plumpton Wall (Cu) is probably that of the Roman camp *Voreda*, and Heddon on the Wall (Nb) is on the line of Hadrian's Wall.

Some places situated on or near a hill are distinguished by a word for "hill", as with Hill Somersal (Db), Hetton le Hill (Du) and Walton on the Hill (Sr); Houghton le Side (Du) from Old English *side* "hill-side"; Toot Baldon (O) from Old English *tōt* "look-out hill"; and Copt Hewick (WRY) from Old English *copped*, perhaps in the sense "peaked hill". Other names indicate the position of the village in a valley, as in Dalton le Dale (Du), Stainton le Vale (L) and Stanford in the Vale (Brk), as well as Hoe Benham (Brk) and Hetton le Hole (Du), both with Old English *hol* "hollow, valley". Those situated in wooded country are often self-explanatory, as with Wood Dalling (Nf) and Woodperry (O), but Sco Ruston (Nf) has Old Norse *skógr* "wood". *Forest* is sometimes used of a woodland district belonging to the king and preserved for hunting, as in Marston in the Forest and Stockton on the Forest (NRY) from the Forest of Galtres, and Hesket in the Forest and Hutton in the Forest (Cu) from Inglewood Forest.

Moor is used of a high tract of uncultivated ground, the usual sense in the North, or of marshland, hence Barnby Moor (Nt), More Crichel (Do), Thornton le Moors (Ch) and Bradley in the Moors (St). *Weald* or *Wold* "open upland, moorland, wasteland" is found in Old Hurst (Hu), Normanby le Wold (L) and Stow on the Wold (Gl). The *Weald* in Eyton upon the Weald Moors and Preston upon the Weald Moors (Sa), however, is misleading for it represents an earlier *wild*, i.e. "on the wild moors". *Heath* "uncultivated land, heather covered land" appears in Normanton le Heath (Lei) and St. Giles on the Heath (D); *marsh* in Marsh Benham (Brk) and Welton le Marsh (L); and *mire* in Ainderby Mires (NRY) and Kirmond le Mire (L). Thorpe in the Fallows (L) is perhaps "Thorpe in the ploughed or arable land", while Ashley Green (Bk) and Brafield on the Green (Nth) were presumably villages noted for their village-greens or commons.

Many places have added the name of the river on or near which they stand. The usual forms appear in Ashton on Mersey (Ch), Adwick upon Dearne (WRY) and Weston by Welland (Nth), but we also have Witton le Wear (Du), and with the river-name used alone, Danby Wiske (NRY), Eye Kettleby (Lei) and Severn Stoke (Wo) from the Wiske, Eye and Severn respectively. Others have the name of a river valley, as in Eaton Dovedale (Db) and Burley in Wharfedale (WRY).

Another group of names adds that of a district, the particular relation of the place to the district being indicated by the use of a preposition. So, there are Ashton under Lyne (La) and Newcastle under Lyme (St), each including the name of a forest, itself perhaps from a Celtic river-name meaning "elmy river". A series of Warwickshire names, comprising Bourton on Dunsmore, Clifton upon Dunsmore, Ryton on Dunsmore and Stretton on Dunsmore, take the affix from Dunsmore Heath "Dunn's moor". Brampton en le Morthen (WRY) comes from an old district name Morthen or Morthing "moor assembly or meeting", and the affix in Kirby in Cleveland (NRY) means "steep district". Occasionally the district name appears without a preposition as in Higham *Upshire* (K) "higher district" and Sutton *Coldfield* (Wa) "open land where charcoal is burnt". In one or two names it is that of a hundred or wapentake as in Boothby *Graffoe* (L) "spur of land with a grove" and Charlton *Horethorne* (So) "grey thorn-tree". Carleton *Forehoe* (Nf), however, is near Forehoe Hills "four barrows", which gave its name also to Forehoe Hundred.

Some names are distinguished by an affix which is itself a place-name, often one which is still in use today, as in Kirby *Knowle* (NRY), which is near Knowle Hill "knoll", and Kirby *Underdale* (ERY), close to Hundle Dale "Hundolf's valley". Kirkby *Ireleth* (La) is adjacent to Ireleth "Irishmen's hill-slope", Perry *Barr* (St) to Great Barr, noted previously, and Stretton *Sugwas* (He) to Sugwas perhaps "sparrow swamp".

More often, however, the added name is no longer used

105

independently, as with Burnham *Deepdale* (Nf) from a now lost, but self-explanatory, Deepdale, Burton *Pidsea* (ERY) "pool (now drained) in the marsh", Martin *Hussingtree* (Wo) "Hūsa's tree", and *Silk* Willoughby (L), the shortened form of a lost *Silkby* "Silki's farm or village".

The largest group of affixes consists of those derived from the name of some early holder of the manor, whether a forename or a surname. Occasionally an Old English forename has survived—Abba in *Ab* Kettleby (Lei), Æffa in *Aff*puddle (Do), Heca in *Egg* Buckland (D), Gōdgȳð (feminine) in *Good* Easter (Ess), Mæðelgār in Tolleshunt *Major* (Ess), as well as Ēadgȳð (feminine) in Stoke *Edith* (He) and *Edith* Weston (R), these last perhaps named from the wife of Edward the Confessor. Some of the personal names are of Scandinavian origin—Hrafnsvartr in Crosby *Ravensworth* (We), Ketill in Strickland *Ketel* (We), Sveinn in Hoyland *Swaine* (WRY), Tola (feminine) in *Tol*puddle (Do), and Vagn in Wootton *Wawen* (Wa)—while Welsh David is found in Culm *Davy* (D) and Owen in Hales*owen* (Wo). Most of the names used in this way, however, were personal names introduced into England through the Normans, many of which were of German origin. Of the more common ones there is Bernard in Holcombe *Burnell* (D), Richard in Askham *Richard* (WRY), Ralph in Brompton *Ralph* (So), Roger in Strickland *Roger* (We), and Walter in *Waters* Upton (Sa), where *Water* represents the regular medieval pronunciation. Feminine names of Norman origin include Agnes in Burton *Agnes* (ERY), while *Mauld's* Meaburn (We) has Mauld, a common medieval form of Matilda. Less common christian names include Everard in Papworth *Everard* (C), Warin in Grendon *Warren* (He), and Otton, the usual French form of Otto, in Belchamp *Otton* (Ess). In almost every case the individual from whom the affix is derived can be traced in early records.

More frequently, however, it is the surname of the family which at one time held the manor. Few of these are of English origin, but examples include Roebuck, originally a nickname, in Appleton *Roebuck* (WRY), Walsh "Welshman" in Shelsley *Walsh* (Wo) and Fleming "man from Flanders" in Stoke Fleming (D). The Salomes of Berrick *Salome* and Britwell *Salome* (O) took their name from Sulham (Brk); the Wallops of Farleigh *Wallop* (Ha) came originally from Wallop in the same county; but the Audleys of Stratton *Audley* (O) seem to have come from Audley (St). Sometimes the surname was derived from some minor place-name, as with those of the families which held *Bank* Newton (WRY) and Weston *Bampfylde* (So), from some "bank" and "bean field" respectively.

A very high proportion of the family names which occur as affixes to older place-names are of French origin, and those interested in the meanings of such names should refer to P. H. Reaney's *A Dictionary of British Surnames*. It will be most convenient to give examples of this type county by county in a list at the end of the chapter. This will also serve to indicate the relative frequency of affixes in various parts of the country, for the distribution of those derived from French family names appears to agree broadly with that of affixes as a whole, except apparently in East Anglia where those of the types already discussed occur fairly frequently. In general terms, as Tait pointed out, affixes from French family names are uncommon in the North and East, except in Yorkshire. They occur increasingly in the Midlands, and are more numerous still in the South, particularly in the South-west, where the high proportion is probably partly to be explained on historical grounds. Here, there were numerous small manors, and where a parish was made up of a number of hamlets the various parts would need to be distinguished in some way from each other.

It is impossible at present to indicate with any degree of accuracy the dates at which affixes of various kinds tend to become common. Full lists of early forms are not yet available for those counties still to be surveyed by the English Place-Name Society, but Ekwall has given in his *Dictionary* the earliest dates he has noted of the affixed forms of the names he includes in this work. Moreover, the present affix in some names is not the only one to have been attached to the name. Some have had earlier affixes which have disappeared.

Leaving aside for the moment those which have the name of an owner or tenant prefixed or added, a survey of the examples given above shows that in the majority the affix, whether English, French or Latin, is first found in the 13th century, and a considerable number of the others in the 14th. Few are found before this date, but among them are Woodditton in 1086, and in the 12th century Chislehampton, Corfe Mullen, Fen Drayton, Over Haddon, Venn Ottery, Waterperry and White Roding. On the other hand, Chipping Wycombe and Potter Somersal (earlier *Nether*) have not been noted before the 15th century, and some do not appear till later still, for example Ault Hucknall (1535), Middleton Stoney (1552), Barnby in the Willows (1575, earlier *on Witham*) and Plumpton Wall (1578).

A remarkably high proportion of the affixes derived from the name of the manorial holder is similarly first recorded in the 13th and 14th century, particularly in the 13th. In some cases the affix is found already before 1200, as for example in Affpuddle (1086), Wootton

Wawen (1138–47), Crosby Ravensworth (about 1160), Stoke Edith (about 1180), and Hooton Pagnell (1192). Only a few are not recorded until after 1400, and these include Newton Tracy (1402), Marks Tey (1439, earlier Tey *Mandeville* from the name of the holder in 1086), Barton Blount (1535, earlier Barton *Bagpuize*), Berrick Salome and Holme Pierrepont (1571), Ashton Keynes (1572), and Hampton Lucy (1606, earlier *Bishops* Hampton).

Some of the individuals and families whose names occur as affixes are known to have been associated with the place long before their names were affixed to the place-name. Many are first recorded as holders or tenants in the 12th or 13th century, less frequently so in the 14th. There is, however, a notable group of which an ancestor is named as tenant in Domesday Book. This includes Barrow Gurney, Bolton Percy, Drayton Parslow, Dunham Massey, Hartley Mauditt, Heanton Punchardon, Holme Lacy, Horsted Keynes, Hurstpierpoint, Kingston Bagpuize, Mansell Lacy, Sampford Arundel and Willingale Spain. In a few noteworthy cases, where the affix is a personal name, the individual was connected with the place even earlier, and this is so in Affpuddle (987), Tolpuddle and Wootton Wawen (both about 1050), and Egg Buckland (in the time of Edward the Confessor).

The following is a representative selection of place-names, county by county, whose affixes are composed of family names of French origin:

Bedfordshire: Aspley *Guise*, Higham *Gobion*, Leighton *Buzzard*, Marston *Moretaine*.

Berkshire: Kingston *Bagpuize*, Ufton *Nervet*.

Buckinghamshire: Drayton *Beauchamp*, Drayton *Parslow*, Milton *Keynes*, Newton *Blossomville*, Preston *Bisset*.

Cambridgeshire: Swaffham *Bulbeck*, Weston *Colville*.

Cheshire: Dunham *Massey*, Minshull *Vernon*.

Cumberland: Newton *Reigny*.

Derbyshire: Barton *Blount*, Marston *Montgomery*, Newton *Solney*.

Devonshire: Aveton *Giffard*, Bere *Ferrers*, Bovey *Tracy*, Buckland *Tout Saints*, Cheriton *Fitzpaine*, Comb*pyne*, Heanton *Punchardon*, Newton *Tracy*, Stoke *Rivers*, Sydenham *Damerel*, Upton *Pyne*.

Dorset: Bradford *Peverell*, Chaldon *Herring*, Clifton *Maybank*, Haselbury *Bryan*, Hinton *Martell*, Kingston *Lacy*, Kingston *Russel*, Langton *Matravers*, Okeford *Fitzpaine*.

Durham: Coatham *Mundeville*, Dalton *Piercy*.

Essex: *Marks* Tey, North Weald *Bassett*, Shellow *Bowells*, Stanford *Rivers*, Stansted *Mountfitchet*, Stapleford *Tawney*, Stondon *Massey*, Theydon *Garnon*, Wendon *Lofts*, Willingale *Spain*.

Gloucestershire: Duntisborne *Rouse*, Guiting *Power*, *Meysey* Hampton, Somerford *Keynes*, Stanley *Pontlarge*.

Hampshire: Barton *Peverel*, Barton *Stacey*, Hartley *Mauditt*, Hartley *Westpall*, Hinton *Admiral*, Sherfield *English*, Shipton *Bellinger*, Weston *Corbett*.

Herefordshire: Eaton *Tregose*, Holme *Lacy*, Mansell *Gamage*, Mansell *Lacy*, Ocle *Pychard*, Weston *Beggard*.

Hertfordshire: *Furneux* Pelham.

Huntingdonshire: Hemingford *Grey*, Offord *Darcy*, Orton *Longueville*.

Kent: Boughton *Malherbe*, Boughton *Monchelsea*, Sutton *Valence*.

Lancashire: Heaton *Norris*, Ince *Blundell*.

Leicestershire: Ashby de la *Zouch*, Aston *Flamville*, Croxton *Kerrial*, Goadby *Marwood*, Kirby *Bellars*, Kirkby *Mallory*, Melton *Mowbray*, Newbold *Verdon*.

Lincolnshire: Boothby *Pagnell*, Mavis *Enderby*, Thornton *Curtis*.

Middlesex: none surviving.

Norfolk: Kirby *Cane*, Swanton *Novers*.

Northamptonshire: Easton *Maudit*, Higham *Ferrers*, Marston *Trussell*, Middleton *Cheney*, Stoke *Albany*, Stoke *Doyle*.

Northumberland: Seaton *Delaval*.

Nottinghamshire: Burton *Joyce*, Colston *Basset*, Holme *Pierrepont*.

Oxfordshire: Ascot *d'Oyley*, Kingston *Blount*, Newton *Purcell*, Rotherfield *Peppard*, Sibford *Gower*, Stoke *Talmage*.

Shropshire: Albright *Hussy*, Aston *Botterell*, Berwick *Maviston*, Eaton *Constantine*, Hope *Bowdler*, Leegomery, Neen *Savage*, Stanton *Lacy*.

Somerset: Barrow *Gurney*, Charlton *Mackrell*, Charlton *Musgrove*, Chilton *Cantelo*, Curry *Mallet*, *Goose* Bradon, Hill *Farrance*, Huish *Champflower*, Kingston *Seymour*, Newton *St. Loe*, Norton *Fitzwarren*, Sampford *Arundel*, Shepton *Mallet*, Stocklinch *Ottersay*, Stogursey (earlier Stoke *Courcy*).

Staffordshire: Clifton *Campville*, Drayton *Basset*, Weston *Coyney*.

Suffolk: Bradfield *St. Clare*, Carlton *Colville*, Stowlangtoft, Thorpe *Morieux*.

Surrey: Stoke *d'Abernon*.

Sussex: Horsted *Keynes*, Herst*monceux*, Hurst*pierpoint*.

Warwickshire: Aston *Cantlow*, Hampton *Lucy*, Morton *Bagot*, Radford *Semele*, Stretton *Baskerville*.

Wiltshire: Alton *Barnes*, Ashton *Giffard*, Ashton *Keynes*, Berwick *Bassett*, Easton *Grey*, Littleton *Pannell*, Marston *Maisey*.

Worcestershire: Bentley *Pauncefote*, Chaddesley *Corbett*, Croome *d'Abitot*, Elmley *Lovett*, Hampton *Lovett*.

Yorkshire: Thorpe *Bassett*, Wharram *Percy* (East Riding); Hutton *Bushell*, Newton *Morrell* (North Riding); Acaster *Malbis*, Allerton *Mauleverer*, Bolton *Percy*, Hooton *Pagnell*, Thorpe *Salvin* (West Riding).

Chapter Ten

---- ★ ----

PLACE-NAMES AND ARCHAEOLOGY

MANY of the place-names in use today give interesting information about the earlier history of the place in question. A particular name may have been given because of the existence there of a Bronze Age sanctuary, an Iron Age hill fort, a Roman camp, a barrow, an old road and so on, and it may be that only the name now remains to testify to the archaeological interest of the place itself. Those names derived from Roman and other roads and ways, as well as those associated with paganism, have been discussed elsewhere. Here, we shall consider names denoting prehistoric, Roman, Anglo-Saxon and Scandinavian sites, and containing elements with such meanings as "fortification", "Roman camp", "earthwork" or "barrow".

In some cases archaeological excavation has given definite information of the date and origin of whatever is commemorated by the name, though it does not of course follow that the namers knew them for what they actually were. In other cases, the early forms of a name suggest a derivation for which archaeological evidence is not yet, and may never be, available. The barrow or earthwork concerned may have been levelled by the plough, or its traces covered by later building, though air photography, or a chance discovery on the ground, may at some future date provide definite evidence for an etymology which at present is deduced only from the early forms of the name.

A large and interesting group is that derived from Old English *ceaster, cæster* "old fortification, Roman camp, town or city". Many of them were in fact originally Roman towns or camps, as were Caistor (L, Nf), Castor (Nth), Chesters (Nb) and Little Chester (Db). As a second element the word often has a similar sense, as in those with a first part derived from a Celtic name, and noted elsewhere. A large group, however, has an Old English personal name as first element, presumably that of the Anglo-Saxon chieftain who first took possession of the site—Anna in Ancaster (L), Cēna in Kenchester (He), Cissi in Chichester (Sx), Ebba or Ebbe in Ebchester (Du), Gōdmund in Godmanchester (Hu), Rudda in

Rudchester (Nb), perhaps Tāda in Tadcaster (WRY), and Yra in Irchester (Nth). Others are named from a nearby river, for example Frocester (Gl) "Frome", Ilchester (So) "*Gifl*, the earlier name of the Yeo", Ribchester (La) "Ribble", Towcester (Nth) "Tove", and Alcester (Wa) "Alne", identical with which is Alchester (O), from a lost river-name *Alne*. The first element of Lanchester (Du) means "long" and of Whitchester (Nb) "white", presumably a reference to the stone buildings; in Porchester (Ha) it denotes its situation "near a port or harbour", Silchester (Ha) perhaps "where willows grow" and Woodchester (Gl) "in a wood", the last a Roman villa. There is also a small but interesting group, where it is a bird-name, as in Outchester (Nb) "owls", Craster (Nb) "crows", and Hincaster (We) "hens or wild birds". These presumably refer to deserted camps frequented by the birds in question, though in the case of the last two the precise nature of the fortification is uncertain. Some early forts, whether Roman or prehistoric, were later apparently used as shelters for animals, as for instance the Roman camp at Binchester (Du), a name having a probable first element *binn* "manger or stall", presumably for cattle. In Bewcastle (Cu) "Roman camp with a booth or temporary shelter", a change from *chester* to *castle* took place after a medieval fortress was built inside the old camp. A similar change has taken place in Horncastle (L) "Roman town on a horn-shaped piece of land (between rivers)", and in the first element of Castleford (WRY) "ford near a Roman camp". The first part of Dorchester (O), where there was a small Roman settlement, is of pre-English origin, but its meaning is unknown.

Ceaster occurs as the first element of several names, such as Casterton (R) and the more common Chesterton "farmstead or village near a (Roman) camp", and most of them are situated near to Roman stations. None is, however, known near Cheshunt (Hrt) perhaps "spring", Chesterfield (Db) "open land" or Chesterton (O), but it may be significant that each is on or close to a Roman road. The exact nature of the camp near Chesterford (Ess) is not known, but the ford here carries the ancient track called Icknield Way. There is a prehistoric camp near Chesterblade (So), the second element of which seems to be Old English *blæd* "blade or leaf" used perhaps in some topographical sense.

The Roman name of Bath (So), *Aquæ Sulis*, has been lost, and the modern name goes back to the dative plural of Old English *bæð* "the baths", i.e. those of the Roman spa. Particularly interesting too is Fawler (O) "multi-coloured, i.e. tessellated, pavement", since the remains of a Romano-British house with such a pavement were discovered there in 1865, and the place presumably took its name from this. Fawler (Brk) has the same etymology, but no tessellated pavement has yet been discovered there, though there is some evidence for Romano-British settlement in the district. The second element in both cases is Old English *flōr*, modern *floor*, and this is the source of Floore (Nth), which may have been named for similar reasons, though here again there is no archaeological evidence to confirm it.

Old English *burh* "fortified place" is also used of a former Roman camp or town, as in Brough (Db, ERY, NRY, We), Burgh Castle (Sf), Burgh by Sands (Cu) and Burrow (by Burrow) (La). As the second element of a compound name it is found with the same sense in Aldborough (WRY) "old", the self-explanatory Littleborough (Nt) and Newbrough (Nb), Goldsborough (NRY), with the personal name Golda, and Richborough (K), of which the meaning of the first element is uncertain, but is apparently pre-English. Mawbray (Cu), also the name of a Roman fort, means "maidens' stronghold" and is therefore comparable with Maiden Castle (Do). Here, too, belongs Canterbury (K) "fort of the *Cantware*, i.e. the people of Kent".

Particularly in the south, *burh* seems to have been frequently applied to prehistoric sites of various kinds. Ashbury (Brk), from the personal name *Æsc*, and Blewbury (Brk), perhaps "variegated", referring to the soil or vegetation, are each apparently named from a neighbouring Neolithic long barrow. Avebury (W), perhaps with a personal name Affa, takes its name from a great Bronze Age sanctuary there, and Tisbury (W), with the personal name Tysse refers to a similar, but now destroyed, sanctuary. The greater number of such names, however, denote Iron Age forts, as with the self-explanatory Littlebury (Ess), Oldbury Camp (K) and Oldbury Castle (W), as well as Hembury Fort (D) "at the high stronghold", which has given its name to the modern village of Broadhembury. Sometimes the first element of such names refers to the trees which grew nearby, as in Whitsbury (Ha) "wych-elm", or Wilbury (Hrt) "willow", while a well-marked group of them describes the animals or birds frequenting the deserted fort—Aconbury (He) "squirrel", Musbury (D, La) "mouse", Oxborough (Nf) "oxen", Conkesbury (Db) and Cornbrough (NRY) "crane", Oubrough (ERY) "owl", Owslebury (Ha) "blackbird", Spettisbury (Do) "woodpecker", and Yarnbury Camp or Castle (W) "eagle". Of these Aconbury, Spettisbury and Yarnbury are known to be Iron Age forts.

Many of the names in *burh* which also take their names from similar forts have as first element an Old English personal name, presumably that of one of the early settlers there. In Buckinghamshire there is Cholesbury "Cēolwald"; in Dorset, Dudsbury "Dudd"; in Hampshire, Exbury "Eohhere", and Tidbury Ring "Tuda"; in Somerset, two examples of Cadbury "Cada", and Maesbury Camp perhaps "Mᴂrec"; in Wiltshire, Barbury Castle "Bera", Chisbury "Cissa", and Ebsbury "Ippi"; in Gloucestershire, Chipping Sodbury "Soppa", and Maugersbury "Mᴂðelgār"; and Hunsbury Hill perhaps "Hūn", in Northamptonshire. An occupational name meaning "ploughman" is the first element of Salmonsbury Camp (Gl), from which Bourton on the Water "farmstead or village near a fort" was named, while that in Hallingbury (Ess) is a folk-name meaning "Heall's people", and in Chisenbury Trendle (W) "Cissa's people", as well as Danbury (Ess) perhaps "dwellers in the woodland pasture". Other names derived from Iron Age forts include Fosbury (W) "hill fort", Torberry Hill (Sx) "fort near a tor", Winkelbury Camp (W), originally *Winterbury*, "fort used in winter", and Ringsbury Camp (W), identical with Ringborough (ERY), "circular fort".

In addition *burh* is used of other sites. Glastonbury (So), an Iron Age lake village, has Old English forms in *burh* and *ēg* "island" side by side, and the first element is probably Celtic, for which the meaning "place where woad grows" has been suggested. Budbury (W) "Budda's fort" referred to a stone circle, now destroyed. Scarborough (NRY) "Skarði's fortification" is said in Icelandic sources to have been founded by a certain Þorgils, nicknamed Skarði, but the site had already been previously occupied, probably by a Roman signal station.

During the Anglo-Saxon period fortifications were built, no doubt, during the struggles between the various kingdoms, and later against the Danes, and it is possible that a good many of the names in *burh* originated in these ways, though documentary evidence which shows that this is the case is seldom available. Shoebury (Ess), however, "shelter, i.e. protecting, fort", may date from 894, and Hertingfordbury (Hrt), "fort of the people of Hertford", as has been suggested, was perhaps constructed by Edward the Elder in 912. Burton (near Bakewell, Db), like many of the Burtons and Bourtons, means "farmstead or village near a fort", and that from which it was named was built by the same king already by 921.

We should note, however, that *burh* could also denote a "fortified house or manor", and even "manor", in place-names, and the first of these is probably found in Kingsbury (Hrt, Mx) and Kingsbury

Episcopi (So). This sense is also likely where the first element refers to a cleric, of which examples are noted elsewhere; an official, as in Shermanbury (Sx) "shireman (perhaps sheriff)"; or a lady, as in Queniborough (Lei), apparently named from a "queen", and in Fladbury (Wo) and perhaps Fledborough (Nt), from the feminine personal name Flæde.

In names given after the Norman Conquest the meaning "manor" is probably to be assumed, and such names are found especially in Bedfordshire, Buckinghamshire, Essex, Hertfordshire and Middlesex. The first element of these may be a personal name or family name, which was not used in England until the Middle English period, as with Basset in Bassetsbury (Bk), Blemund in Bloomsbury (Mx), Juvenal in Jenningsbury (Hrt), Marescal in Mascallsbury (Ess), and Sterr in Starborough Castle (Sr). In others *Bury* has been added to an older place-name, as in Edgware Bury (Mx), Feeringbury (Ess), Melbourn Bury (C), Nazeingbury (Ess), and Orwell Bury (Hrt).

Although we can sometimes indicate the precise sense of *burh* in a particular place-name by archaeological, documentary or other evidence, it is impossible to do so for most of the names containing this element, as scholars have long recognized. In these cases, therefore, it is safest to translate the word as "fortified place" or "fortification", whether the first element is a personal name, or an adjective or noun. The first of these groups is large and includes Aylesbury (Bk) "Ægel", Banbury (O) "Banna", Desborough (Nth) "Dēor", Eynesbury (Hu) "Ēanwulf", Gainsborough (L) "Gegn", Hartlebury (Wo) "Heortla", Mexborough (WRY) "Mēoc", Padbury (Bk) "Padda", Penbury (Gl) "Penda" and Rothbury (Nb) "Hrōða". To the second belong those named from the cardinal points of the compass—Norbury (at least 5 counties) and Northborough (Nth), Sudbury (Db, Mx, Sf) and Sudborough (Nth), Astbury (Ch) and Eastbury (Brk), and Westbury (at least 6 counties) as well as Westborough (L). Nobury (Wo) means "new fortification", and Turnberry (Cu) "circular fort". Lathbury (Bk) was apparently made of "laths", and Stanbury (WRY) of "stone", while Clarborough (Nt) was overgrown with "clover", and Somersbury (Sr) used only in "summer". Limbury (Bd) is "fortification on the River Lea", and Pendlebury (La) "fort on *Pendle*", the latter an older hill-name, perhaps identical with Pendle Hill in the same county. Mixbury (O) means literally "dunghill fort", possibly because an old encampment was used as a place for collecting manure. Medbury (Bd), however, may be a further example of a "maidens' fort", and would therefore be identical in meaning with

Mawbray (Cu), but no traces of an encampment can be seen there today. The Old English compound *eorðburh* "earth-work" usually refers in place-names to a prehistoric camp or site. Arbury Camp (C), for example, is an earthwork of uncertain, but probably of prehistoric, date, while Harborough Banks (Wa) is a pre-Roman camp, as are Arbury Hill Camp (Nth) and Yarborough Camp (L). At Arbury (La, Wa) no traces seem to remain of the earthworks from which the places took their names, but Arbor Low (Db) "earthwork hill" was a Bronze Age sanctuary. It is not always easy, even in early forms, to distinguish this word from *herebeorg* "army shelter", but the latter is apparently the source of Arbury Banks (Hrt), an Iron Age hill fort. Later *herebeorg* developed the sense "lodging", the usual meaning of Harbour in place-names. It is found especially in the compound Cold Harbour "cold (fireless) shelter", a name found in most counties, but which is particularly common in Kent and Sussex. It has been recorded as early as the 14th century, though found most frequently in 16th- and 17th-century sources. Another compound of *here*, *herewīc* "army camp", is the source of Harwich (Ess), perhaps originally, as has been suggested, a Danish camp.

Aldwark (Db, NRY, WRY) and Newark (Nt, Nth), "old" and "new fortification" respectively, have as second element Old English *(ge)weorc*, and so has Southwark (Sr), of which the earliest forms mean "fortification of the people of Surrey". But already by 1023 the first element had been changed to *South-*, from its situation in relation to Old London Bridge. The same word occurs, too, in the simplex name Wark (Nb), and in Workway Drove (W) "way by the fortification", named from a Neolithic enclosure. The corresponding Scandinavian *verk* is found only in Foremark (Db) "old fortification", a name equivalent to the English Aldwark. Near the village are raised earth formations, which have not yet been properly excavated, but no doubt form the "fortification" from which the place is named.

The most famous of all our prehistoric sites, Stonehenge (W), probably means "stone gallows", and it may well be that the stones were thought to resemble a series of gallows. On the other hand, Woodhenge (W) is a modern name given by 20th-century archaeologists in jocular imitation of Stonehenge.

A considerable number of prehistoric sites are now called *Castle*, and these names are almost invariably late. The best known is probably Maiden Castle (Do); but Maiden Castle is found also in Cheshire, Cumberland and Westmorland, and a comparable one is

Maiden Bower (Bd), all alike being Iron Age forts. Maiden Castle is equivalent in meaning with both Mawbray (Cu) and Medbury (Bd), and, though the exact sense of *maiden* is doubtful here, it may in fact mean "impregnable" or denote a place which, like a maiden, was "inviolate". In some cases, of course, the name Maiden Castle could be a borrowing from the Dorset one. Castle Hill is also common for such sites, but more often *castle* has been added to a village name. Bratton Castle (W), Chun Castle (Co), Desborough Castle (Bk), Letcombe Castle (Brk) are all names of Iron Age forts; Rowland's Castle (Brk) is a Belgic enclosure, Hardknot Castle (Cu), a Roman fort, Robert's Castle (Ess), a Danish or Saxon camp, while such names as Bats Castle (So) and Rat's Castle (K) are comparable with similar ones containing terms for birds or animals.

House is occasionally used of barrows—Hob Hurst's House (Db) is a round barrow and Kit's Coty House (K), a Megalithic barrow. *Church*, too, is sometimes used of similar sites; Sunkenchurch is found in several counties, and the comparable Sunkenkirk (near Millom Cu) refers to a stone circle. Another type of place-name almost invariably of archaeological interest is that containing the word *Devil*. Devil's Den (W) is a Megalithic long barrow, as is also The Devil's Bed and Bolster (So). The Devil's Quoits (O) is a Bronze Age sanctuary, The Devil's Chapel (Gl) is the name of Roman iron-workings and The Devil's Arrows (WRY) are standing stones. Devil's Ditch is very common, found for example in Berkshire, Essex, Hampshire and Sussex, each being a linear earthwork, while Devils Dyke (Hrt) is a Belgic frontier ditch and The Devil's Dyke (C), an Anglo-Saxon earthwork. *Ditch* and *Dyke* are, as we should expect, often used of linear and other earthworks, as in Black Ditch (Brk), Danes Dyke (ERY), Grey Ditch (Db), Thieves Dikes (NRY), as well as Offa's Dyke, which marks the old boundary between England and Wales.

Old English *stān* is sometimes used in place-names of a building of stone, presumably indicating that a stone-built dwelling was unusual in Anglo-Saxon times. Occasionally it denotes Roman buildings— Stanchester (Ha) is named from a Roman house; several such villas are known in the parish of Stansted Mountfitchet (Ess), while Stanstead Abbots (Hrt) may also refer to a similar villa. Stanste(a)d means literally "stone place or site". Stanton is usually "stone farmstead" or "farmstead on stony ground", but in one or two cases the name may have archaeological significance. This is certainly likely with Stanton Drew (So), for immediately to the east of the village is a group of megalithic monuments, and with Stanton

116

Harcourt (O), which is apparently named from The Devil's Quoits. The compound *feoðerstān*, literally "four stones", i.e. tetralith, three upright stones with a head stone, is the source of Featherstone (Nb, St, WRY), while *scylfestān*, which seems to have meant "cromlech", has given Shilstone (in Drewssteignton D), from the cromlech now called Spinster's Rock. At least six other examples of Shilston(e) occur in Devonshire, each probably with the same etymology, though no such stones are to be found near them today.

The names of stone circles are equally interesting. Among later ones are The Bridestones (NRY), Druids Circle (WRY), Grey Wethers (D), Nine Ladies (Db), Nine Maidens (Co), Stripple Stones (Co), Twelve Apostles (Co), and Long Meg and her Daughters (Cu), this last a Megalithic circle with Long Meg as an outlier. Old English *trendel* "circle" is certainly used sometimes of archaeological sites, as in Rowtrundle (D), a prehistoric hut circle, The Trundle (Sx), a Neolithic earthwork, later an Iron Age fort, and Chisenbury Trendle (W).

The sites of ancient camps were sometimes used as enclosures for horses, and Old English *stodfald*, modern *studfold*, "horse enclosure", is the source of Stotfold (Bd), a Belgic cemetery, while Stutfall Castle (K) refers to the Roman fort *Lemanis*, which gave its name to Lympne.

Place-names derived from Old English *hlāw* and *beorg* and Scandinavian *haugr*, with a personal name as first element, have been dealt with elsewhere, but there are examples of these words compounded with other elements, also referring to barrows. Henlow (Bd) "wild birds' mound" is a barrow of unknown date, and Bartlow (C), originally "birch-tree mound", was named from Romano-British barrows. Even more numerous are names from *beorg*, which refer to tumuli, Barrow Field and Barrow Hill being common in some counties. Other examples include the simplex Burgh (in Banstead Sr), Plumberow Mount (Ess) "plum-tree", Stoborough (Do) "stone", and Ruberry (K) "rough", while Pimperne Long Barrow (Do), as the name suggests, is a Neolithic long barrow, and was formerly the name of a hundred; Silbury (W), with a first element of doubtful meaning, is the largest archaeological mound in Europe, and Swanborough Tump (W) "peasants' mound" is named from a round barrow. *Tump* is a dialect word meaning "hillock, tumulus", occurring also in Hetty Pegler's Tump (Gl), the name of a long barrow. Scandinavian *haugr* can also be shown to denote a barrow in place-names such as the North Riding Three Howes, Flat Howe and Loose Howe. The first element of this last may be Old English *lūs* or Old Norse *lús* "louse", which is thought to be used in place-names to describe something small. Hoon (Db) is derived from the dative plural of *haugr* and means "at the barrows", taking its name from several nearby tumuli.

Other words, such as Old English *cest* and *līc*, indicate places where a coffin or a body was at some time discovered. The first of these, meaning "chest, coffin", is the source of Chessell Down (Wt) "hill", where there is an Anglo-Saxon cemetery, and perhaps also of Chestham Park (Sx). *Līc* "body, corpse" occurs in all probability in Litchborough (Nth) and Litchardon (D) "corpses' hill", though in neither case is the suggested etymology confirmed by archaeology.

Old English *hord* "treasure" in some names probably refers to places where treasure has been found, or was thought to be buried. There is, for example, an ancient earthwork at Hordle (Ha) "treasure hill", while Hurdlow (Db) "treasure mound" is situated in an area rich in tumuli. A similar interpretation is likely for such names as Gollard (Ha), Goldsworth (in Woking Sr), and the field-names Goldhord and Goldhoard, occurring in many counties, all from *gold-hord* "gold hoard, gold treasure", and also for Mathon (Wo/He) from *maððum* "treasure". Another important element for the archaeologist, as Mr. G. J. Copley has pointed out, is Old English *crocc* "crock, earthenware pot", from which Crock Field (in Newington K) was named. This is on the site of a Romano-British cemetery, and was no doubt named from the vessels which are reported to have been found there.

These examples will show how archaeology can sometimes make it possible to indicate an etymology for a place-name, or to give a more precise meaning to one already known. In the future, the use of air-photography, and more intensive field research may help to explain other names whose interpretation is at present doubtful. On the other hand, the etymological meaning of a place-name may well provide a clue for the archaeologist and suggest to him a promising location for investigation.

Chapter Eleven

———— ★ ————

PLACE-NAMES WITH PAGAN,
MYTHOLOGICAL AND POPULAR ASSOCIATIONS

THE different Anglo-Saxon kingdoms remained pagan for varying periods of time. There is no evidence that the Britons ever
attempted to convert their enemies to Christianity, or that Irish
missionaries were at work in England before the arrival of Augustine
in Kent in 597. The conversion went forward gradually, with
occasional set-backs, throughout the 7th century, but it must be
remembered that the only dates we know are those marking the
acceptance of Christianity by the rulers of the various kingdoms. In
theory, no doubt, the king took his people with him into the fold,
but, in practice, it is likely that the mass baptisms, of which we sometimes hear, were largely nominal, and that the old pagan gods
lingered long, especially in isolated and out-of-the-way districts, and
as late as 700 there were still pagan communities in England. By
this time, however, such relics of paganism are likely to have been
slight and unimportant, and place-names commemorating the older
religion must belong to a much earlier period. As Sir Frank Stenton
has pointed out, where the name of a centre of such worship has
survived, that name must already have been firmly established if it
could remain unchanged despite the victory of Christianity.

Heathen place-names are found in most of those areas in which
Anglo-Saxon settlement is known to have been early, and the clear
picture we have of them is largely due to the work of Sir Frank
Stenton. The most striking feature of the geographical distribution
of such names is their extreme scarcity in Northumbria. As we
should expect, few are found in the most westerly counties, along
the Welsh border, or in Dorset, Devon or Somerset, and they are
rare also in the East Midlands, Lincolnshire and East Anglia.

Place-names connected with the old pagan religion are of three
types. First, there are those names which merely indicate the
former existence of a heathen temple or shrine. Secondly, there are

119

the cult-centres, places dedicated to a particular heathen god. Thirdly, there are the names which suggest the former existence of some kind of sacrificial rite. But in considering the evidence of such names, we should remember that no Anglo-Saxon heathen temple has yet been identified and excavated, and that reference to paganism in Anglo-Saxon literary sources provides a very incomplete picture.

Three Old English words for "heathen temple", "idol", "holy place", *alh*, *hærg*, and *wīg* or *wēoh*, occur in place-names. The first of these is rare, surviving only in Alkham (K) "homestead with a heathen temple". Old English *hærg* is more frequent and appears as the first element in Arrowfield Top (Wo) "meadow, open land", Harrowden (Bd, Nth) "hill", Harrowbank House (Du) "slope" and Harrowick (Bd) "farm". Harrow on the Hill (Mx) is recorded in 767 as *Gumeninga hergae* "heathen temple of the Gumeningas (Guma's people)", and the shrine at Harrow must presumably have belonged to them or been particularly associated with them in some way. This word appears, too, in Peper Harrow (Sr) "Pippera's heathen temple". Scandinavian records show that such temples were sometimes privately owned, their founder and his heirs drawing revenues from them, and a name like Peper Harrow suggests that such a custom was not unknown in this country, even though the evidence for it is slight.

The last of these words is the one most frequently found in place-names—*wīg* "idol, heathen temple". The simplex form is found in Wye (K), Weyhill (Ha), with the later addition of -hill, and Wyham (L), an old dative plural, "at the heathen temples". More commonly, however, it appears as the first element of a compound name, as in Weedon (Bk), Weedon Beck and Weedon Lois (Nth) "hill", Weeford (St) "ford", Weoley Castle (Wo), Wheely Down (Ha), Whiligh and Whyly (Sx), Willey House (Sr) "wood or glade", Wyville (L) "spring or stream", and perhaps Wyfold (O) "fold". It has also survived as the second element of Patchway (in Falmer Sx) "Pæccel's heathen temple", a name comparable with Peper Harrow.

The second group of names consists of those indicating sites dedicated to the pagan gods. Old English *ēs* or *ōs* "heathen god", the latter the first element of the personal name Ōswald, may occur in two place-names, Easole (K) "embankment, ridge", Eisey (W) "island", and in the name of a hundred, Easewrithe (Sx) "thicket", which would have been places "dedicated to the heathen gods".

Other place-names indicate the cult-centres of some particular god or goddess. Frīg, the consort of the god Woden, who has given her name to Friday, is probably found in Fretherne (Gl) "thorn-bush", and Froyle (Ha) "hill", while Frobury (Ha) may originally have been identical with Froyle, but *burh* "fortification" has later been added to it.

Thunor, the god of thunder, corresponding to the Scandinavian Thor, has given his name to Thursday. He also appears in such place-names as Thunderfield (Sr) "open land", Thundridge (Hrt) "ridge", the hundred-name Thurstable (Ess) "pillar or post", as well as Thunderley (Ess), Thundersley (Ess) and Thursley (Sr) "grove sacred to Thunor". All these are in the South of England, and place-names compounded with Thunor appear to be absent from the North and Midlands, which would suggest he was essentially a Saxon or Jutish god.

The name of the war-god *Tig, Tiw*, preserved in Tuesday, also occurs in a few place-names—Tuesley (Sr) "grove", Tuesnoad (K) "piece of woodland", Tysoe (Wa) "hill-spur", and perhaps Tewin (Hrt). This last may be a folk-name meaning "worshippers of Tīw", a group of people who regarded him as their own particular god.

Woden, the English equivalent of the Scandinavian Othin, is the god from whom most of the Anglo-Saxon dynasties traced their descent. His name has given us Wednesday, as well as several place-names in the Midlands and South, but none in the North. So, we have Wednesbury (St) "fortification" and Wednesfield (St) "open land", only five miles apart, Woodnesborough (K) and Wormshill (K) both "hill", and the hundred-name Wenslow (Bd) "hill or barrow", as well as Woden's Barrow or Adam's Grave (W), a Neolithic long barrow. To these can be added Wansdyke, the name of the great British defensive work in Hampshire, Wiltshire and Somerset. Indeed, Woden's importance is clearly established by the fact that, from an early date, earthworks and dykes were attributed to him. Moreover, he is the only one of the Anglo-Saxon gods to whom a nickname was given, since it is probable that, like Othin in Scandinavia, Woden was also called Grīm. This is from a word meaning "mask, disguise" and, as used of the god, probably refers to his habit of appearing in disguise. Grim's Dike (Ha, WRY) and Grim's Ditch (Bk, Ha, O, W) are therefore comparable to Wansdyke, and there is also Grim's Bank (Brk), the name of a linear earthwork, and Grimsbury (O) "fortification attributed to Grīm, i.e. Woden".

The names so far discussed are situated, with very few exceptions, within the area included by a line from Ipswich to Stafford and from Stafford to Weymouth, as Stenton points out. What precise conclusions are to be drawn from this is at present uncertain, but at least it shows that paganism was very strong in the central Midlands and in the central South and South-east.

Other place-names, however, perhaps throw light on certain heathen practices. There is, for example, a small group which has, as first element, an animal-name in the genitive singular with Old English *hēafod* "head" as second element. In place-names *head* often refers to a headland, a promontory or even a hill, as well as to the source of a river, and such names as Hartshead (La, WRY) and Rampside (La) are either from headlands or hills, which were considered to resemble a "hart" and a "ram" respectively, or from places frequented by these animals. But others are hardly to be explained on topographical grounds, and the late Dr. H. Bradley and Professor Bruce Dickins have suggested that in some cases *head* may mean "animal's head". Such names would then have been given to sites where pagan sacrifice of animals took place and where the head of the animal was set on a pole. Animal sacrifice, and also human sacrifice, is in fact known both from the Continent and from Scandinavia, but there is no comparable evidence in English sources. None the less, human sacrifice may well be indicated by the hundred-name Manshead (Bd), and animal sacrifice by the place-names Broxted (Ess), Broxhead (Ha) "badger", Eversheds (Sr) "wild boar", Farcet (Hu) "bull", Shepshed (Lei) "sheep", Swineshead (Bd), Swinesherd (Wo) "swine", and Gateshead (Du), which Bede translates as "(at) the head of the goat".

The burial of the dead, whether cremated or not, in a mound or cemetery accompanied by objects of various kinds, from weapons and jewellery to domestic articles, was also a pagan custom. The practice of cremation had already died out during the pagan period, and, with the conversion to Christianity, the custom of burying objects with the dead also gradually came to an end. Several place-names illustrating the pagan custom have as second element Old English *hlāw*, meaning either "mound" or "hill". In some cases it is difficult to be certain of the exact sense, but in others the meaning "burial-mound, tumulus" is confirmed by the presence of a burial-mound, which has been excavated and dated to the Anglo-Saxon period. A small group of these names has an Old English personal name as first element, and in such cases it seems likely that the tumulus takes its name from the man who was buried there. Several remarkable objects, now preserved in the British Museum, were found in a large tumulus at Taplow (Bk) "Tæppa's burial-mound". Similarly, Cuckamsley (Brk) must have been named "Cwichelm's burial-mound" because a certain Cwichelm was buried there, who is perhaps to be identified with a king of Wessex of that name who died in 593. There can be little doubt that such names belong to the pagan period.

In some counties, for example Dorset and the Isle of Wight, the word *hlāw* is not found, while in others, such as Lincolnshire, Norfolk and Suffolk, it is rare. It is, however, particularly common in Derbyshire, where at least 30 out of over 70 names in -low can so far be shown to denote burial-mounds. A personal name is the first element of 11 of the 30—including Bassa in Baslow, Eatta in Atlow, Hucca in Hucklow, and Tīdi in Tideslow. In other counties only occasional examples have been noted, but the following *may* illustrate the pagan custom of burying the dead in a tumulus—Bledlow (Bk) "Bledda", Cutslow (O) "Cūðen", Hounslow (Mx) "Hund", Longslow (Sa) "Wlanc" and Winterslow (W) "Winter".

Traces of Scandinavian heathenism in English place-names are very slight. Most of the Scandinavians who settled in England during the last quarter of the 9th century were certainly pagan. Although they sacked monasteries in their early raids, Lindisfarne in 793 and Jarrow in 794, their own religion appears to have had little hold on them. *The Anglo-Saxon Chronicle* in the annal for 878 describes how the Danish king Guthrum and his leading followers accepted baptism as part of the terms of peace with Alfred, but there is little evidence of the methods by which the mass of them were converted to Christianity. Nor do we know how long they remained heathen. Few place-names survive to show the sites of Scandinavian pagan temples, but Hoff (We) and Ellough (Sf), both meaning "heathen temple", seem fairly certain examples. The latter of these appears also as first element of Elloughton (ERY) "hill with a heathen temple". Here, too, may belong some of the names derived from *lundr* since this word means "sacred grove" as well as "grove".

The only name of a Scandinavian heathen god, which appears in a modern place-name, is Othin, in Roseberry Topping (NRY), earlier *Othenesberg* "hill dedicated to Othin". The village in which Roseberry is situated was apparently often called *Newton under Oseberry* and the initial R of the modern name comes from the preceding preposition. The second part of the name Topping is merely "hill top".

Most of the English names so far considered were formed during the pagan period. Other names, however, reflect a popular mythology, a belief in the supernatural world of dragons, elves, goblins, demons, giants, dwarfs and monsters. Such creations of the popular imagination lived on long after the introduction of Christianity, and traces of these beliefs still exist today.

In Germanic mythology the dragon is represented as guarding the treasure in the burial-mound, and the theme of a fight against such a dragon dominates the final section of the Old English poem *Beowulf*. According to another Old English poem: "The dragon must be in the mound, the aged one exultant over the treasures". "Dragon's mound" is in fact the meaning of Drakelow (Db, Wo) and Dragley (Beck) (La), while Drake North (in Damerham W) first recorded as *Drakenhorde* in 940–6, means "dragon's treasure", i.e. treasure thought to be guarded by a dragon. The first element of these names, Old English *draca*, modern *drake*, is found also in Drakedale (NRY) "dragon's valley" and Drakenage (Wa) "dragon's edge".

Old English *wyrm*, modern *worm*, means "reptile, snake" and also "dragon", and the latter is the likely meaning in Wormwood Hill (C), formerly *Wormlow*, the name of a tumulus, and so comparable to Drakelow. Elsewhere, however, it is impossible to decide between the various senses of this word.

Giants are particularly associated in place-names with valleys, and Indescombe (D) and Thursden (La) both mean "giant valley", though their etymologies are different. The first element of Thursden survives in Lancashire dialect as *thurse*, and this word is found also in Thirlspot (Cu) "giant's pot or deep hole" and perhaps in Tusmore (O) "giant's pool". *Dwarf* occurs occasionally as in Dwariden (WRY) "valley" and Dwerryhouse (La) "house", but *elf* is fairly frequent in minor names, in association with a hill in Eldon Hill (Db), and with valleys in Alden (La) and Elveden (Sf).

Most supernatural beings of this kind were evil. Old English *scucca* "demon, evil-spirit" is the first element of Shobrooke (D) and Shocklach (Ch) "stream", Shugborough (St) "fortification", Shuckburgh (Wa) and Shucknall (He) both "hill", and Shuckton (Db) "farmstead". The word which survives as dialect *scratch* "devil" is found in Scratchbury Hill (W), a Neolithic camp which was presumably associated with the devil.

Old English words meaning "spectre, ghost" may occur in Grimley (Wo) "wood, glade", Grimshaw (La) "copse", and Shincliffe (Du) "steep slope". The earlier name of Skinburness (Cu), *Skinburgh*, means "fortified place haunted by a demon or spectre", and to this, *ness* "headland" was added later.

Various terms for "goblins" are also used in local names. *Bug* "bogey, boggart" is probably the first element in Bugley (W) "wood, glade"; *hob*, as in *hob*goblin, occurs in Hob Hill (Db) and Hobmoor (ERY) and is especially common in minor names in both Derbyshire and North Yorkshire; and *puck, pook*, as in *Puck of Pook's Hill*, is equally common, particularly in the South, as in Pockford (Sr) "ford", Puckeridge (Hrt) "stream", Puckwell (Wt) "spring" and Purbrook (Ha) "brook".

Finally, though modern *witch* does not seem to occur in old place-names, Old English *hætse*, a word with the same meaning, is found in Hascombe (Sr) and Hescombe (So) "valley", and perhaps also, with reference to a valley, in Hassop (Db) and to a ford in Hessenford (Co).

Note: Dr. Margaret Gelling has twice recently re-examined the group of names discussed in this chapter. She has shown that Whyly is as likely to be identical in etymology with Weeley (Ess) "willow wood or glade", as to have *wig* as first element. She rightly considers the evidence of the early spellings, so far available, to be inconclusive or worse for Alkham, Arrowfield Top, Harrowbank, Harrowick, Thundridge, Tuesnoad, Wormshill, as well as for those thought to be derived from Old English *ēs* and from the name of the goddess *Frīg*. We must, therefore, delete them all from the corpus of likely pagan names. She would, further, interpret Peper Harrow as "the heathen temple of the pipers", commenting that the use of musical instruments in pagan worship seems a reasonable hypothesis. She has also argued forcefully against interpreting any of the animal-head names as reflecting pagan sacrifice, and is without doubt right in advising extreme caution. But *if*, for instance, Manshead cannot be explained on topographical grounds, it is difficult to see how a place-name meaning "the head of a man" is to be interpreted, unless it reflects a pagan custom.

For her discussions, see Margaret Gelling, "Place-Names and Anglo-Saxon Paganism", in *University of Birmingham Historical Journal*, vol. viii, 1961, and "Further Thoughts on Pagan Place-Names", reprinted in *Place-Name Evidence for the Anglo-Saxon Invasion and Scandinavian Settlements*, E. P. N. S., 1975.

Chapter Twelve

------------ ★ ------------

PLACE-NAMES
WITH CHRISTIAN ASSOCIATIONS

GODSTOW (O) "place of God" is the only place-name which without doubt refers to God, and is so-named from the 12th-century abbey of Benedictine nuns there. Old English *god*, however, was used also of a heathen god and in Gadshill (K) and Godshill (Wt) it is difficult to decide between the two senses.

The first element is the name of Our Lord in Christchurch (Ha) "church dedicated to Christ", where there was an Augustinian priory, Chrishall (Ess) "Christ's nook" and Cressage (Sa) "Christ's oak". The first may have been land belonging to the church, but Cressage was perhaps a place where early Christians met for worship before a church had been built. A similar interpretation is likely for Christow (D) "Christian place", no doubt a place with some special, but now unknown, Christian association.

It will have been noticed that two of these names have a second element in -stow, a word which in Old English had the meanings "place, place of assembly, holy place". Its use in hundred-names in the second of these senses has already been dealt with, but the exact meaning in other names is not always so easily distinguished. Halstow (K), however, is "holy place" and the Devonshire Cheristow and Churchstow both mean literally "church place" i.e. place with a church. Occasionally the evidence suggests some such sense as "hermitage" for the word, as in Plemstall (Ch), where the first element is the personal name Plegmund, and an Archbishop of Canterbury of that name (890–914) is said to have lived here as a hermit. Hibaldstow (L) "Hygebald's place" takes its name from the burial there of St. Hygebald, so that the word may have the particular sense "burial-place". On the other hand, a meaning "monastery" is indicated in St. Mary Stow (L), where there was an abbey of Benedictine monks.

But the most common distinctively Christian use of *stow* in place-names is with a saint's name as first element and indicating the

126

existence there of a church dedicated to that particular saint. Edwinstowe (Nt) takes its name from Edwin, king of Northumbria (killed in 632), Felixstowe (Sf) from St. Felix who was responsible for the conversion of East Anglia, and Wistanstow (Sa) from St. Wigstan. Such names are particularly common in Herefordshire, Devonshire and Cornwall, perhaps significantly, all counties which were settled comparatively late by the Anglo-Saxons. In the first there is Bridstow (identical with Bridestowe D) "St. Bridget", Marstow "St. Martin" and Peterstow "St. Peter"; in Devon, Jacobstowe (also Jacobstow Co) "St. Jacob (James)" and Petrockstow (identical with Padstow Co) "St. Petroc"; and in Cornwall, Michaelstow (also Ess) "St. Michael", Morwenstow "St. Morwenna" and Warbstow "St. Werburg".

Old English *stoc* "place" seems to have been used in similar senses and it probably had the specialized meaning "holy place" in Stoke by Nayland (Sf), where there was an Anglo-Saxon monastery, and in Tavistock (D), named from the River Tavy, where there was also an abbey of early foundation.

The usual word for a monastery in Old English is *mynster*, which also means "large church". This is the source of the Kentish Minster (in Sheppey) and Minster (in Thanet), where there were nunneries in Anglo-Saxon times, as well as Minster Lovell (O). Whether there was a monastery here before the Norman Conquest is unknown, but at any rate there must have been a large church, as the name itself indicates. The Lovell, however, commemorates Maud, wife of William *Luvel*, who founded a priory here in the 13th century. Axminster and Exminster in Devon are named from monasteries on the rivers Axe and Exe; Kidderminster (Wo) is "Cydela's monastery", Newminster (Nb) "new monastery", probably founded in 1138, and Westminster (Mx), named from its situation west of London. But, where there is no certain record of the former existence of a monastery of early foundation, it is safest to assume for *mynster* the alternative meaning "church" or "large church", as in a group presumably named from the founder or an early owner—Bēda in Bedminster (So), Bucca in Buckminster (Lei), Ēata in Yetminster (Do), Pippa in Pitminster (So). This is the case also with Charminster (Do), Ilminster (So), Sturminster (Do) and Warminster (W), named from the rivers Cerne, Isle, Stour and Were respectively, as well as the Essex Southminster "south" and Upminster "higher".

The usual English place-name element for "church" is the word *church* itself. This is found in Church (La), and as the first element of a large group, including Cheriton (D, Ha, K, So), Cherrington (Wa),

Chirton (W), Churston Ferrers (D) and Churton (Ch), meaning "village with a church" or "village belonging to a church". As a second element, the first is frequently the name of the founder or of an early owner—Achurch (Nth) "Ása (feminine) or Ási", Alvechurch (Wo) "Ælfgȳð, a lady", Bonchurch (Wt) "Buna", Dunchurch (Wa) "Dunn", Hawkchurch (D) "Hafoc" and Lillechurch (K) "Lilla". A further group has the name of the saint to whom the church was dedicated—Dewchurch "Dewi, i.e. St. David", Kenderchurch "St. Cynidr" and Peterchurch "St. Peter", in Herefordshire. The church was presumably built near a "fen" in Fenchurch (Mx), while the reference in Hanchurch (St) is to its "high" situation. The building itself was of "variegated colours" at Vowchurch (He) and Frome Vauchurch (Do); Whitchurch, a common name, was "white", either from the colour of the stone, or because it was built of stone rather than the commoner wood, which had been used at Woodchurch (Ch, K). Berechurch (Ess) was "made of boards", while Stokenchurch (Bk) was "made of logs", and must therefore have been of the same type of Anglo-Saxon church as that which still partly survives at Greensted juxta Ongar (Ess).

The Scandinavian *kirk* is almost universal in the North and North Midlands in place of the corresponding English *church*. In names like Kirkstall (WRY) and Kirkstead (L) "site of a church", as well as Kirkham (ERY) "homestead with or belonging to a church" and Kirton (L, Nt, Sf) "village with or belonging to a church", where the second element is an English word, *kirk* may well have replaced an original English *church*. But it is compounded with Scandinavian *bȳ* "farm, village" in about 40 cases, according to Professor Hugh Smith, surviving as Kirby and Kirkby and meaning "village with a church". As a second element, the first occasionally denotes the name of the founder or early owner, as in Algarkirk (L) "Alger" and Ormskirk (La) "Orm", but more frequently it is the name of the saint to whom it is dedicated, hence Chadkirk (Ch) "St. Chad", Felixkirk (NRY) "St. Felix" and Romaldkirk (NRY) "St. Rumwald". In Cumberland the order of the elements is often reversed, giving examples of inversion compounds, formed on the pattern of Celtic names. This is the case with Kirkandrews from St. Andrew, Kirkbride (as compared with Bridekirk in the same county) from St. Bride, and Kirksanton from St. Sanctan, a name which has a parallel in Kirk Santon in the Isle of Man.

Both *Church* and *Kirk* have also been added to village names to distinguish them from others of the same name, as with Church Brampton (Nth), Church Enstone (O), Church Lawford (Wa) and

Kirkharle (Nb), Kirkheaton (WRY) and Kirk Langley (Db). Particularly noteworthy is Stowe Nine Churches (Nth), so-named since the lord of the manor of Stowe had the right of presentation to nine churches.

Some places have been named from the saint to whom the church was dedicated without the addition of a word meaning "church". Occasionally the form of the saint's name is in the genitive, as in St. Albans (Hrt), St. Annes (La) and St. Helens (La, Wt). Some are from the names of lesser known saints, especially those of Welsh or Cornish origin, as in the following examples, all, except the last, in Cornwall—St. Austell "Austol", St. Breock "Brioc", St. Clether "Cleder", St. Devereux "Dyfrig", St. Ives "Ia" and St. Weonards (He) "Gwennarth". Indeed, some of the saints are so obscure, that all that is apparently known of them is that they are commemorated in modern place-names. This is the case with the Cornish St. Breward, St. Cleer, St. Endellion, St. Eval, St. Mewan and St. Wenn. In the same county, too, there is a large group consisting simply of the saint-name without an initial St., so Cornelly "St. Cornelius", Illogan "St. Illogan", Mawgan "St. Maugan", Phillack "St. Felicitas", and Zennor "St. Senara". Mevagissey contains the names of two saints "St. Mew (and) St. Ida", while Perranzabuloe means "St. Peran in the sand", for the first element is the saint-name Peran and -zabuloe is the modern form of a medieval Latin addition *in sabulo* "in the sand"; it has in fact been buried at least once in the past. Occasionally the saint-name, used alone, is found outside Cornwall, as for example Botolphs (Sx) "St. Botolph", Clodock (He) "St. Clydog", Ippollitts (Hrt) "St. Hippolytus", and Sellack (He) "St. Suluc".

The patron saint of France has given his name to St. Denys (Ha), while St. Giles, the French form of the Latin St. Egidius, has given St. Giles on the Heath (D). A few places are named from Anglo-Saxon saints: St. Bees (Cu) from Bega, a virgin saint mentioned by Bede; St. Neot (Co) and St. Neots (Hu), from Neot, said to have been buried at Eynesbury and translated to St. Neots nearby in the late 10th century; and St. Osyth (Ess) from the daughter of an under-king of Surrey, who founded a nunnery here.

The name of the saint to whom the church is dedicated has sometimes been prefixed to an older village name, as in Germansweek (D), St. Mary Cray and St. Paul's Cray (K), but usually it is added as in Ayot St. Lawrence and Ayot St. Peter (Hrt), Chalfont St. Giles and Chalfont St. Peter (Bk) and Deeping St. James and Deeping St. Nicholas (L). The form of Papworth St. Agnes (C), however, is misleading, and must be due to popular etymology, for Agnes is the name of a 12th-century holder of the manor of Papworth and not derived from St. Agnes. On the other hand, St. has been lost in Alton Pancras (Do), Stoke Gabriel (D) and Margaret Roding (Ess), since the affixes are from the dedication of the respective churches to St. Pancras, St. Gabriel and St. Margaret.

The French loan-word *chapel* occurs in a few place-names such as Chapel en le Frith (Db) "chapel in the (Peak) Forest", Chapel St. Leonards (L) from its dedication, and Whitechapel (Mx), which can be compared with Whitchurch, already noted. The Northern French form *capel* is found in Capel (K, Sr) and Capel St. Andrew and Capel St. Mary (Sf). Like *church*, *chapel* was sometimes added to older village names, as in Chapel Ascote (Wa), Chapel Brampton (Nth) and Chapel Chorlton (St.).

Where *temple* appears in place-names it usually denotes a place which belonged to the Knights Templars or where they held property, as in the single simplex name Temple (Co), where they had a house, and in Templeton (Brk, D) "manor belonging to the Templars". It has also been prefixed to a village name in Temple Bruer (L), Temple Cowley (O) and Temple Dinsley (Hrt), where the Templars had houses, Temple Normanton (Db) and Temple Sowerby (We), where they held estates, as well as Temple Grafton (Wa). The Templars, however, are not known to have had any associations with Grafton. But most interesting of all is Baldock (Hrt), a place founded by the Templars in the 12th century. It was named from Baghdad, no doubt because of their associations with that city during the Crusades. The modern form, itself, comes from *Baldac*, the Old French form for Baghdad.

The usual word for a hospital in Middle English was *spitel*, and this survives as Spital and Spittle, both common names, perhaps the best known of which is Spital in the Street (L). The only such name of Anglo-Saxon origin is Cotterstock (Nth) "hospital", but unfortunately nothing is known of its early history.

French *hermitage* has given the modern Armitage (St), where a hermitage is recorded from the 13th century. The Old English word, however, was *ānsetl*, literally "dwelling for one", "lonely dwelling", and this is the first element of Ansley (Wa) and Anslow (St), both meaning "glade with a hermitage". One or two place-names are derived from *hermit*, for example Armathwaite (Cu) "hermit clearing", where a house of Benedictine nuns was established in the 12th century, while Scandinavian *papi* "hermit" occurs in Papcastle (Cu), earlier *Papecastre*, "Roman fort inhabited by a hermit".

1 *Extract from Domesday Book of 1086, showing entries for two wapentakes of the North Riding of Yorkshire*

2 *Extracts from the Pipe Rolls of 1195, 1196 and 1197, showing the progressive deterioration of the spelling of Nuthall (Nt), "corner of land where nuts grow"*

The spelling in 1194 (not illustrated) is *Notehala*. In 1195 the scribe, confusing *t* and *c*, wrote *Nuchala*; this is followed in the next year by a misreading of *e* for *c*, thus giving *Nuehala*; then, in 1197, the scribe took the first element in the place-name as being the word "new", and so wrote *Niewehale*

3 *One of the maps compiled c. 1250 by, or for, Matthew Paris of St. Albans, for his* Chronica Maiora *and* Historia Anglorum *and John of Hunger-ford's Chronicle. These are the earliest-known detailed maps of Great Britain, the fullest of which contains 280 place-names*

4 *The south-eastern part of the anonymous map of Great Britain of c. 1335, known as the "Gough map", after its eighteenth-century discoverer, or the "Bodleian map", after its resting-place in Oxford. It shows a great advance on Paris's maps, both in cartographical accuracy and in the number of place-names*

5 *Detail of West Worcestershire and the adjoining part of Herefordshire from the sixteenth-century Sheldon tapestry-map of Warwickshire and Worcestershire, woven at Barcheston by Robert Hyckes*

6 *Central part of John Speed's map of Rutlandshire from his* Theatre of the Empire of Great Britain, *published in 1611*

7 *Detail from Ralph Agas's map of the City of London,* Civitas Londinum, *probably published c. 1591*

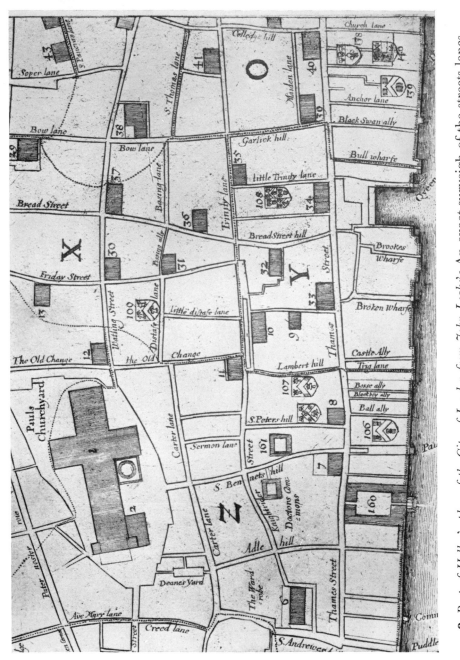

8 *Part of Hollar's plan of the City of London from John Leake's* An exact surveigh of the streets lanes and churches contained within the ruines of the city of London, *published in 1667 after the fire*

The origin and development of the word *cross* have been discussed in Chapter Four. Here, we may note a few additional examples of its occurrence in place-names. As a first element it is found in the common Scandinavian compound name Crosby "village with a cross", and this must also be the meaning of Croston (La), where the second element is Old English *tūn*. Other Scandinavian compounds include Crossthwaite (NRY), Crosthwaite (Cu, We), Crostwick (Nf) "clearing with a cross", and Crossrigg (We) "ridge with a cross". It occurs as the second element, however, in Hoar Cross (St) "grey cross", Shallcross (Db) literally "shackle cross", perhaps a wheel-head cross, and Twycross (Lei) "double cross", which may have been one with four arms used as a signpost. Rey Cross (NRY) apparently means "cross on the cairn", the latter probably marking the boundary between Yorkshire and Westmorland. Minor names derived from wayside crosses, many of which were also boundary marks, are common, particularly Lady Cross or Lady's Cross, one dedicated to Our Lady, and Stump Cross "cross which has lost its head".

Cross is a loan-word, ultimately from Latin *crux*, and the genitive of the Latin word itself has been added to a village name in Ampney Crucis (Gl). *Crux* was also the immediate source of Old French *crois*, which seems to survive only in minor names, apart from its use in the earlier name of Royston (Hrt), where there was formerly an Augustinian priory called *la Crois Roes* "cross of (a lady called) Roheis". Only the last word survived, however, and when a village grew up there in the 13th century *ton* was added, giving the modern Royston.

The usual Old English word for a cross, *rōd*, modern *rood*, however, occurs only occasionally, as in Radstone (Nth) and Rudston (ERY) "rood-stone". The stone from which Rudston took its name still stands in the church-yard. *Rood* is also prefixed once to a village name, Rood Ashton (W). Old English *mǣl* "cross" is the first element of a group of names, including Malden (Sr), Maldon (Ess) and Meldon (Nb) "hill marked with a cross", as well as the second element of the compound *cristelmǣl* "cross". This is the source of Christian Malford (W) "ford with a cross", where the modern form is presumably the result of popular etymology, Christleton (Ch) "village with a cross" and Kismeldon (D) "hill with a cross".

Holy is often used with christian association in place-names such as Holy Island (Nb), on which the priory of Lindisfarne was situated, and Hallington (Nb) "holy valley". It is particularly widespread, in various forms, in the names of springs, hence Halliwell (La),

Halwell (D), Halwill (D), Holwell (O) and the common Holywell, as well as Helliwell (WRY), where Helli- is a distinctively dialectal form. The meaning of all these names, "holy well", is also that of Hallikeld (NRY), which has a Scandinavian word for "spring" as second element. It may be noted that originally Old English *hālig* "holy" had a pagan connotation, but no place-name is known where this must necessarily be the case.

The names of various ecclesiastics occur in place-names, sometimes denoting where they lived, but more often land and property belonging to them. The commonest is *priest*, as in Prescot (La, O), Prescott (Gl) "priests' cottage", Prestwich (La), Prestwick (Nb) "priests' farm", as well as Prestbury (Ch, Gl), the very common Preston, and Purston (Nth, WRY), which probably all mean "priests' manor". Occasionally *priest* has been prefixed to older village names, as in Priest Hutton (La), while *Preston* in Preston Crowmarsh (O) represents a genitive plural "of the priests".

Comparable to Preston Crowmarsh is Monken Hadley (Hrt) "Hadley of the monks (of Walden Abbey)", while *monk* itself has been prefixed in Monk Bretton (WRY), where there was a Cluniac priory, which became a Benedictine monastery in 1280, and Monk-hopton (Sa) which belonged to Wenlock Priory, and added in Toft Monks (Nf), where there was a small Benedictine priory. In early documents these additions are often given Latin forms, and in one case Buckland Monachorum (D), where there was a Cistercian abbey, the Latin genitive plural has survived as a suffix. *Monk*, however, in the genitive plural, occurs as the first element of the place-name Monkton (at least 7 counties) "manor belonging to the monks".

Canon is the first element of an occasional name such as Canonbury (Mx) "manor belonging to the canons (of St. Bartholomew's, London)", and was also prefixed in Canons Ashby (Nth) and Canonsleigh (D), where there were priories of Augustinian canons, while the Latin genitive plural survives in Whitchurch Canonicorum (Do), which belonged to the abbey of St. Wandrille, Normandy.

Places with names containing Old English *hīwan* "household", and also "religious community", can sometimes be shown to have been owned by a religious body of some kind, as in the case of Hainault Forest (Ess) "holt or wood of the religious community", which belonged to the abbey of Barking. Similarly, Henwick (Wo) "farm", Clyst Honiton (D) and some of the Hintons "manor" appear to have been monastic property at one time or another, while Henwood (Wa) "wood belonging to a religious community" was the site of a Benedictine nunnery.

Old English *abbod* "abbot" is the source of Abbotsbury (Do) "abbot's manor", which was a Benedictine abbey, and of Abbotstone (Ha) and Abson (Gl) each meaning "manor belonging to an abbot". The Old French *abbat* was borrowed into English as *abbot* and helped to reinforce the English word. It has been added in names such as Brampton Abbotts (He), Hemingford Abbot (Hu) and Stoke Abbott (Do), while the Latin *abbas* survives in Cerne Abbas and Milton Abbas in Dorset, both Benedictine abbeys. Similarly, *prior* is found as a distinguishing epithet in Alton Priors (W), Ditton Priors (Sa) and Swaffham Prior (C), denoting villages formerly held by a priory.

Charterhouse "house of Carthusian monks", however, is not found in sources independent of place-names till 1534. The word itself is derived from Old French *chartreuse*, and the modern form must be due to popular etymology. In place-names it survives in Charterhouse in Coventry, Finsbury and Hull, and in the suffix of Hinton Charterhouse (So), where as the names suggest there were houses of the Carthusian order.

In the absence of direct evidence on the subject it is not always easy to decide whether place-names containing Nun- as a first element are to be derived from the Old English personal name Nunna or Old English *nunne* "nun". The latter meaning is probable in Nunley (Wa), since it was at one time in the possession of a nunnery, but Nunnington (NRY), Nunton (Nth) "farm, village" and Nunwick (Nb, WRY) "dairy-farm", along with other modern names in Nun-, are probably from the personal name Nunna. There can be no doubt, however, that *nun* has been prefixed in Nuneaton (Wa) and Nunstainton (Du), since each was the site of a nunnery. Similarly, Old English *myncen*, which also means "nun", occurs in Minchin Buckland (So), where there was a priory of the Sisters of St. John of Jerusalem, and in Minchinbarrow (So), from the priory of Benedictine nuns there.

Middle English *ancre* could mean either "anchorite" or "anchoress", but the meaning of Ankerwyke (Bk) is clearly "anchoresses' dwelling", i.e. nunnery, since it was formerly a priory of Benedictine nuns.

Old English *abbodisse* "abbess" is the first element of Abbotstone (W) "manor of the abbess (of Wilton)"; but it is Middle English *abbesse*, a French loan-word, which has been prefixed in Abbess Roding (Ess). Compton Abbas and Melbury Abbas in Dorset, however, have a reduced form of Latin *abbatissa*, i.e. *abbas*.

We have already noted the use of Lady, referring to the Virgin

133

Mary, in Lady Cross, and it is this word which occurs in Lady Halton (Sa), from the dedication of the church. The same word is found also in White Ladies Aston (Wo), so-named because Aston was earlier held by nuns of the Cistercian Order, as was Brewood Black Ladies (St) by the priory of Benedictine nuns.

There is a group of village names distinguished by the addition of the name of the religious house, which at one time held the manor, as with Acaster Selby (WRY) from Selby Abbey, Crowmarsh Battle (O) from Battle Abbey, Hartley Wintney (Ha) from Wintney Priory, Hurstbourne Tarrant (Ha) from Tarrant Abbey, Morton Tinmouth (Du) from Tynemouth Priory, and St. Paul s Walden (Hrt) and Wickham St. Paul's (Ess) from St. Paul's Cathedral, London. Newton Longville (Bk), Offord Cluny (Hu), Tooting Bec (Sr) and Weedon Beck (Nth), however, were once possessed by or were dependent on the church of St. Faith of Longueville, the abbey of Cluny and the abbey of Bec-Hellouin in France respectively.

Where *bishop* occurs in place-names that place usually belonged to a see, as in Bishopstone (Bk, He, Sx, W), Bishopton (Du, WRY), Bishton (Gl, Sa, St) and Bushton (W), as well as Bispham (La) and Bushbury (St), all of which mean "manor held by a bishop". A similar sense is likely for Bishopthorpe (WRY) and Biscathorpe (L), of which the second element is probably the Scandinavian *biskup*. *Bishop* has also been prefixed in Bishop Auckland (Du), Bishops Cannings (W), Bishops Hull (So) and Bishop's Stortford (Hrt). In the early forms of these last, *bishop* was usually rendered by Latin *episcopus*, genitive *episcopi*, and this has survived in Huish Episcopi (So), Kingsbury Episcopi (So) and Wick Episcopi (Wo). In most of these examples the identity of the individual bishop can be established from medieval references. In some early names, however, the first element may rather be from the Old English personal name Biscop. So, Biscot (Bd) is perhaps "Biscop's cottage" and Bishopdale (NRY) "Biscop's valley".

Chapter Thirteen

———— ★ ————

PLACE-NAMES ILLUSTRATING SOCIAL
AND LEGAL CUSTOMS

THE main division in Anglo-Saxon society, if we are to judge from the extant codes of Law, was that between the freeman and the serf. Both these classes were further subdivided, in the one case into freemen of noble birth and ordinary peasant cultivators, in the other into various classes of serfs, though here the reason for the differences is uncertain. Ignoring these last, the Laws of King Alfred divide society below the king into three main classes: (*i*) those of noble birth with more than five hides of land, (*ii*) those of noble birth with less than five hides of land, and (*iii*) the freeman, not of noble birth. These distinctions are peculiar to the Wessex of King Alfred, but similar ones with local variations appear also in the other Anglo-Saxon kingdoms, and an interesting group of place-names reflects these early divisions of society.

The obvious place to begin is with some of the numerous names containing the word *king*, Old English *cyning*. This is frequently combined with *tūn*, probably in the sense "manor", in Kingston already noted, Kineton (Wa) and Kingstone (Brk, He). Other elements appear in Kingsdon (So) and Kingsdown (K) "hill", Kingsley (Ch, Ha, St) "wood or glade", as well as the self-explanatory Kingsbridge (D), Kingsford (Wa), Kingstone (So) and Kingswood (Gl, Sr, Wa). In addition *King* is sometimes prefixed to the names of places held by the crown, as in King's Cliffe (Nth), Kings Newnham (Wa), King's Walden (Hrt) and added in Areley Kings (Wo). In medieval sources this is sometimes translated as Latin *Regis*, the genitive singular, which survives in Bartley Regis (Ha), Grafton Regis (Nth) and Newton Regis (Wa).

The corresponding Scandinavian word *kunungr* has apparently replaced the English one in some Northern and Midland names such as Congerston (Lei), Conington (C, Hu) and Coniston (ERY, La, WRY) "manor", Conisbrough (WRY) also probably "manor", and Coniscliffe (Du) "cliff". It is, however, likely to be original in

135

Coneysthorpe (NRY) and Coneythorpe (WRY) "outlying farm" and Coningsby and Conisby (both L) "farm, village", since the second elements of these names are Scandinavian words.

Royal association is also indicated by place-names which have as first element Old English *cyne* "royal". Kenton (Nb) and Kington (Do, He, W, Wa, Wo) both mean "royal manor" and Kingston on Soar (Nt) "royal stone". It will be noticed that some names derived from *cyne* have a modern form in King-, but such a development, which often took place early, is natural enough in view of the similarity in form and meaning between the two words.

Queen, Old English *cwēn*, is rare in place-names, but may well be the first element of Quainton (Bk) and Quinton (Gl, Nth, Wo) probably meaning "queen's manor". In such cases, however, it is difficult to distinguish *cwēn* from Old English *cwene* "woman", and the latter, in the genitive plural *cwena*, is the source of Quenington (Gl) "women's manor". But there can be no doubt that Middle English *quene* "queen" represents the first element of Quinbury (Hrt) and Queenborough (K) since there is documentary evidence to show that they were respectively named in honour of Maud, wife of King Stephen, and Philippa, wife of Edward III. *Queen* has also been prefixed in Queen Charlton (So) after the manor had been given by Henry VIII to Catherine Parr.

A few places are named from Old English words meaning "prince", such as *fengel* in Finglesham (K) "prince's homestead", and more commonly *æðeling*, found perhaps in Athelington (Sf) and Allington (Do, L, W) "princes' farm", Athelney (So) "princes' island" and Adlingfleet (WRY) "prince's stream".

Next to the king and the members of the royal family was the rank of *aldormann*, modern *alderman*, "nobleman of the highest rank". This occurs in Aldermanbury (Mx) "alderman's manor", the likely meaning also of Aldermaston (Brk) and Alderminster (Wo). During the 10th century, because of the influence of Old Norse *jarl* "nobleman, earl", *aldormann* was replaced as a title by the Old English *eorl*, originally merely "nobleman", which may occur in Arleston (Db) and Earlstone (Ha) "farm"; but there was also a personal name Eorl and this could be the first element of these names. After the Norman Conquest *earl* was the usual title for the great magnates, and as such is prefixed to older names as in Earl Framingham (Nf) from the Earls of Norfolk, Earls Heaton (WRY) from the Earls of Warren and Surrey, and added in Plympton Erle (D) from the Earls of Devon and Winterbourne Earls (W) from the Earls of Salisbury. The usual term in the 9th and 10th century for a member of the lesser nobility was *pegn*, modern *thane*, but the original meaning of the word was "servant" and in Thenford (Nth) "thanes' ford" it is impossible to say in which sense it is used.

Two interesting names, Hestercombe (So) "valley" and Hexham (Nb) "homestead", have as first element Old English *hægstald* and *hagustald* "warrior, bachelor", also probably "owner of an enclosure". This is thought to refer to the younger son of a nobleman who had no share in his father's estate and so had to secure a holding for himself elsewhere.

The usual term for a free peasant below the rank of noble was Old English *ceorl*, modern *churl*, occurring frequently in Charlton, as well as Charleton (D) and Chorlton (Ch, La, St) "farm or village of the churls". In Carleton and Carlton both common names in the Scandinavianized districts, however, the English word has been replaced by the corresponding Old Norse *karl* "freeman of the lower class", which is perhaps the first element of Carlby (L) "farm or village of the free peasants". *Ceorl* is found also in Chorley (Ch, La, St) "wood, glade" as well as the self-explanatory Charlecote (Wa), Charlcote (W), Charlcott (Sa) and Charlwood (Sr). Terms for a servant or serf are very rare in place-names, but there is *gōp* in Gopsall (Lei) "hill" and *esne* in Isombridge (Sa) "bridge".

Two Old English words which need special mention are *cild*, modern *child*, and *cniht*, modern *knight*. The former is used in various senses in place-names. For example, Childwall (La) and Chilwell (Nt) both mean "stream of the children", perhaps because they played there. However, in the common Chilton "farm, village", Chilcote (Lei, Nth) "cottage" and Chilhampton (W) "home farm" the genitive plural *cilda* is compounded with a word for a habitation, and it has been suggested that the *children* in question were perhaps the younger sons of a family to whom a farm or estate had been given as a joint possession. Individual ownership, on the other hand, is indicated by Chilson (O) and Chilston (K), of which the first element is the genitive singular, hence "young man's farm". But the young men who gave their name to Childwick (Hrt) "dairy-farm" were probably oblates of the abbey of St. Albans who, according to a medieval account of the abbey, obtained their milk from this place. Occasionally, *Child* was later prefixed to an older village name, as in Chilfrome (Do) and Childs Ercall (Sa), in some sense now uncertain.

Old English *cniht* similarly means "youth", and Knightsbridge (Mx) is presumably "bridge where young men meet". The word also meant "servant", "retainer of a lord", and either sense is possible in the common Knighton "farm", Knightcote (Wa) "cottage",

Knightley (St) "wood, glade" and Knightwick (Wo) "dairy-farm". The later sense of *knight* "man raised to honourable military rank by the king" does not occur until the 12th century, and so is rarely found in place-names.

Some examples of Scandinavian terms for various ranks of society have already been noted. Others which occur in place-names include *hold*, an officer of high rank in the Danelaw, in Holderness (ERY) "headland of the hold"; *dreng*, a free tenant, probably in Dringhoe (ERY) "hill", Dringhouses (WRY) "houses" and Drointon (St) "farm"; and *leysingi* "freedman", perhaps in Lazenby (NRY) and Lazonby (Cu) "farm", though the first element of the last two could be the nickname Leysingi. Similarly the first element of Bonby (L) and Bomby (We) "farm" could represent either *bondi* "peasant farmer" or the personal name Bondi.

Official titles are also occasionally found in place-names. Old English *dōmere* "judge" is the first element in Damerham (Ha) "enclosure", *tollere* "tax-gatherer" in Tollerton (NRY) "farm", and *(ge)rēfa* "reeve, bailiff" in Reaveley (Nb) "wood, glade" and Reepham (Nf) "homestead". *Sheriff*, literally *shire-reeve*, "chief executive of the king" is the source of Screveton (Nt), Shrewton (W) and Shurton (So) "manor", and of the prefix in Sheriff Hales (Sa) from the sheriff of Shropshire, and Sheriff Hutton (NRY) from a sheriff of York.

Anglo-Saxon law recognized two main categories of land tenure. *Folcland* "folk-land" was held according to folk-right, or customary law, and from it the king drew certain food-rents and customary services. This has given Faulkland (So) and Falkland in minor names and field-names. *Bōcland* "book land", granted by royal book or charter, usually with freedom from some of the customary services, is the source of the common Buckland, a name so far noted only in Hertfordshire and Lincolnshire outside the South of England.

Sir Frank Stenton has pointed out that the *hide*, Old English *hīd*, formed the basis of social organization everywhere in Anglo-Saxon England, except in Kent. *Hide* denoted the amount of land which would support a household, a free family and its dependants, and, as we have seen previously, on an average it seems to have been 120 acres. This word occurs in place-names in the simplex form Hyde (Bd, Ch, Ha, Mx), which Ekwall considers may be translated "homestead consisting of one hide". As the second element of a compound, sometimes in the form -field or -head, however, it is found occasionally with a numeral, as in the Wiltshire Toyd "two",

Fifield Bavant "five" and so-assessed in Domesday Book, and Tinhead "ten". Fifield is paralled by Fifield (O) and Tinhead by the affix in Stokein*teignhead* (D), the name of an area assessed as ten hides in Domesday Book. Two further examples may be added, Nynehead (So) "nine" and Piddle*trenthide* (Do) "thirty", this last also being assessed as thirty hides in Domesday Book.

The names of some places reflect the fact that they were charged with the payment of some particular tax. Galton (Do) "farm" and Yeldham (Ess) "homestead" each have as first element a word meaning "tax". Pennington (Ha, La) and Penton (Ha) probably meant "farm subject to a penny rent", and Galhampton (So), Galmington (D, So), Galmpton (D) and Gammaton (D) "farm of the rent-paying peasants".

Those of others indicate that the ownership of them had at one time or another been in dispute, as in Threapland (Cu, WRY) "disputed land", Threapwood (Ch) and Threepwood (Nb) "disputed wood". This is also the meaning of Callingwood (St), a French-English hybrid. On the other hand, Warley (Ess), literally "agreement wood or glade", presumably records the settlement of such a dispute. Other names denote places communally owned as with Manton (Nt, R, W) "communally owned farm", and the same first element is found in Manea (C), Maney (Wa) "island, well-watered land", Mangreen (Nf) "green", presumably a grassy place, Manley (Ch, D) "wood or glade" and Meanwood (WRY) "wood" Almondbury (WRY), with Scandinavian *almenn* "all men" as first element, presumably means "fortification belonging to the community" and is named from the Iron Age fort there.

Words for different types of criminals are not infrequent in minor names. Old English *sceaða* "thief, criminal" occurs in Scadbury Park (K), a name probably denoting a disused fortification frequented by thieves; *sætere* and *scēacere* "robber" are found respectively in Satterleigh (D) and the Lancashire Shackerley and Shakerley, each meaning "robbers' wood". *Flēming* "fugitive" is thought to occur in Fleam Dyke (C), a post-Roman earthwork, and comparable with Wrekendike (Du), which has *wrecca*, modern *wretch*, "fugitive" as first element. Old English *wearg* "felon" is compounded with *hyll* in Wreighill (Nb), perhaps "hill where criminals are executed", and with *burna* in Warnborough (Ha) "stream where felons are drowned", while Worgret (Do) and Warter (ERY) have *rōd* "cross" and *trēow* "tree" respectively as second element, and denote "gallows". *Gallows* itself is especially frequent in minor names and field-names, but Gawber (WRY) "gallows hill" is an example of

139

the occurrence of the word in the name of a more important place. Here, too, may be mentioned Dethick (Db) "death oak", presumably one on which criminals were hanged. On the other hand, Flamstead (Hrt) is "place of flight", presumably for fugitives and criminals, and it has been pointed out that later a condition of the tenure of the manor was that protection should be given to travellers.

Examples have already been given of names denoting meeting-places connected with local government, especially those which became the names of hundreds and wapentakes. Similar names are not uncommon, though we often have no idea what kind of a meeting was held at the particular place, as with Matlock (Db) "oak at which a meeting is held" and Matlask (Nf) "ash at which a meeting is held". Spellow (La) "speech mound" has as first element Old English *spell* "speech" and so has Spellbrook (Hrt) "speech brook", while Spetchley (Wo) "speech glade" is derived from *spēc*, modern *speech*, and was one of the meeting-places of Oswaldslow Hundred. Another meeting-place of the same hundred was probably Stoulton (Wo) literally "seat farm or village". It has been suggested that in this case it was the seat of the judge or speaker at the hundred court, so that the name would mean "farm or village with or near the speaker's seat". At Mottistone (Wt) "speaker's stone", the stone was a large menhir which still stands on the hill above the village.

Runnymede (Sr) is apparently an old meeting place, which may be the reason why the meeting between John and the Barons, at which Magna Carta was sealed, took place there. As it stands it means "meadow at *Runy*", but *Runy* was originally "island where a council is held".

Old English and Scandinavian *þing* "meeting, assembly" occur as the first element of several names. The English word is found in Thinghill (He) "hill", Tingrith (Bd) "stream", and also in Finedon (Nth) "valley" and Fingest (Bk) "wooded hill", in which F- for earlier Th- is a late dialectal development. The Scandinavian form is found more particularly in the compounds *þinghaugr* "assembly mound or hill" and *þingvǫllr* "assembly field". The first is the source of Fingay Hill (NRY), perhaps the meeting-place of the whole Riding, and the second has given Thingwall (Ch, La) and Dingbell Hill (Nb), as well as Tynwald, the court of the Isle of Man.

Chapter Fourteen

————— ★ —————

ENGLISH SETTLEMENT-NAMES

THE names dealt with here are those of settlements and do not include those of natural features which later became the names of towns, villages, farms, etc. The four principal elements from which they are derived normally survive as *ton*, *ham*, *wick* and *worth* and, though *wick* and *worth* occur also as simplex names, they appear chiefly as the final element of compounds. In such cases the first element may be a personal name, a term indicating personal or group ownership, a word descriptive of situation, shape, size, and so on, or some term for an animal or bird, or for a crop, plant or tree. Thousands of such names occur and only a selection of them can be discussed here.

Old English *tūn*, modern *town* (cognate with German *Zaun* "hedge"), is the commonest of all place-name elements. In early names it seems to have had the sense "farmstead", but later it developed the meaning "hamlet, village". This is the likely sense when it was added to a Celtic name, as in Cruckton (Sa) and Helston (Co), or to an older English topographical name, as in Claverton (So), where the first part is identical with Clatford (Ha), Milverton (Wa), with Milver- identical with the common Milford "mill ford", and Throckmorton (Wo) from Throckmor- "drain pool". A similar meaning, or even that of "manor", is to be assumed when the first element is a post-Conquest personal name or surname, or a term for an ecclesiastic or for royalty, examples of which are noted in the relevant chapters.

For most names, however, it is safer to assume a meaning "farmstead", especially when the first element is a personal name. The number of such compounds is very large; for example, there are 230 in Devon alone, of which some 60 are said to have been given after the Norman Conquest; on the other hand, only one has been noted in Surrey. Occasionally, the same name is repeated in different counties, so that Wessington (Db), Wistaston (Ch), Wisteston (He) and Wiston (Sx) all mean "Wīgstān's farmstead". Further examples of this type of name will be found at the end of the chapter, but here

141

a small and interesting group may be noted, which the references in Domesday Book suggest is named from the holder of the estate in the time of Edward the Confessor. This includes Alston (D) "Alwine", Blackmanstone (K) "Blæcmann", Osmaston by Derby (Db) "Ōsmund", Shearston (So) "Sigerēd" and Afflington (Do) "Ælfrūn", this last the name of a lady.

Some "farmsteads or villages" were named from groups of people, as with Bickerton (Ch, He, Nb, WRY) "bee-keepers", Fisherton (D, W), Fiskerton (Nt) "fishermen", Mangerton (Do) "traders", Potterton (WRY) "potters", Salterton (W) "salters", Sapperton (Db, Gl, L, Sx) "soap-makers", Shepperton (Mx) "shepherds", Smeaton (NRY, WRY) and Smeeton (Lei) "smiths", and Tuckerton (So) "tuckers, i.e. cloth-fullers".

Not infrequently the first element denotes the situation as in the common Norton, Sutton, Weston, Easton and most of the Astons, identical with which is Eston (NRY), as well as Norlington (Sx) "towards the north", Westerton (Sx) "western" and Westmeston (Sx) "westmost". Middleton is a very common name of English origin, while Melton (L, Lei, WRY), which also means "middle farmstead", has a first element from the corresponding Scandinavian word. There is also Netherton (Nb, Wo) "lower farmstead", Overton (Ch, Db, Ha, R, Sa, W) "higher farmstead", and Otherton (St, Wo) "the other farm", perhaps named in relation to some earlier settlement. Heaton (La, Nb, WRY) is "high farm", while Hampton (Ch, Sa), Hampton in Arden (Wa), Great Hampton (Wo), Wolverhampton (St, with Wolver- added later from the name of an early woman owner Wulfrūn), Heanton (D), Hinton (Brk, Gl, Ha, So), all come from Old English *Hēantūne* "at the high farm". Almost equally common are such names as Langton, found in many counties, Lanton (Nb), Launton (O), Longton (La, St), Longtown (Cu) "long", compared with Scampton (L), with a first element from Old Norse *skammr* "short". Gratton (Db) and Gretton (Nth), Mickleton (Gl, NRY), Middleton (He) and Storeton (Ch) all mean "big farm", Alton (Db, Lei) and Olton (Wa) "old farm", and Newton, a very common name, Newington (Gl, K, Mx, O, Sr) and Niton (Wt) "new farm". Some of these last may represent an Old English dative form *æt Niwantūne*, and the -*n*- of the inflectional form survives in Naunton (Gl, Wo) and Newnton (W). The first element is also an adjective in Grinton (NRY) "green" and Whitton (Du, Mx, Nb, Sa, Sf) "white", though a personal name Hwīta is possible in some of the Whittons. Horton "muddy, dirty farm" is also common, and this is similarly the meaning of Gorton (La), Sherrington (W) and Slipton

(Nth). The first element, however, means "clay" in Clayton (La, St, Sx, WRY) and Cleeton (ERY), "gravel" in Girton (C, Nt), and "sand" in Sancton (ERY), Santon (Cu, L, Nf) and Manton (L).

Many farmsteads or villages were named from a river, as with Charwelton (Nth, Cherwell), Crediton (D, Creedy), Glympton (O, Glyme), Itchington (Wa, Itchen), Linton (Nb, Lyne), Lonton (NRY, Lune) and Tamerton (D, Tamar). In others, including Beighton (Db), Betchton (Ch), Brockton (Sa), Brocton (St), Brunton (Nb), Eaton (Bk, Brk, He, Nt, O, W), Eaton Socon (Bd), Water Eaton (St), Fletton (Hu) and Flitton (Bd), the first element means "river" or "brook". Here, too, may be included Alton (Ha), Alton Pancras (Do), and the Wiltshire Alton Barnes and Alton Priors "farmstead near the source of the river" and Mitton (La, Wo, WRY) and Myton (NRY, Wa) "near the river confluence". Marten (W), Merton (D, Nf, O) and the common Martin and Marton are all from Old English *mere* "mere, pool"; Eaton (Ch, Db, Lei), Church Eaton (St), Eaton Bray (Bd) and Eton (Bk) from *ēg* "island, low-lying land partly surrounded by stream"; Hampton (He, Mx, Wa) from *hamm* "enclosure, water-meadow"; and Huyton (La), Hyton (Cu) from *hȳð* "landing-place".

Some have been named from a "valley", as with the common Compton, Dalton and Denton, while comparable names include Clotton (Ch), Cloughton (NRY) "clough", Corton (Do, So) "gap, pass", Dorton (Bk) "door, pass", Hopton, which occurs in several counties, "small valley", and Yatton (He, W) "gate, gap". Those place-names in the Midlands and South with a first element derived from Old English *halh*, such as Halloughton (Nt, Wa), Haughton (Sa), Holton (O, So) also belong here, for this word seems to have been used in these areas in the sense "narrow valley". In the North, however, it has given dialectal *haugh* "flat land by a river, water-meadow", and this is the meaning in Haighton (La), Halton (La), Haughton (Du, La, Nb) and Westhoughton (La). But in other names with forms similar to some of these the exact sense is uncertain.

The first element of some names in *tūn* is a word for a "hill", as in Hilton (Db, Hu, NRY, St) and Hulton (La, St), Downton (He, Sa, W) and Dunton (Ess, Lei, Nf, Wa), as well as Clapton and Clopton, found in a number of counties, "hill or hillock", the common Clifton "cliff, slope", Hoghton (La), Hooton (Ch, WRY), and Hutton, in many counties, "hill-spur", Neston (W) "ness, headland", and Shelton and Shilton, both occurring several times, "shelf, ledge".

Other names derived from terms for natural features include

Morton and Moreton, each represented by many examples, as well as Murton (Du, Nb, NRY) "moor or marsh", and Slapton (Bk, D, Nth) "slippery place". Woodton (Nf), Wootton, in many Midland and Southern counties, and Wotton (Bk, Gl, Sr) all mean "farmstead in the wood", while the common Grafton is "farmstead near the grove".

The farm or village was sometimes named from a neighbouring building—a "mill" in Millington (Ch, ERY) and Milton (Cu, Db, Nt, St), and a church with a "steeple" in Steepleton (Do).

A large number, however, must have been noted for the animals kept there, judging from the first element of the names. It is "sheep" in Shepton (So) and Shipton (Do, Gl, Ha, O, Sa), "rams" in Rampton (C, Nt), "cattle" in Natton (Gl), Netton (W) and Notton (Do, W), "calves" in Calton (Db, St, WRY), Cawton (NRY), Chawton (Ha), Kelton (Cu), as well as Calverton (Bk, Nt) from the genitive plural, "swine" in Swinton (La, NRY, WRY), "boars" in Everton (Bd, La, Nt), and perhaps "mules" in Moulton (Ch, L, NRY, Nth, Sf), while Hunton (Ha) means "farm for hounds" and Doughton (Gl, Nf) "duck farm". Two other names which may be mentioned here are Butterton (near Newcastle St) "butter farm" and Honiton (near South Molton D) "honey farm". Occasionally the first element is the name of a wild animal or bird, as in Darton (WRY) which has been translated "enclosure for deer" and "deer park", Foxton (C, Lei, NRY) "fox", Dufton (We) "dove" and Storrington (Sx) "stork".

Other farms were named from the crops grown there, as with the common Barton "barley farm", and Soberton (Ha), Surbiton (Sr) "southern barley farm". In some cases, however, Barton means "outlying grange", and this is particularly likely with those Bartons which were monastic property. "Flax" was grown at Flaxton (NRY), as also at Linton (C, Db, ERY, He), "hay" at Hayton (Cu, ERY, Nt, Sa), and "rye" at Royton (La), Ruyton (Sa) and Ryton (Du, Sa, Wa). Garston (Ha, Hrt) must have been especially noted for "grass", and this name has been rendered "meadow" and "grass enclosure", Faxton (Nth) for "coarse grass", Claverton (Ch) for "clover", and Foddington (So) and Grassington (WRY) for their "grazing".

Old English *tūn* is frequently compounded with terms for other plants, especially "broom" as in the common Brampton, Branton (WRY), Brompton (ERY, Mx, NRY, Sa), and "leek" in Latton (Ess, W), Laughton (Lei, Sx, WRY) and Leighton (Bd, Ch, Hu, La, Sa). Less frequent are "bent-grass" in Beeston (Nf, Nt, WRY), "wild-saffron" in Crafton (Bk), "fern" in Farrington (So), "brooklime" in Lemmington (Nb), "moss" in Moston (La, Sa), "rushes" in Sefton (La), "thistles" in Thistleton (R), and "woad" in Watton (Hrt).

The first element of many of those from the name of a tree is self-explanatory, as with Ashton (Ch, Gl, La, So, W), Elmton (Db), Mappleton (Db, ERY) and Treeton (WRY), and the common Thornton. Less obvious are Acton (Ch, He, Mx, Sa, St), Aighton (La) and Aughton (ERY, La, WRY) "oak", Allerton (La), Ellerton (ERY, NRY), Ollerton (Ch, Nt), Orleton (He, Wo) and Owlerton (WRY) all "alder", and Saighton (Ch), Salton (NRY) "sallow". Perton (St), Pirton (Hrt, Wo), Puriton (So), Purton (Gl, W) and Pyrton (O) mean "pear-tree farm", Plompton (WRY) and Plumpton (Cu, La, Nth, Sx) "plum-tree farm", and Appleton, a common name, "apple-tree farm". But Old English *æppeltūn* also means "orchard" and this may have been the original sense of some of the Appletons.

Somerton (L, Nf, O, So) and Winterton (Nf), identical with which is Winderton (Wa), certainly denote the seasonal uses of the farms. But the exact meaning of Drayton, found frequently, is uncertain, though the first element is Old English *dræg* "dray, cart", and also "drag, portage". It is, however, impossible to be certain of the exact sense in all the names. Similarly, Hampton (Gl, O), Hampton Lovett (Wo), Highampton (D) and Littlehampton (Sx), from Old English *hāmtūn*, the last two with later prefixes, may have denoted an enclosure in which a homestead stood, a home farm, the village proper as distinct from the outlying parts, or the chief manor of a large estate. Other examples of *hāmtūn*, with a self-explanatory first element, include Bridgehampton (So), Brookhampton (Wa, Wo), Fenhampton (He), Netherhampton (W) and Shorthampton (O). Again, Market Weighton (ERY), Wighton (Nf), Witton (Ch, Wa, Wo) and Wyton (Hu) are all from Old English *wīctūn*, which may have meant "homestead", "dwelling-place", or perhaps "farm near a village".

A further group of names in -*tūn* consists of a personal name followed by a medial -*ing*-, as in Paddington (Mx), Old English *Pad(d)ingtūn*. Such names are to be distinguished from those like Hoddington (Ha), Old English *Hod(d)ingatūn* "farmstead or village of Hod(d)a's people", in which the first element is the genitive plural of a folk-name. These will have early Middle English forms in -*ingeton*, but those with the medial -*ing*- will have only -*ington*. The interpretation of such names is disputed, but the current view,

145

held by the English Place-Name Society editors, is that the *-ing-* is a connective particle, so that Paddington would mean "farmstead associated with Pad(d)a" or that it was a suffix, so that the earlier name was *Padding* "place associated with Pad(d)a", to which at a later date was added *tūn*, perhaps with the sense "estate". Examples of this common formation are given at the end of the chapter.

Old English *tūn* occurs only rarely as a first element, but there is Towneley (La) "glade belonging to the village, i.e. Burnley". It is, of course, found frequently in such later and self-explanatory names as Town End and Town Head. Elsewhere, it forms part of the Old English compounds *tūnstall* "site of a farm, farmstead", the source of the common Tunstall, Dunstall (L, St), and *tūnstede* "farmstead" in Tunstead (Db, La, Nf).

Examples of Old English *hām* "homestead, village", in which the first element is the genitive plural of an Old English folk-name, appear in an earlier chapter. Such names belong to an early period in the Anglo-Saxon settlement of Britain, and it has been shown that other names containing this element are, as a group, even earlier. They are certainly common in the East, but uncommon in the West, where Anglo-Saxon settlement was comparatively late.

As with *tūn*, *hām* occurs frequently with a personal name as first element and a selection of these is given at the end of this chapter. But the first element is often descriptive of situation in Northam (D) and Norham (Nb), Southam (Gl, Wa), Eastham (Ch, Wo) and Middleham (Du, NRY); of age in Newham (Nb), the common Newnham, and Nuneham (O); of size in the Surrey Mitcham and Mickleham "big", and Medmenham (Bk) "middle-sized". It should be noted, however, that some of these names, as well as some of those which follow, may alternatively be derived from Old English *hamm* "enclosure, water-meadow", since it is often very difficult to separate these two elements unless very early spellings are known.

Some were named from a river, as with Cockerham (La), Irlam (La), Measham (Lei) and Trentham (St) from the Cocker, Irwell, Mease and Trent respectively, while Burnham (Ess, Nf) and Fleetham (Nb) both mean "homestead on the stream". Brigham (ERY) is "homestead near the bridge", and Wareham (Do) "near the weir". From other natural features there are Barham (Hu), Downham (C, Ess, Nf, Sf), Dunham (Ch, Nf), Peckham (K, Sr) and Clapham (Bd, Sr, Sx), all with words meaning "hill"; Dalham (K, Sf) "valley", Sulham (Brk) "narrow valley", Woodham (Ess, Sr) "wood", and Saham (Nf) and Seaham (Du) "lake, sea".

A number of "homesteads" were named from the animals kept

there, as with Gotham (Nt) "goats", Horsham (Nf, Sx) "horses", Neatham (Ha) "cattle", Shipham (So) "sheep" and Studham (Bd) "stud, herd of horses", while Flitcham (Nf) refers to the "flitches of bacon" it produced. Occasionally, the first element is the name of a wild animal or bird as in the self-explanatory Foxham (W) and Fincham (Nf).

Others are from the crops or other plants which grew there—"beans" at Banham (Nf), "bent grass" at Bentham (Gl, WRY), "broom" at Bramham (WRY), "clover" at Claverham (So), "dill" at Dilham (Nf), "fern" at Fareham (Ha), Farnham (Bk, Do, Ess, Sf, WRY) and "grass" at Gresham (Nf). Names from trees are rare, but include Bookham (Sr) "beech", Elmham (Nf, Sf) "elm" and Mapledurham (Ha, O) "maple". The common Needham "needy homestead", however, was probably named from the unproductive land there.

The Old English compound *wīchām* has been shown to denote a small settlement in the neighbourhood of, or associated with a Roman *vicus*, as in Wickham (Brk, Ess, Hrt, Sf), Wykeham (L, NRY) and Wykham (O). Another compound *hāmstede* "site of a dwelling" occurs in Hampstead (Brk, Mx), Hamstead (St, Wt), Hempstead (Ess), as well as Great Berkhamsted (Hrt) "birch-tree", Wilshamstead (Bd) either the personal name Winel or Wil, and Hemel Hempstead (Hrt), where *Hemel* "broken country" refers to the uneven nature of the neighbouring area.

Old English *wīc* had a variety of meanings. It might denote a "dwelling" or "building where food or goods were prepared", as for example "fish" in Fishwick (D, La), with which can be compared Fisherwick (St) "fishermen's dwelling", "charcoal" in Colwich (St) and perhaps Colwick (Nt) and "salt" in Saltwick (Nb). A similar meaning may occur in Kepwick (NRY) with a first element Old English *cēap* "trade, market", hence "building for trade", though this name has been translated "market-place".

A number of names containing this element have as first element the name of a farm-animal or produce. It is likely that in such cases the word meant "farm", especially "dairy-farm", and this may well be its usual meaning in place-names. So, there is Bulwick (Nth) "bull", Calwich (St) "calf", Cowick (D, WRY) "cow", Hardwick and Hardwicke, found in most counties, "herd", Oxwick (Nf) "ox", Shapwick (Do, So), Shopwyke (Sx) "sheep"; the common Butterwick "butter", Casewick (L), Cheswick (Nb), Chiswick (Ess, Mx) "cheese", Spitchwick (D) "bacon", Woolwich (K) "wool"; as well as Bewick (ERY, Nb) "bee farm". Barwick (Nf, So, WRY), the common Berwick and Borwick (La) mean literally "barley farm", but the compound is probably used here in the sense "grange, outlying part of an estate or manor".

Sometimes the "farm" was named from its owner and a selection of these, derived from personal names, is given at the end of the chapter. But *wīc* was still used to form new place-names in the Middle English period, for Battleswick (Ess) is from the *Bataille* family and Stilesweek (D) from the *Stoyls*.

Wick occurs in other compounds such as Southweek (D), the common Southwick, Eastwick (Hrt, Sr, Sx) and Astwick (Bd, Nth), Westweek (D), Westwick (C, Du, Nf, WRY), Middlewich (Ch), and Hewick (WRY) "high farm"; Newick (Sx) and Aldwych (Mx), Aldwick (Hrt), Haultwick (Hrt) "old farm"; and the self-explanatory Greenwich (K), Greenwick (WRY). It is occasionally named from a nearby river as with the Northumberland Alnwick and Lowick on the Aln and Low, but there is also Flitwick (Bd) "near a stream". Denwick (Nb), Fenwick (Nb, NRY) and Morwick (Nb), however, are from other natural features, a "valley", "fen" and "marsh", while Gratwich (St) means "farm on gravelly ground", Papplewick (Nt) "in a pebbly place", Sandwich (K) "on sand" and Standerwick (So) "on stony ground".

Particularly interesting is the fact that *wīc* has sometimes been added to a village name, as in Cookbury Wick (D), Eton Wick (Bk), Hackney Wick (Mx) and Writtle Wick (Ess), probably denoting "outlying farm or dairy-farm belonging to Cookbury", and so on.

The basic sense of Old English *worð* seems to have been "enclosure"; but at an early date it had developed a meaning "homestead", the likely one in most place-names where the first element is a personal name, as it is in about three-quarters of all names derived from this word. Out of 23 modern names containing *worth* in Surrey, 15 were named from their owners, and this is perhaps the case in another five; in Essex the relative numbers are 26 out of 34, in Derbyshire 9 out of 12, and similar proportions are found in most counties. Examples of these are given at the end of the chapter. Littleworth (W, Wa), Longworth (La) and Southworth (La) are self-explanatory, while Heworth (Db, Du, NRY) means "high homestead" and Rowarth (Db) "enclosure on rough ground", but in the Berkshire Littleworth and Longworth the adjective is a later addition. Stanworth (La) may denote a stone-built homestead or one on stony ground, but Greatworth (Nth) was a "homestead on gravelly soil". Edgeworth (Gl, La) was named from its situation on an "edge or hillside" and Tamworth (St) from the River Tame.

148

Lindsworth (Wo) is named from the "lime-tree", and "cole or cabbage", "nettles" and "reeds" grew at Colworth (Bd), Nettleworth (Nt) and Redworth (Du) respectively. Five similar names, Ashworth "ash-tree", Dilworth "dill", Hollingworth (also Ch) "holly" and Farnworth (twice) "fern", occur in Lancashire, where the proportion containing a personal name is well below the usual average. Here, as well as in the West Riding, many are still the names of small places. It has been suggested that *worth* continued to be used to form place-names longer in the North than in other areas, and this might well account for the different pattern found there. In the South-west and the West Midlands, the word is found only rarely, if at all; instead, its place is taken by derivatives, of similar meaning, *worðig* and *worðign*. Of these, the first is confined mainly to Devon, with only occasional examples from others of the south-western counties. Early spellings in *-worth* and *-worthy*, however, occur for the same name, so that it is sometimes difficult to be certain which is the original form.

Among the more interesting examples (all in Devon, except where stated) are Curworthy "mill", Smallworthy "narrow", Widworthy "wide, spacious", Yalworthy "old", and Wringworthy (also Co) which may mean "enclosure with a press, i.e. for cheese or cider". The first element is an Old English personal name in Beaworthy "Bǣga or Bēaga", Elworthy (So) "Ella", Halsworthy and Holsworthy "Heald", Hockworthy "Hocca" and Wembworthy "Wemba". It is clear, however, that *worthy* was still in living use after the Norman Conquest for Ditsworthy seems to be from a Middle English personal name Durke and Gulworthy from a family called *Golle*.

Old English *worðign* is almost entirely confined to the West Midlands and Devon, where in early forms it is sometimes found indiscriminately with *-worth* and *-worthy*. Apart from Devon, it is chiefly found in Herefordshire and Shropshire, with only occasional examples elsewhere. As a simplex name it survives as Worden (D) and Worthen (D, Sa); in compounds it often has a modern form -wardine, though other endings occur, in Bradworthy (D) "broad, spacious", Harden (St) "high", Northenden (Ch) "north", as well as Brockworth (Gl) "brook", Ridgwardine (Sa) "ridge", Stanwardine (Sa) "stone". The Herefordshire Leintwardine and Lugwardine are names from the rivers Lent and Lugg; Marden (He) is perhaps "enclosure belonging to Maund" and Wrockwardine (Sa) "near The Wrekin". In others the first element is a personal name—Bēda in Bedwardine (Wo), Bēdel in Belswardyne (Sa), Ella in Ellerdine (Sa) and Pēoda in Pedwardine (He). There is, however, no place-name derived from *worðign*, which can be shown to have been formed after the Norman Conquest, though the word was still in everyday use in the 13th century.

Place-names in *tūn*, of which the first element is an Old English personal name, include:

Acton (Nb, Sf), Acton Turville (Gl) "Acca", Alfriston (Sx) "Ælfrīc", Chapel Allerton (So) "Ælfweard", Alphamstone (Ess) "Ælfhelm", Alverstone (Wt) "Ælfrēd", Amaston (Sa) and Ambaston (Db) "Ēanbald", Atherstone on Stour (Wa) and Edstone (Wa) "Ēadrīc", Bacton (He, Nf, Sf) "Bacca", Barmpton (Du) "Beornmund", Barnston (Ess, Nt) "Beorn", Bayton (Wo) "Bǣga", Breaston (Db) "Brægd", Brixton (Sr) "Beorhtsige", Brixton (W) "Beorhtrīc", Cayton (NRY, WRY) "Cǣga", Colaton (D) "Cola", Durweston (Do) "Dēorwine", Edmonton (Mx) "Ēadhelm", Edwalton (Nt) "Ēadwald", Hadstone (Nb) "Hæddi", Harlton (C) "Herela", Harmston (L) "Heremōd", Hexton (Hrt) "Hēahstān", Hoxton (Mx) "Hōc", Kilmeston (Ha) "Cynehelm", Kimbolton (He, Hu) "Cynebald", Kinvaston (St) "Cynewald", Lullingstone (K) "Lulling", Lupton (We) "Hluppa", Picton (Ch, NRY) "Pīca", Pillaton (Co) "Pīla", Selmeston (Sx) "Sigehelm", Simpson (Bk) "Sigewine", Tilton (Lei) "Tila", Wigginton (Hrt, O) and Wigton (Cu) "Wicga", Wilbarston (Nth) "Wilbeorht", Woolverstone (Sf) "Wulfhere" and Wyboston (Bd) "Wīgbald", all *masculine* names.

Abberton (Ess) and Edburton (Sx) "Ēadburg", Aylton (He) "Æðelgifu", Chellington (Bd) "Cēolwynn", Knayton (NRY), Kneeton (Nt) and Kniveton (Db) "Cēngifu", Leverton (Brk) "Lēofwaru", Sevington (K) "Sǣgifu", Wollerton (Sa) "Wulfrūn", Wolterton (Nf) "Wulfðrȳð", all *feminine* names.

Further examples of the Paddington type, "farmstead associated with Pad(d)a", or "place associated with Pad(d)a", with *tūn*, perhaps in the sense "estate" added later, include the following, in which only the personal name which occurs as first element is given:

Aldington (Wo) "Ealda", Avington (Brk, Ha) "Afa", Bavington (Nb) "Babba", Beddington (Sr) "Beadda", Bovington (Do) "Bofa", Bridlington (ERY) "Berhtel", Cardington (Bd) "Cēnrēd", Cockington (D) "Cocca", Coddington (Ch, Db, He, Nt) "Codda or Cotta", Covington (Hu) "Cufa", Denton (Nth) "Dudda", Diddington (Hu) and Doddington (C, K, L, Nb, Nth) "Dudda", Donington (L, Lei, Sa) "Dunn", Eckington (Db, Wo) "Ecca or Ecci", Evington (Gl) "Geofa", Folkington (Sx) "Folca", Hullavington (W) "Hūnlāf", Kensington (Mx) "Cynesige", Kidlington (O) "Cydela", Killington (We) "Cylla", Kirklington (NRY, Nt) and Kirtlington (O) "Cyrtla", Lillington (Wa) "Lilla", Luddington (Wa) "Luda", Pilkington (La) "Pīleca", Puckington (So)

"Pūca", Snoddington (Ha) "Snodd", Waddington (WRY) "Wada", Wallington (Hrt) "Wændel", Wallington (Nb) "Walh", Wennington (Ess) "Wynna", Whittington (Db, La, Nb, St, Wa, Wo) "Hwīta", Workington (Cu) "Weorc or Wyrc" and Paignton (D) "Pǣga". The usual early 19th-century spelling of the last was Paington and the modern form is said to have been adopted by the Railway Company after 1850.

Place-names in -hām compounded with an Old English personal name include:

Biddenham (Bd) "Bȳda", Bilham (WRY) "Billa", Bloxham (O) "Blocc", Bluntisham (Hu) "Blunt", Bodenham (He) "Boda", Cadnam (Ha) and Cadenham (W) "Cada", Chippenham (C) "Cippa", Dagenham (Ess) "Dæcca", Edenham (L) "Ēada", Edmondsham (Do) "Ēadmund", Egham (Sr) "Ecga", Epsom (Sr) "Ebbi", Hailsham (Sx) "Hægel", Haversham (Bk) "Hæfer", Heversham (We) "Hēahfrið", Loudham (Sf) and Lowdham (Nt) "Hlūda", Masham (NRY) "Mæssa", Oakham (R) and Ockham (Sr) "Occa", Pickenham (Nf) "Pīca", Puttenham (Hrt, Sr) "Putta", Rodmersham (K) "Hrōðmǣr", Strensham (Wo) "Strenge", Tatham (La) "Tāta", Tickenham (So) "Tica", Wappenham (Nth) "Wæppa", all *masculine* names; and Alpraham (Ch) "Alhburg" and Wilbraham (C) "Wilburg", both *feminine*.

Place-names derived from *wīc* with a personal name as first element:

Alswick (Hrt), Astwick (Hrt) and Elswick (Nb) "Ælfsige", Baswich (St) "Beorcol", Canwick (L) "Cana", Chadwich (Wo) and Chadwick (Wa) "Ceadel", Earswick (NRY) "Eðelrīc", Elwick (Du, Nb) "Ella", Elswick (La) "Eðelsige", Heckmondwike (WRY) "Hēahmund", Ipswich (Sf) "Gip(e)", Orgarswick (K) "Ordgār", Pattiswick (Ess) "Pætti", Postwick (Nf) "Poss", Wadswick (W) "Wæddi", Winwick (Hu, Nth) "Wina", Wistanswick (Sa) "Wīgstān", all Old English *masculine* names; and Goodwick (Bd) "Gōdgifu", a *feminine* name.

Beswick (ERY) "Besi", Renwick (Cu) "Hrafn" and Sedgwick (We) "Siggi", in each case very probably a Scandinavian *masculine* name.

A representative selection of the large group of place-names composed of an Old English personal name and *worð* comprises:

Ainsworth (La) "Ǣgen", Backworth (Nb) "Bacca", Badgeworth (Gl) and Badgworth (So) "Bæcga", Badsworth (WRY) "Bæddi", Bayworth (Brk) "Bǣga", Bedworth (Wa) "Bēda", Betchworth (Sr) "Becci", Blidworth (Nt) "Bliða", Bloxworth (Do) "Blocc", Brinkworth (W) "Brynca", Brixworth (Nth) "Bricel or Beorhtel", Chatsworth (Db) "Ceatt", Culworth (Nth) "Cūla", Elworth (Ch, Do) "Ella", Fittleworth (Sx) "Fitela", Handsworth (St) "Hūn", Handsworth (WRY) "Handel", Harmondsworth (Mx) "Heremōd", Hunstanworth

(Du) "Hūnstān", Ickworth (Sf) "Ica or Icca", Idsworth (Ha) "Iddi", Ingworth (Nf) "Inga", Inworth (Ess) "Ina", Kensworth (Bd) "Cægin", Kibworth (Lei) "Cybba", Ludworth (Ch, Du) "Luda", Lulworth (Do) "Lulla", Marsworth (Bk) "Mæssa", Mereworth (K) "Mǣra", Molesworth (Hu) "Mul", Paddlesworth (K) "Pæddel", Papworth (C) "Pappa", Pebworth (Gl) "Pybba", Pickworth (L, R) "Pīca", Rickmansworth (Hrt) "Rīcmǣr", Tetsworth (O) "Tǣtel", Wadsworth (WRY) "Wæddi", Wadworth (WRY) "Wada", Whitworth (Du, La) "Hwīta", Wirksworth (Db) "Weorc or Wyrc", all *masculine* names, and Kenilworth (Wa) from the *feminine* Cynehild.

Chapter Fifteen

————— ★ —————

ROADS AND WAYS

THE most important of the old roads in England are Ermine Street, Watling Street, Ryknield Street, the Fosse Way, Akeman Street and Icknield Way. Except for the last, which is a prehistoric trackway, all are Roman roads.

In Roman Britain, there was a network of roads, covering over 5,000 miles. London was the centre of the system, with eight roads radiating from the city. Others, however, intersected and linked the main roads, joining towns and forts in the various parts of the country. Some utilized in part even older trackways, such as the Icknield Way, but most were laid out by the Romans themselves for purposes of military and civil government. The system of Roman roads, so far as it is known, is of course given in the Ordnance Survey Map of Roman Britain, but most maps mark at any rate the more important ones. They are also treated in considerable detail in the large single-volume edition of Ivan D. Margary's *Roman Roads in Britain*.

Whether the Romans themselves gave names to the roads they built is unknown, and certainly if they did none of them has survived. Most of the modern names are of Old English origin, and in Anglo-Saxon times these were the only metalled roads in the country, though prehistoric trackways like Icknield Way were also important routes. Indeed, the importance of these roads and tracks is suggested in that, under William the Conqueror at latest, the special privileges of the King's Peace protected travellers on Ermine Street, Fosse Way, Watling Street and Icknield Way. Because of these legal privileges and because of the special importance of these particular roads, the custom grew up of giving their names to other roads which had nothing to do with them, hence, the appearance of such names as Ermine Street, Watling Street, etc., applied to roads which had no connexion with the originals. This practice is not, as has been suggested, due merely to modern antiquarians, since some such transferred names are recorded as early as the 13th century.

The word *street* occurs in four of the six road-names mentioned,

153

and it is found also as the first element of some place-names. Modern *street* comes from Old English *strēt* (*strǣt*), itself borrowed from Latin *strata*, and meaning "paved road, Roman road". Indeed, its normal sense in place-names is "paved way", very often "Roman road", as in the following examples.

Watling Street is the name of the main road from Dover to London, through Canterbury and Rochester. From London it goes to Wroxeter, by way of St. Albans, Towcester, High Cross and Wall. It may follow the line of an older route from the coast towards Wheathampstead, near St. Albans (Hrt), the centre of an important British tribe called the Catuvellauni. Originally, Watling Street was simply a local name for the road in the neighbourhood of St. Albans. It appears in Old English as *Wæclinga strǣt* and *Wætlinga strǣt*, and though the latter has given the modern name, *Wæclinga strǣt* is closer to the original one. The Anglo-Saxon name of St. Albans was *Wæclingaceaster* "Roman fort of the Wæclingas (Wacol's people)", and it is clear that Watling Street takes its name from the same folk-group. From this application the name was gradually extended to the whole road. The original Watling Street has also given its name to another Roman road, that which runs north and south through Wroxeter, from Chester in the north to Monmouth in the South. This particular extension of the name was perhaps inevitable, since Watling Street itself terminated at Wroxeter. In other cases, however, the name has been applied to roads which had no connexion at all with it. That from York to Corbridge is called Watling Street, particularly in the North Riding, as also parts of the Roman roads between Manchester and Ribchester, and between Ribchester and Poulton le Fylde.

Ermine Street runs from London to the Humber near Winteringham, through Braughing, Chesterton and Lincoln. Beyond the Humber it continued from the Roman fort at Brough to York, though this section of the road is no longer called Ermine Street. The origin of the name is similar to that of Watling Street. In Old English it is *Earninga strǣt* "Roman road of the Earningas (Earn's people)". These people also gave their name to Arrington (C) "farm or village of the Earningas", which is situated on Ermine Street. Again, like Watling Street, the name must originally have been used locally, but by the time of the Norman Conquest it had been extended to the whole length of the road. Ermine Street, too, has given its name to another quite independent Roman road, that from Silchester to Gloucester, and variously spelt Ermine Street and Irmine Street.

The south-west terminus of the Fosse Way is not known for

certain, but it is likely to have been near Axmouth (D). From there it went by way of Ilchester, Bath, Cirencester, High Cross and Leicester to Lincoln, where it joined Ermine Street. The name is ultimately derived from Latin *fossa* "ditch", presumably with reference to a prominent ditch on one or both sides of the road. Originally the ditch or ditches may have been defensive, and it has been suggested that Fosse Way may have been a frontier line protected by forts. In all the early sources it is referred to as *Fosse*, occasionally as *Fosse Street*, and the modern name does not seem to have been used before the 15th century.

The fourth of the privileged roads was the prehistoric Icknield Way, which connected the Wash with Salisbury Plain. It seems to have run from near Hunstanton by way of Newmarket, Dunstable, the Thames at Streatley, and then south-west into Dorset. Its meaning is unknown, and it may well be pre-English. The name was also transferred to another road now called Icknield Street or Ryknield Street. It is first described, under the latter name, by Ranulf Higden (d. 1364) as running from St. Davids in Wales to York, by Worcester, Birmingham and Lichfield, though it is found in the form Icknield Street in documents from the end of the 12th century. It has more recently been considered to be a branch from Fosse Way at Bourton on the Water, through Alcester, Birmingham, Wall, Little Chester and Chesterfield to Templeborough, near Rotherham. The change in the name from Icknield to Ricknield is probably due to the fact that in the Middle English phrase *at ther Icknilde strete* the final *-r* of the oblique case of the definite article has been mistakenly assumed to belong to the following syllable. Locally Ryknield Street south of Bidford (Wa) is Buckle Street "Burghild's Roman road", perhaps named from Burghild, a daughter of Cenwulf, king of Mercia (796–821). Another stretch of the same road in Warwickshire is called Haydon Way, literally "head way", i.e. chief way.

The most important east-west road in the South Midlands was Akeman Street. It is now the name of the branch road from the Fosse Way at Cirencester, which continues the Bath–Cirencester road to Alchester and Tring, and which probably originally joined Watling Street at St. Albans. But in Anglo-Saxon times the road from Bath to Cirencester was not called Fosse Way as it is today. The name Akeman Street suggests that the entire road through the South Midlands to Bath was earlier called by that name, since the meaning is perhaps "Acemann's Roman road", and it can hardly be merely coincidence that the earlier Anglo-Saxon name for Bath itself was *Acemannes ceaster* perhaps "Acemann's Roman fort". It

155

would seem likely, therefore, that Bath and the important road running from it were named after the same man. Again, an originally local name has become that of the road along its entire length. As with the others, the name was transferred to an independent road, from Cambridge to Ely and Denver (Nf).

Wool Street, part of the Roman road in Cambridgeshire sometimes called Via Devana, seems to mean "wolves' road", no doubt one particularly frequented by wolves. Via Devana is not a genuine Latin name, but was invented by an 18th-century Professor of Geology in the University of Cambridge, who believed that the road which is thought to run from Colchester to Cambridge and Godmanchester (Hu), led ultimately to Chester, the Romano-British *Deva*.

Other names for short stretches of Roman roads are Devil's Causeway, Devil being commonly used of ancient sites or roads; Maiden Way, a name perhaps comparable with Lover's Lane; and Peddars Way, in East Anglia, "pedlar's road".

Stone Street, from Canterbury to Lympne (K), and again from Halesworth to Woodton (Nf), and Stane Street, from London to Chichester (Sx) and from Braughing to Colchester (Ess), both mean "stone, i.e. paved, road". The latter, however, is not a genuinely old form, but an antiquarian reintroduction. Had the name been continuously used it would have given Stone or Stan in Modern English. On the other hand, Stane would have been the regular development in the North, and the Roman road from Manchester to Wigan was probably earlier known as Stany Street "stony road", for Stanystreet survives as the name of a place in Worsley (La). Here, too, belongs Stanegate, the name of the road from Corbridge to Carvoran and on to Carlisle. This also means "stone road", with the second element from Old Norse *gata* "road". This word was also used of Roman roads in Derbyshire; Batham Gate "road to the baths" led from Brough to Buxton, while Doctor's Gate, which appears in the 17th century as *Doctor Talbotes Gate*, from an unidentified Doctor Talbot, went from Brough to Melandra, near Glossop.

High Street, in the sense "important road", is sometimes used of Roman roads, as is the self-explanatory King Street. But in the past Roman roads were often simply called Street or The Street and although few of them retain this form the name has occasionally been given to villages on or near them, such as Streat (Sx) and the more common Street. Strete Raleigh (D), on the other hand, was probably named from an ancient trackway. In addition, Street, sometimes preceded by the French (*en*) *le*, has been added to the names of villages, such as Barton le Street (NRY), Chester le Street (Du), Thorpe le Street (ERY), while the English form appears in Spital in the Street (L), all situated on Roman roads.

The ford on a Roman road is responsible for Startforth (NRY), Strefford (Sa) and the common Stratford and Stretford. Other places have similarly been named from these roads, with a first element *strǣt* or *strēt*. So, Stratton and Stretton, found in many counties, as well as Sturton (L, Nb, Nt, WRY) mean "farmstead or village near the Roman road". Stratton (So) and Stretton (Wa) are further distinguished, the former as "on the Fosse", the latter as "under Fosse", both with reference to Fosse Way. The English word for "homestead" occurs in Streatham (Sr) and Stretham (C), and that for "glade" in Streatley (Bd, Brk), Streetly (C, Wa) and Strelley (Nt), while Streatlam (Du) comes from the dative plural of the compound which has given Streatley. Other examples of places named from Roman roads include Stratfield (Brk, Ha) "open land" and Stradsett (Nf) "place".

One particular stretch of Roman road, the continuation of the London–Silchester road to Old Sarum (W), is called Port Way. This is a common name, more often used of old trackways, some of prehistoric date, as are those in Derbyshire and Devonshire still known in places as Port Way. In most cases, however, the name is no longer used of the track itself and survives only in the names of farms. The meaning is "way leading to a town", though it is rarely possible today to be certain which town is meant.

Hare Street appears as a name for parts of Roman roads and of ancient trackways, and it has been noted, for example, twice in Hertfordshire, three times in Essex and four times in Wiltshire. The similar Hare Way, however, seems to have survived only in field-names. Both mean literally "army road", i.e. a road wide enough for an army to march along, and so "highway". A similar compound, with the same meaning, survives in field-names as Harepath, and this was originally the first part of Harpford (D, So) "ford which carried a highway".

The four commonest names for roads and tracks of post-Roman origin are Broad Way, Hollow Way, Ridge Way and Salt Way. As with all names containing *way*, the meaning varies from "road" to "small track". Salt Way was particularly common in Worcestershire and it has been shown that there were formerly a dozen tracks of this name leading from the neighbourhood of Droitwich, the only district in the Midlands where salt was produced in any quantity during the

157

Middle Ages. Some still survive in that county, while the former existence of others is indicated by modern farms with this name. Salt Way is, of course, found in other counties, both where salt-works were to be found and elsewhere, and it indicates a track used by the pack horses which transported the salt. In the Danelaw and the North generally the more usual name seems to have been Saltergate "salt-merchants' road", where the first element is the occupational name *Salter*. Here, too, we may note Salterford (Nt), Salterforth (WRY) "salt-merchants' ford" and Salters Bridge (St) "salt-merchants' bridge"; these fords and the bridge must have been on routes formerly used by salt-merchants.

Broad Way, Hollow Way and Ridge Way are common in almost every county, and numerous villages and farms are named from them. More important examples include Bradway (Db) and Broadway (So, Wo) "broad road", Holloway (Db, Mx, Sr, W) and Holway (So) "road in a hollow" or "sunken road"; and Ridgeway (Db, K) and Rudgeway (St) "way along a ridge". Some of these last take their names from ancient trackways, like the one still called Ridge Way (Brk–W).

Way is, of course, common, especially in the names of villages situated close to ancient roads and tracks. Among the more interesting compound names are Barkway (Hrt) "birch-tree way", Garmondsway (Du) "Gārmund's road", Halsway (So) "road through the pass", Radway (Wa) and Rodway (So) "road suitable for riding", identical with the modern *roadway*, and Redway (Wt) and Roundway (W) "cleared road". The various Stanways (Ess, Gl, He) "paved road" are usually near a Roman road, as also is Stantway (Gl) "stony road".

The use of Scandinavian *gata* "way, road" in compounds with *stone* has already been noted. This word is common in the North and North Midlands where it seems to take the place of *way*. Some road-names containing *gate* indicate the place to or from which the road leads, and these have occasionally been transferred to villages along the route. So, Galgate (La) is apparently "road to or from Galloway", Deeping Gate (Nth) "to Deeping (L), Spaldinggate (L) "to Spalding". Other examples include Dorket (Nt) "road in the valley", Holgate (ERY) "road running through a hollow" or "sunken road", comparable with Holloway, and Clappersgate (We) "road to the bridge", of which the first element is identical with dialect *clapper* "rough bridge". *Gate* has also been prefixed to two village-names, in each case with reference to its situation on a Roman road— Gate Fulford (ERY), on the main Doncaster–York road, and Gate Helmsley (NRY) on that from York to Malton.

Various words which originally meant "a going, passage" have developed a sense "way, road". Modern English *fare* with the meaning "track, way" survives only in dialect and very occasionally in such names as Denver (Nf) "Danes' track or passage" and Laver (Ess) literally "stream passage", hence ford. Similarly *gang* in the sense "way, road" survives only in dialects, and could be derived either from an English or Scandinavian word. The English word is no doubt the source in Blackgang Chine (Wt), but in the North *gang* may well represent the Scandinavian word, as in Summergangs (ERY) "path(s) which could be used only in summer" and the common Outgang (Cu, Db, ERY, Nt) "way out", very often the way out from the common field of a village.

Modern *lane* is common everywhere in minor names and street-names, but rare in place-names. One or two interesting examples, however, are found, like Laneham (Nt), from the dative plural "at the lanes", a place where several old tracks meet, and Markland (La) "boundary lane", not "boundary land" as the modern form would suggest. *Path* is also uncommon in place-names, but occurs in Gappah (D) "path for goats", Horsepath (O) "for horses", and Sticklepath (D) "steep path". In the North, a dialect variant *peth*, is found in Urpeth (Du) "bison path", perhaps used of the indigenous wild ox, and Hudspeth (Nb) "Hodd's path", but in Gamelspath (Nb) from the Scandinavian personal name Gamel, the dialectal form has been replaced by standard English *path*.

Old English *stīg* and Scandinavian *stígr* "path" both appear as *sty*. They cannot now be separated and are often confused with *sty* "pen". But the sense "path" seems certain in Bransty (Cu) "steep path" and Corpusty (Nf) and Thorfinsty (La), from the Scandinavian personal names Korpr and Thorfinnr. An English compound *ānstiga* "path for one", "narrow footpath" is common in Anstey, and Ansty (Wa).

One or two words of French origin are used in road-names, the commonest being *caucie* "embankment, raised way", surviving in dialects as *causey*. The latter has been superseded in standard English, as also in many place-names, by *causeway* in which the ending is due to popular etymology. Causey, however, is very common in minor names and there are also numerous examples of Causeway.

Modern English *drove* "a herd" is used, particularly in the Fenland, of a cattle road, and as such is common in minor names and field-names in both Cambridgeshire and Lincolnshire, though it is by no means confined to these two counties. Similarly, the word which survives in dialects as *went* "path, way", is found in some place-names, often with the numeral *four*, as in Four Want Ways (Hrt), The Four Wents (Ess) and Fourwents (Sr), as a term for cross-roads. Another word, *leat*, originally meaning "junction (of roads)", survives in dialects also as a "channel for water", the sense required for Longleat (W) "long water-course"; but the original meaning is found in Radlett (Hrt) "road junction", a place situated at an old cross-road on Watling Street. Dialect *twitchel* "narrow passage" is found with this sense in street-names, but it earlier meant "cross-roads" as in Twitchen (D), Twitchill (Db) and Tytchney (Wo).

There are also a few names containing the word *mile*, as for example Milemead (D), literally "a mile distance", situated about a mile from Tavistock. Similarly Mile End (Ess, Mx) means "end of a mile"; the Essex place is about one mile from Colchester, while the more famous Mile End in Middlesex is about a mile from Aldgate on the old London–Colchester road.

Chapter Sixteen

—————— ★ ——————

RIVERS, RIVER-CROSSINGS
AND MARSHLAND

IN addition to those names still used of rivers and streams, there are many others which, though originally river-names, survive only as the names of villages or towns. No distinction will be made here between the two types and only those of English or Scandinavian origin will be considered. Many such names are simply adjectives, or more often derivatives of adjectives, descriptive of the particular river, as with Blyth (Nb, Nt, Sf) and Blythe (St, Wa) from Old English *bliðe*, modern *blithe*, "pleasant, gentle, merry", i.e. "the gentle or merry river or stream". Others of similar origin are Brun (La) "brown", Rede (Nb) "red" and Skerne (Du) "clear". Cave (ERY) and Tale (D) both mean "swift", Stour (C–Ess, K, O–Wa, St–Wo, W–Ha) "strong" and Tove (Nth) "slow". Belah or Beela (We), a mountain stream, seems to be derived from an adjective meaning "roaring". Hamble (Ha), Waver (Cu), Weaver (Ch), Wantsum (K), Wensum (Nf) and Worf (Sa) each means "winding one", with which can be compared Manifold (St) literally "with many folds", i.e. "winding". Loud (La), Lud (L), from which Louth (L) is named, as well as Lyd (D), Lyde (He, So) mean "loud river", Writtle (Ess) is "babbling one"; and Idle (Nt–L) is from Old English *īdel* "idle". Sid (D) is "broad one", and Meden (Nt) and Medina (Wt) "middle one", the first the middle of three streams, the Medina flowing across the middle of the Isle of Wight. From Scandinavian adjectives are derived Bain (L, NRY) probably "straight", Blean (NRY) and Bleng (Cu) "dark", Gaunless (Du) "useless", and Skell (WRY) "resounding".

Other river-names are derivatives of nouns or verbs. Here belong such names as Greet (Nt) "gravel", Mease (Lei–St) and Meese (St–Sa) "moss", Piddle (Do, from which Affpuddle, Tolpuddle etc. are named) "marsh", Sheaf (WRY) "boundary"; Lymm (Ch) perhaps "roaring", Smite (Lei–Nt, Wa, Wo) perhaps "dirty", and Swale (K, NRY), Swallow (L) "rushing". One or two comparable names of Scandinavian origin include Sprint (We), a derivative of a verb meaning "jump, start", appropriate enough for a mountain stream, and Wreak (Lei) probably "twisted", i.e. winding.

A few Old English river-names formed in a similar way, but with the addition of -ing, include Guiting (Gl) "torrent", Leeming (NRY) perhaps "gleaming river", Wantage (Brk), earlier *Waneting*, which has been translated as "intermittent stream", and Wenning (WRY–La) "dark river".

Another type of river-name is that formed from the name of a nearby village or town—called back-formation. Some of these developed in the early Modern English period as their forms indicate, e.g. Chelmer (Ess) from Chelmsford, earlier *Chelmersford*, and Wandle (Sr) from Wandsworth, earlier *Wandelsworth*. Other examples include Alde (Sf) from Aldeburgh, Arun (Sx) Arundel, Lark (Sf–C) Lackford (Sf), Plym (D) Plympton, Tas (Nf) Tasburgh and Yare (Wt) Yarmouth. Here may also be noted Isis (O), first recorded as *Isa* and *Ise* in the 14th century. It has been suggested that *Ise* is from Tam*ise* (i.e. Thames), a name which was at that time thought to have been a compound derived from Thame, one of the streams at the head of the Thames, and a hypothetical name *Ise*. Isis is presumably simply a Latinization of *Ise*.

The largest groups of river-names of English origin are those derived from Old English *brōc* and *burna*, modern *brook* and *burn*. The geographical distribution of these names, as well as other general considerations, would suggest that *burna* was common in the early Anglo-Saxon period and was later replaced by *brōc*. Its meaning is "stream" and also "spring", but in local names the former was undoubtedly the usual sense. *Brōc* "brook, stream" is common in most parts of the country except the Danelaw, but unlike *burna* few places of importance have names containing the word. For example, while the simplex Bourne is fairly common, there is only Brook (K, Wt) and Brooke (Nf, R). Eastbourne and Westbourne (Sx) were originally also simplex names to which the distinguishing East- and West- were added. Both *brook* and *burn* are the sources of numerous compound names, sometimes each is found with the same first element, more often with a similar meaning. The first element may describe the water as in Colburn (NRY) and Colebrook (D) "cool", Saltburn (NRY) "salt", Sherbourne (Wa), Sherburn (Du, ERY, WRY), Shirburn (O) and Shirebrook (Db) "clear", Whitbourne (He) "white", as well as several which denote a dirty or muddy stream, e.g. Fulbrook (Bk, O, Wa), Harborne (St), Shernborne

(Nf) and Skidbrook (L). In others, it refers to the bed—Cheselbourne (Do) "gravel", Claybrooke (Lei) "clay", Sambourn (Wa) and Sambrook (Sa) "sand", and Stainburn (Cu) and Stambourne (Ess) "stone"; or to the course or speed, as in Gisburn (WRY) perhaps "gushing", Webburn (D) "raging", and Woburn (Bd, Sr, W), Wooburn (Bk), Wombourn (St) and Wambrook (So), which have the same meaning as Cringlebrook (La) and Wrangbrook (WRY) "winding brook". A few are named from natural features, such as a "valley" in Combrook (Wa), a "fen or marsh" in Morborne (Hu), a "meadow" in Umborne (D) and Wimborne (Do). Holborn (Mx) and Holbrook (Db, Do) may belong here also, for the meaning is perhaps "brook running in a hollow" though a possible interpretation is "deep brook", as in Daybrook (Nt). The common Cuttle Brook apparently has the same meaning as the self-explanatory Millbrook (Bd, Ha), Milborne (Do, So), Milbourne (Nb) and Milburn (We). A further group of names of identical meaning includes Marlbrook (Sa), Meersbrook (WRY), Tachbrook (Wa) and Tyburn (Mx), all "boundary brook". Drybrook (Gl) and Dryburn (Cu, Nb) were so-named because they soon became dry, while Winterborne (Do), Winterbourne (Brk, Gl, Sx, W) and Winterburn (WRY) must have flowed only in winter. Honeybourne (Gl, Wo) may denote a stream running through rich land, or simply indicate that honey was found along the banks.

In some cases the brook and burn were named from animals or birds, as in Hartburn (Du, Nb), Hindburn (La), Lambourn (Brk), Otterbourne (Ha), Otterburn (Nb, WRY), Roeburn (La) and Birdbrook (Ess), as well as Gadbrook (Sr) "goat", Shipbourne (K) "sheep", Somborne (Ha), Swinburn (Nb) and Swinbrook (O) "swine", Tichborne (Ha) "kid"; Cranborne (Do), Cranbourne (Ha), Cranbrook (K) and Cornbrook (La) "crane or heron", Enborne (Brk) "duck", Gosbrook (St) and Gusborne (K) "goose", and Kidbrook (K) and Kidbrooke (Sx) "kite". One or two others were noted for their fish, as with Fishbourne (Sx, Wt), Fishburn (Du) and Roachburn (Cu), and there is also Auburn (ERY) "eel stream". The first element of a further group denotes the kind of vegetation which grew nearby, as in Ashbourne (Db), Ashburn (Sx), Rushbrooke (Sf), Sedgebrook (L), and also Fairbourne (K) and Fairburn (WRY) "fern", Golborne (Ch, La) "marsh-marigold", Radbourn (Wa), Redbourn (Hrt), Redbourne (L) and Rodbourne (W) "reeds".

In some cases the stream was named from the man who presumably owned the land through which it flowed—Bedburn (Du)

"Bēda", Chatburn (La) "Ceatta", Cottesbrooke (Nth) "Cott",
Leybourne (K) "Lylla", Lilbourne (Nth) and Lilburn (Nb)
"Lilla", Ockbrook (Db) and Ogbourne (W) "Occa", Tedburn
(D) "Tetta" and Tilbrook (Hu) "Tila". A few others are from
folk-names, as with Bolingbroke (L), Hassenbrook (Ess), Holling-
bourne (K) and Pangbourne (Brk) named from "the people of"
Bulla, Hassa, Hōla and Pǣga respectively, as well as Sittingbourne
(K) "stream of the *Sīdingas* (perhaps 'the dwellers on the slope')".
One further name which may be mentioned is Marylebone (Mx),
earlier called Tyburn. In the 15th century this was changed to
Maryburn "stream of St. Mary", from the dedication of a new church
there. Then in the 17th century, a medial -le- was inserted, perhaps
as has been suggested on the analogy of a name like St. Mary le Bow.
The modern form has developed from this word, with the substitution of -bone for -borne.

Old English *ēa* "river, stream", is the source of several river-
names with a modern ending -ey or -y, as in Ebony (K) "Ebba's
stream", Freshney (L) "fresh river", Mersey (Ch–La) "boundary
river", Pevensey (Sx) "Pefen's river", Waveney (Sf/Nf) "river
flowing through a quaking bog", and Romney (K), of which the
first element is uncertain. Also formed from this element are Caldew
(Cu) "cold river" and Hipper (Db) "river where osiers grow".
Reeth (NRY) and Ryde (Wt) come from Old English *rið* "stream",
an element rate in the North and North Midlands. It occurs in a
variety of forms as the second element, of which the first may be the
name of an animal or bird, as in Shepreth (C) "sheep" and Rawreth
(Ess) "heron". That in Coldrey (Ha) means "coal", presumably
"black", while Chaureth (Ess), Childrey (Brk) and Meagre (Hu)
are from the Old English personal names Ceawa, Cilla and Mǣðelgār
respectively. Another word found chiefly in river-names in the South
and South Midlands is *lacu*, modern dialectal *lake*, "stream, water-
course", the source of Lake (W), the self-explanatory Darklake (D)
and Fishlake (WRY), as well as Charlock (Nth) "cold stream" and
Shiplake (O), Shiplate (So) "sheep stream". It also occurs in
Fenlake (Bd) and Venlake (D) "stream flowing through fen" and
Medlock (La) "through meadowland".

Old English *wæter*, modern *water*, denotes both a stream and a lake
in local names. In the first of these senses it occurs in such self-
explanatory names as the common Blackwater, Broadwater (Sx),
Freshwater (Wt) and Loudwater (Bk). Later it is sometimes added
in stream-names formed from place-names like Pendle Water (La),
a usage which can be compared with that of *River*, a French loan-

word, now frequently prefixed to older river-names, and which is itself almost unknown in early names.

In the North, *Water* is of course often used of a lake, as in Coniston Water (La), from the place-name Coniston, Elterwater (Cu) "swan lake" and Ullswater (Cu–We) "Úlfr's lake".

Other Old English elements occur less frequently in the names of streams; *lœcc*, modern dialectal *latch*, *letch*, "stream, bog", and usually used of a "sluggish stream" has given Leach (Gl), from which Eastleach and Northleach are named, and Cranage (Ch) "crow stream"; *hlynn* "torrent" has given Lyn (D), as well as Croglin (Cu) perhaps "torrent with a bend"; and *wisce* "marshy meadow", used of a river, presumably in the sense of "marshy river", is found in Erewash (Db/Nt) "wandering marshy river".

The two important Scandinavian terms for "river, stream" are *á* and *bekkr*. The former of these is much the less frequent, but has given Brathay (We–La) "broad river", Greta (Cu), Greeta (WRY–La) "rocky stream", and Rawthey (WRY–We), Rothay (We) "trout stream". Numerous names derived from *bekkr* are found in the North and North Midlands. The *beck* is sometimes named with reference to the water or the bed, as in Fulbeck (L, Nt) "foul", Skirbeck (L) "clear", Drybeck (Cu, We) and Holbeck (ERY, Nt, WRY) comparable with Dryburn and Holborn respectively, as well as Routenbeck (Cu) "roaring stream", and Welbeck (Nt) presumably "stream which rises from a spring". Gosbeck (Sf) is "goose stream", Troutbeck (Cu, We) is self-explanatory, while Birkbeck (We), Ellerbeck (La, NRY) and Maplebeck (Nt) are named from the birch, alder and maple respectively.

In local names *well* is used both of a stream and a spring, though in most cases it seems to denote the latter. The modern form is usually *well*, but a dialectal variant *wall* is sometimes found in the West Midlands. A meaning "stream or river" is very likely for some names, such as Cawkwell (L) "chalk", Chadwell (Lei) "cold", Cromwell (Nt) "winding", Irwell (La) "wandering" and Shingle-well (K) "pebble". In Barle (So) and Shorwell (Wt) the first element means "hill", in Hopwell (Db) "valley", while Shadwell (Nf) is "boundary stream". Roel (Gl) was named from the "roe" and Tathwell (L) the "toad", while others were occasionally named from a man—Doggod in Dowdeswell (Gl), Brand in Brauncewell (L) and Wogga in Ogwell (D).

Since it is often impossible to decide in which sense this common element was used it is more convenient to take the other examples together, though it will sometimes be clear from the meaning that it denotes a spring. This is certainly so in Twywell (Nth) and Sywell (Nth) from the numerals "two" and "seven" respectively. The first element often indicates some feature of the spring or stream—"black, dark" in Blackwell (Bk, Db, Nt), "blind, i.e. hidden" in the common Blindwell, "clear" in Brightwell (Brk, O) and Britwell (Bk, O), "cold" in Cauldwell (Bd, Nt), Chadwell (Bk, Ess, Hrt) and Caldwall (Wo), "loud" in Ludwell (Db, Nth, O, W), "babbling" in Prittlewell (Ess), "red" in Radwell (Bk, Hrt), "shallow" in Shadwell (Mx), and "white, clear" in Whitwell (C, Db, NRY, Wt). There is also a large group including Carswell (Brk), Caswell (Do, Nth), Causewell (Hrt), Crasswall (He), Cresswell (Db, Nb, St) and Kerswell (D) denoting a stream or spring where cress grew. As we might expect, many springs were named from their owner—Badeca in Bakewell (Db), Cāfhere in Caverswall (St), Eoppa in Epwell (O), Hersa in Harswell (ERY), Hūdel in Hudswell (NRY) and Offa in Offwell (D). Hardwell (Brk) and Orwell Bury (Hrt) were originally identical names meaning "treasure spring", though the exact significance is uncertain. A further pair of names, Maidwell (Nth) "maidens' spring" and Bridwell (D) probably "brides' spring" may possibly have been associated with fertility rites.

Several terms used specifically of a "spring" also occur occasionally in place-names, as for example *funta*, a Celtic loan-word in Old English. This is a rare element found only in the southern half of England where it survives as -hunt in Boarhunt (Ha) "near a fortification" and Chadshunt (Wa) and Tolleshunt (Ess) from the Old English personal names Ceadel and Toll. Fovant (W) and Havant (Ha) are also from personal names, Fobba and Hāma, while Teffont (W) means "boundary spring". Old English *celde* "spring" is rarer still, but is the source of the Kentish Bapchild and Honeychild, named from Bacca and Hūna respectively. The corresponding Scandinavian *kelda* is rather more frequent in minor names, but occurs also in Threlkeld (Cu) "thralls' spring" and Trinkeld (La) "Þrándr's spring". Another Old Norse word *brunnr* "spring", but also "stream", is apparently represented by the East Riding, Eastburn, Kirkburn and Southburn, all named from the same stream.

Fleet (Do, Ha, L, Mx) comes from Old English *flēot*, modern *fleet*, "estuary, inlet, creek" and also "stream", as do Northfleet and Southfleet (K), Benfleet (Ess) "creek marked by a beam", Hunslet (WRY) "Hūn's stream", Surfleet (L) "sour creek or stream", Wainfleet (L), literally "wagon stream", "one which could be crossed by a wagon" and Herringfleet (Sf) "stream of the *Herelingas* (Herela's people)".

Ewell (K, Sr), Ewelme (O), Ewen (Gl) and Toller Whelme (Do) all mean "source of a stream or river", the last two those of the Thames and *Toller* (now the Hooke) respectively. With these can be compared Dove Head (Db) and Ribble Head (La), as well as other names in which *head* is used in the same sense. On the other hand, Wearmouth (Du), Weymouth (Do) and Yarmouth (Nf) are named from the estuaries of the respective rivers. Portsmouth (Ha), however, means "mouth of the *Port*", *Port* being the old name of the harbour there, and Yarmouth (Wt) is apparently "gravel estuary". Emmott (La) is "junction of the rivers or streams", as also are Meeth (D) and Mytham Bridge (Db), and a comparable Scandinavian name is Beckermet (Cu). Old English *twisla* "fork of a river, junction of streams" is found in the Lancashire Entwistle and Oswaldtwistle from the personal names Enna and Ōswald.

Hythe (K), as well as Greenhithe (K), is derived from Old English *hȳð* "landing-place". Earith (Hu) and Erith (K) mean "gravelly landing-place"; "chalk or limestone" was landed at Chelsea (Mx); "lambs" and "cattle" respectively at Lambeth (Sr) and Rotherhithe (Sr), while those at Putney (Sr) and Stepney (Mx) were owned by Putta and Stybba. Maidenhead (Brk) is "maidens' landing-place", presumably because young women gathered there. Another word with a similar meaning, Old English *stæð*, has given Stathe (So) and Bickerstaffe (La) "beekeepers' landing-place", but Staithes (NRY), Statham (Ch) from the dative plural, and the Lancashire Croxteth and Toxteth owned by Krókr and Tóki, are probably from the corresponding Scandinavian word.

Old English *ēgland*, modern *island*, rarely occurs in place-names, but the first part of this compound, *ēg*, is common. Besides meaning "island" it also denotes land partly surrounded by water, for example by two streams, or dry ground in fenland, or even well-watered land. It is found in one of these senses in the common Eye, Eyam (Db) from the dative plural, and in numerous compound names. Many of these have as first element the name of the owner — Bardsea (La), Bardsey (WRY) "Beornrēd", Battersea (Sr) "Beaduric", Bermondsey (Sr) "Beornmund", Chitty (K) "Citta", Hackney (Mx) "Haca", Gate Helmsley (NRY) "Hemele", Olney (Bk) "Olla", Romsey (Ha) "Rūm" and Whittlesey (C) "Wittel". Others have the name of an animal or bird, as in the self-explanatory Hart (Du), Harty (K), Horsey (Nf, So), Oxney (K, Nth), Chickney (Ess), as well as Chalvey (Bk) "calf" and Quy (C) "cow", while Dorney (Bk) is "island where humble-bees are found". "Peas" grew at Pusey (Brk), "rushes" at Bunny (Nt) and "wild-garlic" at

Ramsey (Ess, Hu). The first element of Thorney (C, Mx, Sf, So, Sx) is self-explanatory; that in Sidney (Sr) means "broad", in Mersea (Ess) "the sea" and in Quaveney (C) "quaking bog". Lundy (D) "puffin island" and Haxey (L) "Hákr's island", however, are from the corresponding Scandinavian word. But the common Old Norse term for an "island" is *holmr*, the source of Holme, though the word is used also in other senses similar to those for *ēg*. Occasionally, it was named from an early owner, Balki in Balkholme (ERY), Gaukr in Gauxholme (La) and Wulfstān in Wolstenholme (La). Sometimes, the first element denotes the animals which grazed there, as with Oxenholme (We), Studholme (Cu) and Tupholme (L), though Tupholme may be from the personal name Tupi; or what grew there as in Haverholme (L) "oats", Heigholme (ERY) "hay", and the self-explanatory Brackenholm (ERY) and Peaseholme (La). There is also Conisholme (L) "king's island", Oldham (La) "old island", and Stockholm (ERY) "island cleared of trees", comparable with Stockholm in Sweden.

Pool and *Mere* are common in place-names. The first refers not only to a pool or pond, but sometimes to a pool in a river, and occasionally to a stream. It is the source of Pool (D), Poole (Ch, Do, Gl), Blackpool (La), Drypool (ERY), and also Wimpole (C) "Wina's pool" and Liverpool (La), originally the name of a now dried-up tidal creek, perhaps meaning "pool with thick water". The *pool* in Skippool (La) certainly denoted a stream—"ship stream"—and the place named from it was formerly an important harbour. Maer (St), Meare (So) and Mere (Ch, L, W) are all from Old English *mere* "pool". Among the numerous compounds containing this word are Ringmer (Sx) "circular pool", Tangmere (Sx) perhaps "shaped like a pair of tongs", Holmer (Bk, He) "in a hollow" and Buttermere (Cu) of which the Butter- may refer to good land around the lake. A large number of these names have as first element the name of an animal or bird, as in Boulmer (Nb) and Bulmer (Ess) "bull", Catmore (Brk) "wild cat", Ilmer (Bk) "hedgehog", Woolmer (Ha) "wolf", Anmer (Nf) "duck", Bridgemere (Ch) "bird", Cranmere (Sa) "crane", Cromer (Hrt, Nf) "crow", while Frogmore (D, Do, Hrt) was noted for its frogs, Almer (Do) and Elmer (Sx) for eels, and Pickmere (Ch) for pike. In other names the reference is to the vegetation growing there—Redmere (C) "reeds" Rushmere (Sf) "rushes" and Grasmere (We) "grass", whether in the lake itself or simply on its banks. Only rarely is the pool named from an early owner, as in Badlesmere (K) "Bæddel", Ellesmere (Sa) "Elli" and Patmore (Hrt) "Peatta".

Ford, Old English *ford*, is one of the common place-name elements, as we might expect. In view of its importance to the early settlers it is not surprising that a large number were named from some early owner or neighbour, Ægel in Aylesford (K), Basa in Basford (Nt), Cēolmǣr in Chelmsford (Ess), Docc in Doxford (Nb), Ella in Elford (Nb, St), Ica in Ickford (Bk), Steorta in Stortford (Hrt) and Wifel in Wilsford (L, W), all the names of men, but Alford (So) is from a lady called Aldgȳð. Occasionally, however, the ford was named from a group of people as in Hemingford (Hu) "Hemma's people", and Shillingford (O) "Sciella's people".

The Ditch- in Ditchford (Wa, Wo) "dyke ford" refers to Fosse Way which crosses the stream here, and others, including Farforth (L), Styford (Nb), Wayford (So) and Wentford (Sf), have as first element a word meaning "way or road". A further group has been named from the river the ford crosses, as with Brentford (Mx), Dartford (K) and Lydford (D) across the Brent, Darent and Lyd, while Yafforth (NRY) means "river ford".

The common Barford and also Barforth (NRY) mean "barley ford", one particularly used when the barley harvest was taken in, and comparable with Heyford (Nth, O) "hay ford". Others were named from the vegetation found there—"broom" at Bramford (Sf), Brampford (D), "chag" at Chagford (D), "burdock" at Clatford (Ha) and probably "marsh-marigolds" at Guildford (Sr). The sites of others were no doubt marked by trees, as at Ashford (D, Db, Sa), Boxford (Sf), Oakford (D), as well as Pyrford (Sr) "pear-tree", Salford (Bd, La) "sallow" and Widford (Ess, Hrt, O) "withy".

A considerable number are from the animals which used them or were found near them, for example Catford (K), Catforth (La) "wild cats", Gateford (Nt), Gateforth (WRY) "goats", Nafford (Wo) and Rutherford (NRY) "cattle", Rochford (Ess, Wo) "raches, i.e. hunting dogs", Shefford (Bd, Brk), Shifford (O) "sheep", Swinford (Brk, Lei, Wo), Kingswinford (St) "swine", as well as Hartford (Ch, Nb), Hartforth (NRY), Horsford (Nf) and Horsforth (WRY). Others are from birds, as with Carnforth (La), Cranford (Mx, Nth), Cransford (Sf) "cranes or herons", Gosford (D, O, Wa), Gosforth (Cu, Nb) "geese", Ketford (Gl) "kites" and the self-explanatory Buntingford (Hrt).

The ford was "long" at Langford and Longford, both common names, "wide" at Romford (Ess), "deep" at Defford (Wo), Deptford (K, W), Diptford (D), and "shallow" at Shadforth (Du), Shalford (Ess, Sr) and Shelford (Nt). The water was "clear" at

Sherford (D), "slaggy, i.e. muddy" at Slaggyford (Nb) and "foul" at Fulford, a name found in many counties. The path across was "rough" at Rufford (La, Nt) and Rufforth (WRY), covered with "cinders" at Cinderford (Gl) and with "loose stones" at Clatterford (Wt). There was "chalk" at Chalford (Gl, O) and "stones" at Stainforth (WRY), Stamford (L, Mx, Nb), Stamford Bridge (ERY), Stowford (W) and the common Stanford; and either the bottom or the water was "red" at Radford (D, Nt, Wa, Wo) and Retford (Nt). Somerford (Ch, Gl, St, W) could only be used in summer and Efford (Co, D, Ha) at ebb-tide.

The ford at Maidford (Nth) was specially associated with "maidens", those at Lattiford (So) and Latherford (St) with "beggars", and that at Glandford (Nf) with "revelry". Freeford (St), as the name seems to suggest, was presumably free from toll, while Tetford (L) and Thetford (C, Nf) denote a "public ford".

Other terms for "ford" appear only very occasionally. Old English wæd is the source of Wade (Sf), Biggleswade (Bd) "Biccel's ford", and Iwade (K) "yew-tree ford". The corresponding Scandinavian vað is rather more frequent, however, in the North and North Midlands, as in Waithe (L) and Wath (NRY, WRY). In compounds it sometimes survives as -with; so, there is Langwith (Db/Nt, ERY) "long ford" and the self-explanatory Sandwith (Cu). Solway (Cu) probably means "ford marked by a pillar", which would be Lochmaben Stone, a large granite boulder which stood at the Scottish end of the ford.

Later, of course, the bridge largely took the place of the ford; but, as is to be expected, *bridge* occurs less frequently than *ford* in the names of important places. The usual modern form is *bridge*, but *brigg* is not uncommon in some areas due to Scandinavian influence (or even to the corresponding Scandinavian *bryggja*, which however means "jetty, quay"), as in Brigg (L), formerly *Glanford Brigg* of which the first part is identical with Glandford (Nf). Though the usual meaning is "bridge", occasionally it may refer to a causeway or to a raised track through marshland, as in Bridgend (L). In some cases the bridge was apparently built or owned by an individual as with Abridge (Ess) "Æffa", Curbridge (O) "Creoda", Harbridge (Ha) "Hearda" and Tonbridge (K) "Tunna". Others were named from the river it crossed as in Bainbridge (NRY), Doveridge, earlier *Dovebridge* (Db), Stourbridge (Wo) and Weybridge (Sr). A number refer to the shape of the bridge or to the material from which it was constructed: hence, Stonebridge (Mx) and Stanbridge (Bd, Do, Ha,

Sx), and Woodbridge (Do, Sf), as well as Stockbridge (Do, Ha, La, WRY), Stocksbridge (WRY) "log bridge" and Stockenbridge (D) "bridge made of logs". Felbrigg (Nf) and Fell Briggs (NRY), Thelbridge (D), Elbridge, earlier *Thelbridge* (K, Sx) and Shide Bridge (Wt) all mean "plank bridge", and Leather Bridge (Wo) must have been named from some special use of leather in its construction. Ironbridge (Ess), however, is misleading, for it means "ewes' bridge", and so belongs to the same group as Bulbridge (W) and Cowbridge (Ess, W). Ivybridge (D) was covered with ivy; Botolph Bridge (Hu) is named from the dedication of the nearby church of Orton to St. Botolph, patron saint of wayfarers; and Wakebridge (Db) may mean "bridge where the wake or annual festival is held". Pennybridge is common in later names for a bridge with a penny toll, and an early example is Pennybridge (near Wadhurst Sx), first recorded in 1438. The meaning "causeway" is likely where the first element has the sense "brushwood" or "made of brushwood", as in Ricebridge (Sr), Risebridge (Du, Ess) and Rising Bridge (Nth), or where it denotes a "fen" as in Fambridge (Ess) or a "muddy place" as in Slimbridge (Gl).

One or two other names of bridges may be noted. Pontefract (WRY), originally French *Pontfreit* "broken bridge", was Latinized in early sources as *Pontefracto* (the ablative case) and the modern form comes from this. Grampound (Co) and Grandpont (O) both mean "great bridge", but that from which Grandpont was named was originally a causeway and not a bridge in the usual modern sense of the word.

The term for "marshland" most common in place-names is *marsh* itself (Old English *mersc*), as in Marsh (Bk, Sa), Saltmarsh (He) and Wildmarsh (Mx). Stodmarsh (K) was named from a "stud or herd of horses" and Bickmarsh (Wa) and Killarmarsh (Db) from the personal names Bica and Cynewald. *Fen* is frequent in *Fen*land names, where it is often added to a river- or village- name, as in the Cambridgeshire Ouse Fen and Wisbech High Fen. When it occurs in the South-west, however, it often survives as Venn (D, Do). It is also the source of a surprising number with a personal name as first element, Gedda in Edvin Loach (He), Mǣrhard in Mason (Nb), Mūl in Mousen (Wo) and Hrōða in Ratfyn (W), as well as others like Fulfen (Ess, St) "foul marsh" and Redfern (Wa) perhaps "winding marsh".

Slough (Bk), from Old English *slōh*, has its obvious meaning, and a derivative of the same word has given Slaughter (Gl) "muddy place". Old English *wæsse* "swamp, wet place" is found most frequently in the West Midlands, as in Buildwas (Sa) "near or with a building", Hopwas (St) "in a valley" and Rotherwas (He) "for cattle", as well as Alrewas (St) "alder swamp" and Alderwasley (Db), originally identical with Alrewas and to which *lēah* "wood, glade" was added later.

Old English *wisce* probably means "marshy meadow" and is the source of Cranwich (Sf) and Glydwish (Sx), frequented by the "crane or heron" and "kite" respectively, and of Dulwich (Sr) and Lysways (St) where "dill" and "reeds" grew. Strood (K), Stroud (Gl) and Stroud Green (Mx) come from *strōd* "marshy land overgrown with brushwood"; the second element also of Gostrode (Sr) "marshy land where geese are found".

In those areas settled by Scandinavians Old Norse *kjarr* is a common term for "marshy land". It survives in dialects as *carr* "plantation of alders in a low-lying place", with which can be compared Aldercar (Db, Nt) and Ellerker (ERY) "marshy land where alders grow". "Reeds" and "willows" grew at Redcar (NRY) and Selker (Cu), while Trencar (NRY) was frequented by "cranes" and Altcar (La) was named from the River Alt. Old Norse *mýrr*, modern *mire*, though well-represented in minor and field-names, is otherwise uncommon, but is found in Knavesmire in York "Knǫrr's marshy ground"; and a unique name of Scandinavian origin, Thirsk (NRY), may be included here, for it is derived from Old Norse *þresk* "fen".

Chapter Seventeen

--------- ★ ---------

HILLS AND VALLEYS

NOT infrequently a name originally given to some particular hill or valley later came to be applied to a near-by farm or village, but these are not habitative names proper, and will therefore be considered here along with those which are still only used of natural features.

Hill itself is very common in place-names, and is found in that form in most counties, though occasionally *Hull* occurs in the West and South-west. The most interesting of the names having the simplex form is that of the place called Hill and Moor (Wo), denoting a hill above a *moor* or marsh. The word is, of course, the second element of a large number of compounds, with the first element sometimes denoting the shape, as in Coppull (La) "with a peak" and Cropwell (Nt) "with a crop or hump", or the steepness, in Stapenhill (St), as well as Shottle (Db) "hill with a steep slope". Windhill (WRY) and Windle (La) mean "windy hill", and Snodhill (He) may be "snowy hill", while Wardle (Ch, La) and Warthill (NRY) are "watch, i.e. look-out, hill", the meaning also of the common Toothill, Tothill, Tottle and Tuttle. The first element is an adjective in Grindle (Sa) "green", Hernhill (K) "grey", Whittle (La, Nb) and Whitle (Db) "white"; Clennell (Nb) "clean", perhaps a hill free from weeds, etc., the common Hungerhill "barren", and Wildhill (Hrt) "uncultivated". Many of the names containing *hill*, which later became the names of villages, have a personal name as first element, Hengest in Hinxhill (K), Ocga in Ogle (Nb), Pohha in Poughill (Co, D), Snodd in Snodshill (W), Tāta in Tatenhill (St), Wyrma in Wormhill (Db), and a folk-name "Sunna's people" in Sunninghill (Brk). In others, however, it denotes the crops which grew there, as with the common Wheathill, as well as Bearl (Nb) "barley", Haverhill (Sf) "oats", Pishill (O) "peas", Ryhill (ERY, WRY), Ryal (Nb) and Ryle (Nb) "rye", while "broom" grew at Broomhill, frequently found as a minor name, and "woad" at Odell (Bd). Those in which it is a tree-name are usually self-explanatory, hence Ashill (So), Birchill and Thornhill,

173

both found in most counties, as are some of those derived from the name of an animal or bird, Catshill (Wo), Harthill (Ch, Db, WRY), Hawkhill (Nb), though less obvious are Coole (Ch) and Keele (St) "cows", Gledhill (WRY) "kite", and note also Beal (Nb) "bee hill".

Old English *dūn*, modern *down*, as used in place-names can denote anything from a slight slope to a steep hill. It is uncommon as a simplex name Down, and is usually distinguished in some way, as in East Down and West Down (D). In compounds, the first element is frequently a personal name, Æbba, or the feminine Æbbe in Abingdon (Brk), Bealda in Baldon (O), Cærda in Charndon (Bk), Cissa in Chessington (Sr), Ēalāc in Elkstone (St) and Ilkeston (Db), Wærma in Warndon (Wo), Winebeald in Wimbledon (Sr) and a folk-name "Billa's people" in Billington (La).

Some hills are named from the animals or birds found there, as with Cauldon (St), Chaldon (Do, Sr) "calves", Everdon (Nth) "boars", Horton (Gl) "harts" and Swindon (St, W), Swinden (Gl) "swine"; others from the crops or plants growing there, "hay" at Haydon (Do, So, W), "rye" at Raydon (Sf), Reydon (Sf), "wheat" at Whaddon (Bk, C, Gl), "clover" at Claverdon (Wa), "broom" at Brandon, found in several counties, and Bromden (Sa), and "fern" at Faringdon (Brk, Do, Ha, O), while Black Heddon (Nb) means "heather-covered hill". The first element denotes the colour of the hill in Fallowdon (Nb) "fallow, yellow", Fawdon (Nb) "multi-coloured", Grendon (Bk, D, Nth, Wa), Grindon (Du, Nb, St) "green", and Blackdown (Do, Wa) "black", identical with which is Blagdon (D, Do, So); or the type of surface or soil in Clandon (Sr) "clean", perhaps free from weeds, etc., Rowden (He) "rough", Smithdown (La) "smooth", Standen (Wt), Standon (Hrt, Sr) and Stondon (Bd, Ess), "stone", as well as the self-explanatory Claydon (Bk, O) and Sandon (Brk, Ess, Hrt, St). Headon (Nt), Hendon (Mx) and High Down (Sx) all mean "high hill", and Shenington (O) is "beautiful hill".

There is also a group of names including Hambledon (Do, Ha, Sr), Hambleton (NRY, R), Hameldon (La), Humbledon (Du) and Hammerton (Db), meaning literally "maimed or mutilated hill". It has been suggested that the first element is used in the sense "bare", or perhaps more often "flat-topped", for many of these hills have rough flat tops. Others are similarly named from their shape, such as Bowden (D, Db) "like a bow", Neasden (Mx) "like a nose" and Edgton (Sa) "having an edge". Weldon (Nth) is a hill "with a spring" and Laindon (Ess) "near the *Lea*", a lost stream-name, identical with the River Lea in the same county. Warden, a common name, means "look-out hill", Burden (WRY), Great Burdon (Du) and Burradon (Nb) "hill with a fortification", and Boldon (Du) "hill with a dwelling".

Modern *cliff*, Old English *clif*, is common enough in place-names, but the topography of the places so-called makes it clear that it could refer to a slope or a steep slope, as well as an escarpment or precipice. As a simplex name, it survives in the common Cliff and Cliffe, but Clive is also found. Among the many compounds is the self-explanatory Redcliff, a name occurring frequently, and identical with which is Radcliffe (La, Nt), Radclive (Bk), Ratcliff (Mx) and Ratcliffe (Lei, Nt). Briercliffe (La) was named from "briars", Catsley (Do) and Gatley (Ch) from "wild cats" and "goats" and Arncliffe (WRY) from "eagles". Occasionally the "cliff" was named from a near-by river as with Avoncliff (W), while Wycliffe (NRY) may be "cliff in a river bend", and Scarcliffe (Db) "cliff with a gap or pass". A personal name, however, occurs only occasionally as first element, but there is Austcliff (Wo) "Alstān" and Hockliffe (Bd) "Hocga".

Old English *beorg* and *hlāw* and Old Norse *haugr* sometimes denote burial-mounds, but the words are also used of natural mounds or hills. From the singular of *beorg* there is Barrow (R) and Barugh (NRY, WRY), and from the plural the Westmorland Barras and Barwise. This word survives as -barrow, -berry, -borough, -bury or -ber as the second element of compounds, and each is illustrated in the following examples, of which the first element may be the name of a tree, as in Mappleborough (Wa), Thornborough (Bk) and Limber (L) "lime-tree hill"; a crop in the Leicestershire Market Harborough "oats" and Whatborough "wheat", or some other plant in Brackenborough (L), and Farmborough (So), Farnborough (Brk, Ha, K, Wa) "fern". Occasionally it is a bird, as in Finborough (Sf), Finburgh (Wa) "wood-pecker", and Kaber (We) "jackdaw". The first element of Grandborough (Bk, Wa) means "green", Whitbarrow (Cu) "white" and Mickleborough (Nt) "big". But in others it denotes the type of soil, hence Chiselborough (So) "gravel", Singleborough (Bk) "shingle", and Stanborough (Hrt) "stone", while the *cockle* in Cocklebury (W), identical with which is Cockleberry (NRY), perhaps refers to the fossils in the stones there.

Old English *hlāw* is used of a natural feature in Lewes (Sx), originally singular, and in the compounds Horelaw (La) "grey", the Derbyshire Callow "cold", Grindlow "green", Shardlow "with a gap", Wardlow "look-out" and Ludlow (Sa), which has been translated "hill by the rapid". In Heatherslow (Nb) the first element means "stag", and in Cushat Law (Nb) "wood-pigeon". Similarly, Old Norse *haugr* means "hill" or "mound" in Blacko (La) "black", Scallow (Cu) "bare" and Ulpha (Cu) "wolf", while Clitheroe (La) is "hill with loose stones", almost certainly referring to the loose limestone of the prominent hill there.

The basic sense of Old English *hōh* in place-names is "spur of land", but the spur may vary from a slight rise to a steep ridge. It survives as Hoe, Hoo and Hooe in simplex names, but the *h-* is sometimes lost when it occurs as the second element of a compound. The first element is frequently a personal name, Æga in Aynho (Nth), Bill in Belsay (Nb), Fleca in Flecknoe (Wa), Wata in Watnall (Nt) and Wifa in Wivenhoe (Ess), and in several names it is a folk-name, "Ifa's people" in Ivinghoe (Bk), "Pydda's people" in Piddinghoe (Sx), as well as Bengeo (Hrt) "dwellers on the Beane", and Farthinghoe (Nth) "dwellers among the ferns". Other examples of *hōh* include Langenhoe (Ess) "long" and Sharpenhoe (Bd) "sharp", Sharrow (WRY) "boundary" and Wellow (L) "spring".

Rudge is a common dialectal form of Old English *hrycg*, which appears in the standard language as *ridge*, but Rigg, from the corresponding Scandinavian word, occurs in the North. Among the numerous compounds containing the English word are Brantridge (Sx) "steep", identical in meaning with Stickeridge (D), Rowridge (Wt) "rough", and the self-explanatory Brownridge (Nb) and Longridge (La). Ditteridge (W) means "ridge near the dyke", apparently a reference to Fosse Way, and Melkridge (Nb) "milk ridge", presumably one which had pasturage giving plenty of milk. "Eagles" were to be seen at Eridge (Sx) and "hawks" at Hawkridge (Brk, So) and Hawridge (Bk), while Totteridge (Hrt) and Waldridge (Bk) were named from early owners Tāta and Wealda. The Scandinavian word, however, is the source of Castlerigg (Cu) "ridge with a castle", Crossrigg (We) "with a cross" and Wheyrigg (Cu) "with a sheepfold", as well as Lambrigg (We) and Whelprigg (We) where "lambs" and "whelps" were to be found, and Haverigg (Cu) and Loughrigg (We) where "oats" and "leeks" respectively grew. Linch (Sx) and Lynch (So) are derived from Old English *hlinc* "ridge, bank", as are Barlinch (So) "where barley grows", Sandling (K) "sandy slope" and Sydling (Do) "broad ridge".

Old English *ofer*, *ufer* "ridge, hill, slope" seems to be most common in the Midlands, as in Over (Ch) and Littleover and Mickleover (Db), both named from the same ridge, with the prefixes as later additions. Original compounds of this word include Heanor (Db), Hennor (He) "high ridge", the self-explanatory Longnor (St), and Bicknor (Gl, He), Hadzor (Wo) and Tittensor (St) from the personal names Bica, Headd and Titta. Calver (Db) means "calf slope", while Ashover (Db), Birchover (Db), Bircher (He) and Okeover (St) were named from the ash, birch and oak. Often in the early forms the related word _ōfer_ "bank, river-bank, shore" cannot be distinguished from _ofer_, but the topography will usually indicate which is the correct etymology. This is certainly the source of Over (C), Northover (So), Westover (So, Wt), and Hedsor (Bk) "Hedde's bank". Very often, too, the early forms of _ōfer_ can be confused with those of _ōra_ "shore, river-bank, slope, hillside", which has probably given Oare (Brk, K, W), Ore (Sx), Bicknor (K), Bognor (Sx) and Pinner (Mx) from the personal names Bica, Bucge (feminine) and Pinna respectively, as well as Pershore (Wo) "bank where osiers grow", Wardour (W) "look-out slope" and Windsor (Brk, Do), Winsor (D, Ha) perhaps "river-bank with a windlass".

For the most part Old English _scelf_ and _scylfe_ "rock, ledge, shelving land" denote a ledge of land, shelving land or plateau in place-names such as Shelf (Db, WRY), Shelve (Sa), Bashall (WRY) "ridge", and Hunshelf (WRY), Minshull (Ch) and Tibshelf (Db) from the names of early owners Hūn, Monn and Tibba. The corresponding Scandinavian word, however, has given Raskelf (NRY) "roe-deer", Hinderskelfe (NRY) from the feminine name Hildr, and Ulleskelf (WRY) from the masculine Úlfr.

Ness (Ch, Sa, NRY) and Naze, common in minor names, are derived from Old English _næss_, _ness_, modern _ness_, which was used not only of a promontory or headland, but also of a projecting piece of high land. It occurs, too, in Foulness (Ess) "birds", Sharpness (Gl) and Sharp Ness (K) "sharp, pointed", Sheerness (K) "bright", and Totnes (D) and Wrabness (Ess) from the early owners Totta and Wrabba. The corresponding Scandinavian _nes_ will often give similar early forms, and could equally well be the source of Bowness (Cu) "bow-shaped headland", but is certainly found in Skegness (L) "Skeggi's promontory".

Tor, Old English _torr_ "rock, rocky peak, hill", a Celtic loan-word, is almost entirely restricted in early names to the South-west of England. In addition, it is not uncommon in Derbyshire, though usually only in names first recorded after 1500. The names containing this element are still often those of natural features or of very small places, as in the following (all in Devon except where stated): Black Tor, Hound Tor, Pig Tor (Db), Rough Tor (also Co), identical with which are Router and Rowtor (Db), and Scobitor, Vobster (So) and Worminster (So) with the personal names Sceobba, Fobb and Wyrm as first element.

Other Old English words occur less frequently in place-names denoting hills and the like; *cnoll*, modern *knoll*, appears in Bigknowle (Sx), Chetnole (Do) and Edge Knoll (Du) from Bibba, Ceatta and Ĕadin, the names of early owners, as well as the common minor name Knowle, and Knole (K); similarly *copp*, modern *cop*, "hill-top, peak" and probably also in the more general sense of "hill", has given the Lancashire Copp, Pickup "hill with a point", and Warcop (We) "hill with a cairn or beacon". This is also the second element of *setcopp*, perhaps "flat-topped hill", the source of Sidcup (K), while Old Norse *setberg*, also "flat-topped hill", has given Sadberge (Du) and Sedbergh (WRY). Lydd (K) and Lydham (Sa) both represent the dative plural of *hlid* "slope", though in the first the ending was lost. The related *hlið*, with similar meaning, is found in Adgarley (La) "Ĕadgār's slope", but is sometimes indistinguishable from Old Norse *hlíð*. The latter, however, is the source of Lyth (We), Lythe (La, NRY), Kellet (La) and Kelleth (We) "slope with a spring", and Hanlith (WRY) "Hagne's slope", from a Scandinavian personal name.

Except in minor names *peak*, Old English *pēac* "hill", occurs only rarely, as in Peak (Db), while Old English *scora*, modern *shore*, "river-bank, steep slope or rock", appears in the Lancashire Shore, and Helmshore apparently "steep ridge with a cattle-shed". Sharples, in the same county, seems to mean "steep place", as does Steep (Ha) and probably Shorne (K).

Scandinavian words also occasionally found include *brekka* "slope, hill", a term associated with Norwegian, as distinct from Danish, settlement in England. It has given, besides Breck, Norbreck and Norbrick "north", Warbreck "with a cairn or beacon" and Swarbrick from the personal name Svartr, all in Lancashire, and Haverbrack (We) "where oats grow". The same is true of Old Norse *fjall, fell* "hill, mountain", which occurs chiefly in the North-west, as in Bow Fell (We) "bow-shaped", Harter Fell (Cu) "of the hart", Whinfell (Cu, We) "where whin grows", and Mell Fell (Cu, We) and Sca Fell (Cu), where *fell* has been added to old hill-names, apparently meaning "bare hill" and "bald hill" respectively.

In some hill-names an ordinary word is used in a transferred topographical sense. This is the case with *edge*, Old English *ecg*, denoting the edge of a hill, a hill-side, or an escarpment, as in Alderley Edge (Ch), Lincoln Edge (L), and especially in Lancashire and the hilly districts of the West Midlands where Edge is a common minor name. In addition, there is the self-explanatory Brownedge (La), Harnage (Sa) and also Stanedge (Db, La) "stony", Heage (Db) "high", and Hathersage (Db) "Hæfer's edge". *Head* is similarly used of a "headland, spit of land" in Birkenhead (Ch) "birch-covered", Read (La) "where roe-deer are found", Thicket (ERY) "thick, dense", presumably with vegetation and the Westmorland Arnside and Burnside from the personal names Earnwulf and Brūnwulf. From the corresponding Scandinavian word there is Sellet (La) "headland with a shieling", and Whitehaven (Cu) "white headland", to which *haven* "harbour" was added later. Old English *bile* "*bill*, beak" is used of a headland or promontory in Amble (Nb) "Anna's headland", while in Portland Bill (Do) it has been added to an older name.

Old English *hēap*, modern *heap*, used of a hill, has given Heap (La), but Professor Ekwall considers that Shap (We), derived from the same word, owes its name to the ruins of the prehistoric stone-circle there. Hett (Du) comes from Old English *hætt*, modern *hat*, and *horn* is sometimes used of a horn-shaped hill, as in Hartshorne (Db) "stag's horn-shaped hill". Similarly Old English *stīgrāp*, modern *stirrup*, is the source of Styrrup (Nt), from a hill with the fancied shape of a stirrup, while *stigel* "stile" has given dialectal *steel* "ridge", the sense required for Steel (Nb) and Steel Fell (We). Preen (Sa) is apparently derived from Old English *prēon* "brooch", again presumably from some fancied shape of the ridge there, and Clegg (La) is from Old Norse *kleggi* "haystack", used here of a hill.

A word commonly used in this way is Old English *sīde*, modern *side*, denoting a hill-side, as in the common and self-explanatory Brownside, Birkenside (Nb) "birch-covered", Whernside (WRY) presumably "where millstones are quarried", and a group, including Facit (La), Fawcett (We), Fawside (Du) and Phoside (Db), meaning "multi-coloured hill-side".

Of the numerous place-name elements denoting a "valley", *valley* itself is rare, and *vale*, also a French loan-word occurs infrequently. Noteworthy, however, are Merevale (Wa) "pleasant valley", and the North Riding Jervaulx and Rievaulx "valley of the Ure" and "valley of the Rye" respectively, the last apparently a translation of the English *Ryedale*. *Dale*, on the other hand, is common enough, particularly in the Scandinavianized areas of the country and occasionally elsewhere. Recent research has suggested that Old English *dæl* "dale" was not a common place-name element, and that the subsequent increasing use of *dale* was due to the influence of the corresponding Old Norse *dalr*. The similarity of the two words often makes it impossible to be certain which of them is the source of particular names. But it is probably the English word in Silverdale (La) "silver" from the colour of the rocks, the common Deepdale and Debdale (Nth) "deep", Edale (Db) "land between streams", and Sterndale (Db) "stony". A few contain an Old English term for animals, as in Cowdale (Db), Kiddal (WRY) "cows", and Withersdale (Sf) "wether", and for a plant in Farndale (NRY) "fern", but the first element could be either English or Scandinavian in Mosedale (Cu) "moss" and Westerdale (NRY) "western". *Dalr* is, however, likely where the first element is a Scandinavian word, as in Borrowdale (Cu, We) literally "valley of the fortification", Bowderdale (Cu) "valley of the booth", Wasdale (Cu, We) "valley of the lake", Grisdale (We), of which the first element means "young pigs", Uldale (Cu) "wolves", and probably Matterdale (Cu) "where madder grows" and Birkdale (La) "where birches grow". This is similarly the case where the first element is a Scandinavian personal name, Bannandi in Bannisdale (We), Blesi in Bleasdale (La), Skelmer in Skelmersdale (La), as well as Patric, an Irish name, in Patterdale (We).

The usual Old English term for a valley was *denu*, as in Dene or Dean, common minor names in many southern counties, as well as the Sussex Eastdean and Westdean, originally simplex names later distinguished by East- and West-. In the North, however, this element is comparatively rare, but in some names it may later have been replaced by *dale*. This is certainly the case with Chippingdale (La) named from the village of Chipping, Lothersdale (WRY) "robber's valley", and Rivelindale (WRY), from the stream-name Rivelin "rivulet". Compound names derived from *denu* are common, and though the usual form is *den*, there is also *don* and even *ton*. In some cases the first element denotes the nature of the ground, "gravel" in Chisledon (W), "dirt, mud" in Horden (Du), "mud" in Sladen (La); or the shape, "like a sack" in Ballidon (Db), "like a trough" in Trawden (La); others are named from a natural feature such as a "brook" in Brogden (WRY), while Marden (Nb), Marden Ash (Ess) and Marsden (La) all mean "boundary valley". The first element is an adjective in Blagdon (Nb) "black", Bradden (Nth) "broad", Dibden (Ha, K) and Dipton (Du, Nb) "deep", Holden (La, WRY) and Howden (Nb, WRY) "hollow", Marden Park (Sr), Meriden (Wa) and Merriden (Sr) "pleasant", Shalden (Ha) "shallow" and Sudden (La) "south". Occasionally *denu* has been added to an older name, now lost, as in Arlecdon (Cu), with

Arlec- "eagle stream", and Todmorden (WRY), of which Todmor-may mean "Totta's boundary". A large number, however, are named from an early owner, Bæssel in Basildon (Brk), a lady called Bucge in Buckden (Hu), Ceadd in Chaddesden (Db), Citta in Chidden (Ha), Ecga in Egdean (Sx), Helma in Helmdon (Nth) and Walsa in Walsden (La), or from a group of people, as in Essendon (Hrt) "Ēsla's people" and Rottingdean (Sx) "Rōta's people". Others are from the animals found there, "wild cats" in Catton (Nb), "foxes" in Foxton (Du, Nb), "sheep" in Shipden (Nf) and Skibeden (WRY), "swine" in Swinden (WRY) and "wethers" in Wetherden (Sf). Barden (WRY) was a valley where "barley" grew, Hebden (WRY) where "hips" were found and Croydon (Sr) where "wild saffron" grew. Similarly, other valleys were named from the trees which grew there, "hazels" in Hesleden (Du), "sallows" in Sawdon (NRY) and "yews" in Yewden (Bk).

Old English *cumb* "hollow, valley", a Celtic loan-word, has given the modern Comb, Combe, Coomb and Coombe and also Cowm (La) and Culm Davy (D). In compounds the first element is some-times an adjective, as in Darncombe (NRY) "hidden", Holcombe, a common name, and Hollacombe (D) "hollow", Shalcombe (Wt) "shallow", while Whitcombe (Do), Widcombe (D, So), Witcomb (W), Witcombe (Gl) and Wydcombe (Wt) all mean "wide valley". Ashcombe (D), Thorncombe (Do) and Withycombe (D, So), identical with which are the Devonshire Widdecombe and Widdi-combe, were named from the particular tree growing there, as was Appuldurcomb (Wt) "apple-tree" and Boscombe (W) "box-tree", while "wheat" grew at Whatcombe (Do). As with *denu*, the *coomb* was often named from an early owner with a personal name of Old English origin, Ielfrēd, a variant of Ælfrēd, in Ilfracombe (D), Babba in Babbacombe (D), Ceawa in Chalcombe (Nth), Titta in Tidcombe (W) and Wifil in Wiveliscombe (So), but in Devon it is sometimes of Celtic origin, as with Branoc in Branscombe and Caradoc in Croscombe.

The usual meaning of Old English *hop* in place-names is that of a small enclosed valley, or of a smaller valley branching out of the main one, the sense of the northern dialectal *hope*. This word is the source of the common Hope, and of compounds chiefly found in the North, such as Langhope (Nb) "long", Ryhope (Du) "rugged" and Middop (WRY), which probably means "(place) amidst the valleys". In a few cases the *hope* was named from an early owner, for example Alsop (Db) "Ælli", Eccup (WRY) "Ecca", Glossop (Db) "Glott", Worksop (Nt) "Weorc or Wyrc", or from a folk-group as in Ratlinghope (Sa) "Rōtel's people". Stanhope (Du) and Stanshope (St) probably both mean "stony valley"; Bacup (La) is "valley below the back or ridge", and Pontop (Du) "valley of Pont Burn". Swinhope (L) and Oxenhope (WRY) were named from the "swine" and "oxen" which grazed there, while "ash-trees" grew at Ashop (Db), "broom" at Broomhope (Nb) and "cress" at Kershope (Cu).

In those parts of the North occupied by Norwegian settlers *gill* "ravine, deep narrow valley" is common, especially in minor names. There is Howgill (WRY) "hollow ravine", Skell Gill (WRY) from the River Skell, the self-explanatory Thieves Gill (NRY); one or two from the names of owners, Admergil (WRY) "Ēadmǣr", Garrigill (Cu) "Gerard" and Scargill (NRY) probably "Skakari"; and several from animals or birds, such as Reagill (We) "fox", Rosgill (We) "horse", and Gaisgill (We) and Gazegill (WRY) "goose". Occasionally this word has later been used of swallow holes, as in Gaping Ghyll near Ingleborough (WRY), the spelling *ghyll*, which sometimes occurs, being a pseudo-archaism, apparently due to its use by the poet Wordsworth.

Other elements occur less frequently. Old English *botm*, *boðm* "valley bottom", found particularly in the North and North Midlands where Bottom and Bothom are common minor names, is found in the self-explanatory Broadbottom (Ch), Longbottom (WRY) and Ramsbottom (La). Another word also occurring chiefly in the North is *clōh*, modern *clough*, "deep valley", as in the Lancashire Meerclough "boundary clough" and Loveclough, from the personal name Lufu. On the other hand, *cinu*, modern *chine*, "ravine" is especially common along the South coast and in the Isle of Wight, where there is Blackgang Chine, Linstone Chine and Shanklin Chine; while *corf* "gap, pass" seems to be restricted to the West and South-west, as in Corfe (Do, So), Corve (Wt), as well as Corve (Sa), now the name of a river.

Old English *hol* or *holh* "hole, hollow", also used in place-names of a valley, has given Hoole (Ch), the self-explanatory Greenhalgh (La), and Ible (Db), Ingol (La), Lapal (Wo) from the personal names Ibba, Inga and Hlappa respectively. *Slæd*, modern *slade*, "valley" is represented now by the minor name Slade, Greenslade (Wa) "green valley", Castlett (Gl) "wild-cat valley" and Chapmanslade (W) "merchants' valley".

Old Norse *slakki* "shallow valley" occurs principally in areas settled by men of Norwegian stock and has given Slack (Cu, La, WRY) and the self-explanatory Castle Slack and Dead Man's Slack in Cumberland.

As was the case with terms denoting hills, several words are used in a topographical sense "valley". Modern *gate*, Old English *geat*, sometimes means "gap in hills, pass, deep ravine" as in Symond's Yat (He) and Ayot (Hu) from the personal names Sigemund and Æga respectively, and in the compound *windgeat* "pass or gap through which the wind sweeps", which has given Winnats (Db), Windgate (Du), Wingates (Nb), and the affix in Compton Wyniates (Wa). A similar development of meaning to "pass, gap" has occurred in the place-name use of *dor* "large door, gate", as in Dore (WRY), and of *duru* "door", the second element of Lodore (Cu) "low pass", the lower gap into Borrowdale. Old English *cēodor*, a derivative of *cēod* "pouch, bag", and denoting a "gorge" is no doubt the source of Cheddar (So), while Beedon (Brk) appears to be from Old English *byden* "tub, butt", with a meaning "valley". With this can be compared the use of *tub*, presumably in a similar sense, in Buttertubs Pass (WRY). Chettle (Do) is from *cetel* "kettle" in the transferred sense of "deep valley"; Chew (La) from *cēo* "gill of a fish", i.e. perhaps "narrow valley"; while Bowling (WRY) is probably formed from *bolla* "bowl" and the suffix *-ing*, meaning "place in a bowl or depression". Similarly the Old English or Old Norse *hals* "neck" occasionally denotes a pass through hills, as in Hawes (NRY), and in several Cumberland names such as Butter-mere Hause and Esk Hause, but in other names it is used of a neck of land between valleys, the sense required by the topography of Halse (D, So). Here, too, may be noted one or two place-names derived from Old English *trōg*, modern *trough*, as in Trough in several northern counties, Trows (Nb) and The Trough of Bowland (WRY–La), in each used of a "valley like a trough".

Chapter Eighteen

———— ★ ————

WOODS, CLEARINGS AND OPEN LAND

NUMEROUS terms for "wood", both English and Scandinavian, occur in place-names. *Wood*, itself, is common, but few
of the names derived from it are those of important places. Woodham
(Du) "at the woods" is from the dative plural, and of the numerous
compounds those named from the cardinal points of the compass
are frequently found. Heywood (La) means "high wood", but
Heywood (W) and Haywood (Ha, Nt, Sa, St) are "enclosure wood"
or "enclosed wood", as in Lockwood (WRY). Broadwood (D, So)
is probably "large wood" rather than "broad wood", and Small-
wood (Ch) "narrow wood" and not "small wood" as the modern
form might suggest. The first element is often the name of the trees
growing there, as we should expect, and Ashwood (St), Hazelwood
(Db) and Hazlewood (WRY) are self-explanatory, but Ewood
(WRY) and Linwood (Ha, L) were named from the "yew" and
"lime" respectively. Others are from the animals or birds found
there—"hares" in Harewood (He, WRY), Harwood (La, Nb)
"eagles" in Arnwood (Ha), "jackdaws" in Cawood (La, WRY) and
"cranes" in Cornwood (D, Wo).

In some cases the wood was named from some natural feature, as
in Dunwood (Ha) "hill", Ewood (La) "river", Hockerwood (Nt)
"hump of ground" and Hopwood (La, Wo) "valley"; others from
the nature of the ground, "level" in Evenwood (Du), "foul" in
Fulwood (La, Nt), "stone, i.e. stony" in Stowood (O), and "wet"
in Weetwood (Nb). Occasionally the wood was named from its
owner, Inta in Intwood (Nf), Paca in Packwood (Wa) and a lady
Gōdgifu in Goodwood (Sx). There are also Brandwood (La),
Brentwood (Ess) and Burntwood (St), each meaning "burnt wood",
and Stobswood (Nb), which seems to be "wood of the stump", no
doubt one which had been cleared, as well as Sherwood (Nt) "shire
wood", perhaps so-named because it was near the shire boundary.

Forest, a French loan word, on the other hand, is rare. It occurs,
however, in The New Forest (Ha), first recorded in 1086, when it
had been newly created as a royal forest. But usually this word has

been added to older names as in Epping Forest (Ess), Inglewood Forest (Cu), Peak Forest (Db), Rockingham Forest (Nth) and Selwood Forest (So–W). Most of these represent the old royal forests of the Middle Ages and though used as game reserves were not necessarily forests in the modern sense of the word. Old English (ge)fyrhð is also used of a wood, or of woodland, and in such a name as Duffield Frith (Db) it indicated a district subject to the medieval forest law. It usually survives as Frith, but in some areas of the Midlands and South also as Thrift, as in Marston Thrift (Bd). This element is rarely found in the names of villages, but an example is Pirbright (Sr) "pear-tree wood".

Old English wald, weald, also "forest, woodland", denoted especially high forest land, but later, in Middle English, was used of high wasteland. The earlier meaning, however, is probably the usual one in place-names such as The Weald (K–Ha), Weald (O), North Weald and South Weald (Ess), as well as Wield (Ha), Old (Nth), a dialectal form, and The Cotswolds (Gl) "Cōd's woodland". The Wolds (ERY, L, Lei, Nt), however, denotes rather a tract of high open land. Wold is also found in a number of other names, including several in (Nf) and (Sf) such as the self-explanatory Northwold and Southwold, Methwold "middle" and Hockwold "where hocks grow". Occasionally it is compounded with a personal name, Cuha in Coxwold (NRY), Secgge in Six Hills (Nt), formerly Seggeswold, Swīðbeorht in Sibertswold (K), and with a folk-name "Esa's people" in Easingwold (NRY).

Holt, from Old English holt "wood", is found widely in the Midlands and South, especially in minor names and field-names. The simplex form Holt is common and in compounds the word sometimes occurs with the name of a tree as first element as in Bircholt (K), as well as Esholt (WRY) "ash" and Occold (Sf) "oak". Eversholt (Bd) is "boar wood" and Gledholt (WRY) "kite wood". Bergholt (Ess) and Linkenholt (Ha) both mean "wood on the hill(s)". Sparsholt (Brk, Ha) is apparently "wood where spear shafts were cut", while throcks were obtained from Throckenholt (C), though exactly what a throck was is uncertain—perhaps the piece of wood to which the ploughshare was fastened.

Old English sceaga, modern shaw, "small wood" is comparatively rare in the South Midlands and South, but fairly common further North, where Shaw occurs often as a minor name. The shaw was only occasionally named from its owner, but Audenshaw (La), Barnshaw (Ch) and Huntshaw (D) have the Old English personal names Aldwine, Beornwulf and Hūn as first element. It is also found compounded with an animal name in Ottershaw (Sr), and Ickornshaw (WRY) "squirrel", and with the name of a bird in Crawshaw Booth "crow" and Dunnockshaw, from dialectal *dunnock* "hedge-sparrow", both in Lancashire, while in the same county is Bickershaw "bee-keepers' wood", as well as Bradshaw (also Db, WRY) "broad or large wood", Brunshaw "wood by the River Brun", and the self-explanatory Openshaw. The first element is the name of a tree in Aldershaw (St), while in Birkenshaw (WRY), Oakenshaw (WRY) and Ollerenshaw (Db) it is an adjective meaning "growing with birches", "oak-trees", and "alders" respectively.

In a previous chapter we noted that Bare and Barrow were derived from Old English *bearu* "wood" or "grove", and this is the source also of Beer (D, Do) and Bere (Do). *Bearu* is particularly common in the South-west, especially in minor names; 14 examples have been noted from Dorset and over 100 from Devon, of which about one-fifth were named from the owner, e.g. Ægel in Aylesbeare, Centel in Kentisbeare, Locc in Loxbeare, as well as Secg in Sedgeberrow (Wo). The birds found there are recorded in Crowborough (St) and Larkbeare (D), as well as Kigbeare (D) "jackdaw" and Rockbeare (D) "rook". "Timber" was cut at Timsbury (So) and spear "shafts" at Shebbear (D).

It is difficult to distinguish between Old English *grǣfe* and *grāf*, both meaning "grove", even in early forms of place-names, but the former occurs fairly frequently in the West Midlands. It is the second element of Bromsgrove (Wo) "Brēme's grove", Congreve (St) "grove in a valley", Ramsgreave (La) "ram's grove" and Youlgreave (Db) "yellow grove". While *grǣfe* often survives as -greave, especially in minor names, *grāf* occurs in modern forms as Grove, and -grave is not unusual when it is the second element of a compound name. The first element may be the name of an animal, "hare" in Hargrave (Ch, Nth, Sf) and "mouse" in Musgrave (We), a tree in Boxgrave (Sx), or a natural or topographical feature in Gargrave (WRY) "triangular piece of land" and Warpsgrove (O) "bridle-way". Staplegrove (So) was a grove where "posts" were cut; Blagrove (Brk) means "black grove" and Leagrave (Bd) "light or bright grave"; and a few are named from an early owner, Cotta in Cotgrave (Nt) and Fygla in Filgrave (Bk).

There are several Scandinavian terms for "wood" in English place-names. Old Norse *skógr* occurs in compounds such as Briscoe (NRY), Hessleskew (ERY) and Thurnscoe (WRY), named from the birch, hazel and thorn respectively. Swinscoe (St) means "wood for swine", Litherskew (NRY) "wood of the slope", Myerscough

(La) "mire wood" and Haddiscoe (Nf) "Hadd's wood". Old Norse *viðr* "wood" is the second element of Askwith (WRY) "ash wood", Blawith (La) "black wood", Hartwith (WRY) "hart wood" and Skirwith (Cu), identical in meaning with Sherwood.

Old Norse *lundr* "small wood, grove", sometimes "sacred grove", is the source of the common Lound and Lund as well as Lunt (La). As a second element it frequently appears as -land, as in Hasland (Db), Plumbland (Cu) and Shrubland (Sf), named from the hazel, plum-tree and shrubs respectively. Rowland (Db) means "grove where roe-deer are found", Timberland (L) "grove from which timber is cut", and others are from the name of an early owner, Boie in Boyland (Nf), Snell in Snelland (L) and Tóli in Toseland (Hu).

Modern English *hurst* or *hirst* is derived from Old English *hyrst*, which had a variety of meanings "copse, wood", "hillock", "wooded hill", and it is often difficult to determine the exact sense in which it is used in a given place-name. In one or other of these senses it occurs in Ashurst (K, Sx), Buckhurst (Ess, Sx), Ewhurst (Ha, Sr, Sx), Lyndhurst (Ha) and Salehurst (Sx), from the ash, beech, yew, lime and sallow respectively, while the first element of Nuthurst (La, Sx, Wa) and of Fernhurst (Sx) is self-explanatory. It is the name of an animal in Deerhurst (Gl) and Hartest (Sf), as well as Brockhurst (Wa) "badger", Gayhurst (Bk) "goat", Ticehurst (Sx) and Tickenhurst (K) "kid", and of a bird in Crowhurst (Sr) and Hawkhurst (K), identical with which is Haycrust (Sa). Sandhurst (Brk, Gl, K) and Stonyhurst (La) are self-explanatory, and Midhurst (Sx) means "middle hurst". The first element of Collyhurst (La) appears to mean "coaly", presumably from charcoal burning. In several cases the hurst was named from its owner, Bada in Bathurst (Sx), Billing in Billingshurst (Sx), Broca in Brockenhurst (Ha) and Cibba in Chippinghurst (O), while Doddinghurst (Ess) and Warminghurst (Sx) are derived from folk-names—"Dudda's people" and "Wyrm's people" respectively.

Another very common element, of which the meaning in individual names is often difficult to determine, is Old English *lēah*, modern *lea*, "wood", and also "glade, clearing in a wood", "piece of open land, meadow". It seems likely that in the older place-names containing this word it usually had the sense "glade, i.e. open land, in a wood", but sometimes "wood, forest". In this connexion it is worthy of note that The Weald (K–Ha) is recorded in Old English as *Andredesleage*, as well as *Andredesweald*. As a simplex name it is widespread in such forms as Lea, Lee and Leigh, and it is also found as the second element of hundreds of other place-names.

As we should expect with so common a place-name element, the first part is often a personal name, and the following list provides a representative selection: Alderley (Ch) "Ealdrēd", Barnsley (WRY) "Beorn", Beckley (K, O) "Be(o)cca", Bletchley (Bk) "Blecca", Cholmondeley (Ch) and Chulmleigh (D) "Cēolmund", Cowley (Bk, O) "Cufa", Dudley (Wo) "Dudda", Hockley (Ess) "Hocca", Kimberley (Nt) "Cynemǣr", Kinnerley (Sa) and Kinnersley (He, Wo) "Cyneheard", Knowsley (La) "Cēnwulf", Loxley (St, Wa) "Locc", Otley (Sf, WRY) "Otta", Wembley (Mx) "Wemba", Wensley (NRY) "Wendel", Willesley (Lei) "Wifel" and Wymondley (Hrt) "Wilmund", each a masculine name. A few feminine names also occur: Ælfgȳð in Alveley (Sa), Aldgȳð in Audley (St) and Cyneburg in Kimberley (Nf). Several are derived from folknames, as in Chiddingly (Sx) "Citta's people", Knottingley (WRY) "Cnotta's people" and Madingley (C) "Māda's people", as well as Finningley (Nt) "fen dwellers".

Practically every kind of tree native to this country appears in names in -ley: the alder (Alderley Gl), the ash (the common Ashley), the aspen (Apsley Bd, Aspley Bd, St, Wa, Espley Nb), the birch (Berkeley Gl, Berkley So), the box (Boxley K), the bramble (Bromley Mx), the elm (Almeley He, Elmley K, Wo), the hawthorn (Hatherleigh D, Hatherley Gl), the hazel (Haseley O, Wa, Wt), the lime (Lindley WRY), the maple (Mapperley Db), the oak (Acle Nf, Eagle L, Oakleigh K, and the common Oakley), the plum (Plumley Ch), the spruce (Sapley Hu), the thorn (Thorley Hrt, Wt, Thornley Du), the willow (Willey Ch, He, Wa), the withy (Weethley Wa, Widley Ha, Withiel So), the wych-elm (Weekley Nth) and the yew (Uley Gl).

Other names denote the crops which grew there: flax (Flaxley Gl, WRY, and Lilley Hrt, Linley Sa, Lindley Lei, WRY), hay (Fawley Ha, He, Filleigh D, and Hailey Hrt, O), oats (Oteley Sa) and wheat (Whatley So and the common Wheatley). Similarly, many are derived from the names of other plants: bent grass (Bentley in many counties), broom (Bramley Db, Ha, Sr, WRY, Bromley Ess, Hrt, K, St, Broomley Nb), chag (Chailey Sx), clover (Claverley Sa, Cloverley Sa), fern (Fairley Sa, Fairlight Sx, Farnley WRY, the common Farleigh and Farley), furze (Farsley WRY, Freseley Wa), gale (Gailey St and Wyrley St), reeds (Reedley La, Ridley Ess, K, Rodley Gl), teasel (Tasley Sa), as well as Hadleigh (Ess, Sf), Hadley (Hrt, Sa), Headley (Ha, Sr, Wo, WRY) and Hedley (Du, Nb) all meaning "glade overgrown with heather".

Lēah is also commonly found with the name of an animal, whether domesticated or wild: beaver (Bewerley WRY), boar (Barley La, WRY, Barlow Db and Everley NRY, W), bull (Booley Sa), calf (Callaly Nb, Calveley Ch), deer (Darley Db, Durley Ha), goat (Gateley Nf), hind (Hiendley WRY, Hindley La), horse (Horsley in many counties), sheep (the common Shipley), stud, herd of horses (Stoodleigh D, Studley O, W, Wa, WRY), wether (Waresley Hu) and wolf (Woolley Brk, Db, Hu, WRY). Here, too, may be included Birley (Db) "glade with a byre", Loseley (Sr) "with a shed or pigsty", Osterley (Mx) "with a sheepfold", as well as Butterleigh (D) and Butterley (Db, He) "butter glade", presumably rich land producing good butter, rather than one where butter was made.

Occasionally it was named from an insect, as in Brisley (Nf) "gad-fly", Hamsterley (Du) "corn-weevil", Midgley (WRY) "midge" and Beeleigh (Ess), Beoley (Wo) "bees", with which can be compared Honiley (Wa) "honey wood or glade". More frequently it is the name of a bird: crane or heron (Corley Wa), crow (Crawley Bk, Ess, Ha), eagle (Arley Ch, La, Wa, Wo, Areley Kings Wo, Earnley Sx), finch (Finkley Ha), hawk (Hawkley Ha), kite (Kitley D) and shrike (Shrigley Ch).

Two common names, Staveley and Yardley, have as first element words meaning "stave" and "rod" respectively, and presumably denote woods from which these were cut. Others have a word denoting a natural feature, for example Chinley (Db) "deep valley", Cleveleys (La) "slope", Dingley (Nth) "dingle", the common Morley "moor or marsh", Shelley (Ess, Sf, WRY) "shelving land", while Marley (D) means "boundary wood or glade". Sometimes the nature of the ground is indicated, as in Evenley (Nth) "level", Hardley (Ha, Wt) "hard", the common Rowley "rough", Slaley (Nb) "mud", Softley (Du, Nb) "soft" and Stanley, in many counties, "stone, i.e. stony". Smalley (Db, La) and the common Langley denote the shape of the *lea*, "narrow" and "long" respectively; while from the size there is Bradle (Do), Bradley, in almost every county, "spacious" and Mickley (Db, Nb) "big"; and from their "high" situation Hanley, Handley and Henley, each of which is repeated in various parts of the country.

The common Scandinavian term in English place-names for a "clearing" is Old Norse *þveit*, surviving in the North as *thwaite* "forest clearing, meadow in a low situation". It occurs in Thwaite (Nf, Sf) and very often in minor names in the North as Thwaite or Thwaites. Occasionally as the second element of a compound name it has been replaced by *field*, so that there is Brackenfield (Db) originally identical with Brackenthwaite (Cu) "bracken clearing" and Stainfield (L) with Stonethwaite (Cu) "stony clearing". It is also sometimes replaced by *wood*, as in Eastwood (Nt) identical with the self-explanatory Easthwaite (Cu), and Storwood (ERY) "brushwood clearing". *Thwaite* occurs also with a variety of first elements, chiefly of Scandinavian origin; terms for animals in Calthwaite (Cu) "calves" and Storthwaite (NRY) "stirks"; for crops or other plants in Heathwaite (La), Haythwaite (NRY) "hay", Haverthwaite (La) "oats", Linethwaite (Cu) "flax", Branthwaite (Cu) "broom" and Seathwaite (Cu) "sedge"; and for trees in Applethwaite (Cu, We), Hawthornthwaite (La), as well as Roundthwaite (We) "mountain ash" and Slaithwaite (WRY) "sloe". Braithwaite (Cu, NRY, WRY) means "broad clearing" and Micklethwaite (WRY) "big clearing", while Castlethwaite (We) is "near a castle", Huthwaite (Nt, NRY) "on a spur of land" and Seathwaite (La) "near a lake". There is also a small group named from an early owner, e.g. Allithwaite (La) "Eilifr", Finsthwaite (La) "Finnr" and Gunthwaite (WRY) "Gunnhildr (a feminine name)".

An element chiefly found in Kent and Sussex, and very occasionally also in Essex and Surrey, is Old English *denn* "woodland pasture", usually pasture for swine, though in some cases the place-names refer to other animals. The following examples are all found in Kent, unless otherwise stated. A number have a personal name as first element: Bethersden "Beadurīc", Biddenden "Bid(d)a", Chillenden "Ciolla" and Rolvenden "Hrōðwulf"; others a folk-name, Otterden "Oter's people" and Tenterden "the people of Thanet", who had rights of pasture there. Cowden and Marden were woodland pastures for "cows" and "mares" respectively, and Playden (Sx), literally "play pasture", was presumably where animals played. Iden (Sx) was noted for its "yew trees", and Smarden for its rich land, for the first element means "fat, grease, butter".

Several terms for "enclosure" occur in place-names. Old English *(ge)hæg* "fence, enclosure" is the source of Hay and Hey, common in minor names, and it is the second element of Rowney (Bd, Hrt) "rough enclosure" and Woodhay (Brk) "enclosure in the wood", as well as Oxhey (Hrt), which is self-explanatory, and Broxa (NRY) and Idridgehay (Db), from Brocc and Ēadrīc, the names of early owners. In Middle English the word can mean "part of a forest fenced off for hunting" and this is sense in Harthay (Hu), where harts were hunted, and in minor names in parts of Derbyshire. This element is especially common in Dorset and Devon, in the last of which there are about 250 examples, many derived from the name of the medieval owner or holder, and it has been suggested that the term is used here of a farm or holding.

Old English *haga* "hedge, enclosure" and the corresponding Old Norse *hagi* "enclosure, pasture" cannot be separated when the element occurs in the Scandinavianized areas of England. The Scandinavian word, however, is perhaps to be assumed where the first element is also Scandinavian. One or other of these is the source of Haigh (La, WRY), Haugh (L) and Hough on the Hill (L). The enclosure was for a "herd of horse" in Stodday (La) and for "cows" in Whaw (NRY). Breary (WRY) means "briar enclosure" and Thorney (Nt) and Thornhaugh (Nth) "thorn enclosure", while Galphay (WRY) is "gallows enclosure".

Outside the South-east and South-east Midlands Old English *camp* "enclosed piece of land" is rare. It survives as -camp but also as -combe in compound names such as Addiscombe (Sr), Ruscombe (Brk) and Warningcamp (Sx), from the personal names Æddi, Rōt and perhaps Wærna respectively, and also Bulcamp (Sf) "bull enclosure", Maplescombe (K) "maple-tree enclosure" and Swanscombe (K) "swineherd's enclosure".

It is difficult to distinguish Old English *hamm* "enclosure", fairly common in the South and South Midlands, from Old English *hām* "homestead". This word seems later to have denoted "a water-meadow", "flat low-lying pasture, land near a river", and, because of the situations of many place-names so-named, it was thought that one or other of these meanings was to be assumed in the place-names. However, it has been shown recently that the etymological meaning is "enclosure", as in Ham, a common name, Hamp (So) and East Ham and West Ham (Ess). In compound names the first element is sometimes an animal name, Dyrham (Gl) "deer", Hartham (W) and Otterham (Co), the last two self-explanatory, or a bird name, Cranham (Gl) "crane or heron" and Elvetham (Ha) "swan". Others are named from a crop, plant or tree, as with Barkham (Brk) "birch", Farnham (Sr) "fern", Feltham (So) "hay", Marcham (Brk) "wild celery" and Witcham (C) "wych-elm", while Marchington (St) was originally identical with Marcham and Old English *tūn* "farmstead, village" was added later. In a few cases the *hamm* was named from an early owner, Ægen in Eynsham (O), Cippa in Chippenham (Gl, W), Eof in Evesham (Wo), Fecca in Feckenham (Wo) and Passa in Passenham (Nth). Sydenham (D, O, So) is "large *hamm*", while the first element of Grittenham (W) means "gravelly" and of Sandown (Wt) "sand, i.e. sandy".

Of the common terms for "open land", *land* itself occurs frequently, though it was in fact used in various senses in place-names. In Cumberland, Holland (L) and Copeland (Cu) "bought land" it certainly refers to a large area of land, but in many other names it denoted a much smaller one. In compounds, the *land* is named from an early owner, e.g. Bēga in Byland (NRY), Cada in Cadlands (Ha), Cydda in Kidland (Nb), Dot in Dotland (Nb) and Þórólfr in Thurland (La). Others are from some natural feature, as in Brookland (K), which is self-explanatory, and Bowland (La), perhaps from a "bow" or bend in the River Ribble; from a building in Burland (ERY) "byre"; or from the animals found there, Strickland (We) "stirk", Studland (Do) "herd of horses", Swilland (Sf) "swine" and Yaverland (Wt) "boar". Leyland (La) means "fallow land", Redland (Gl) "cleared land", the common Newland and Newlands "land newly brought into cultivation", and Portland (Do) presumably "land around the harbour".

The commonest place-name element for "open land", however, is Old English *feld*, modern *field*, used in place-names of "open country" or "cleared space in woodland". This word is frequently compounded with a personal name, as in Alstonfield (St) "Ælfstān", Canfield (Ess) "Cana", Caversfield (O) "Cāfhere", Hurdsfield (Ch) "Hygerēd", Luffield (Bk) "Luffa", and Wethersfield (Ess) "Wihthere", and occasionally also with a folk-name, as in Bassingfield (Nt) "Bassa's people", Finchingfield (Ess) "Finc's people" and Itchingfield (Sx) "Ecci's people".

There is also a group the first element of which is the name of an animal, "wild cat" in Catsfield (Nf), "deer" in Darfield (WRY), "kid" in Titchfield (Ha), "lamb" in Enfield (Mx), "sheep" in Sheffield (Sx) and "wether" in Withersfield (Sf), and note also Austerfield (WRY) "open land with a sheepfold"; or a bird, "dove" in Duffield (Db, ERY), "duck" in Dukinfield (Ch), "eagle" in Yarnfield (St, W) and "jackdaw" in Cavil (ERY); while Netherfield (Sx) is "open land infested by adders" and Dronfield (Db) "by drones". In others it denotes crops, as in Hayfield (Db), and Whatfield (Sf) "wheat", or plants as in Bentfield (Ess) "bent-grass", Bramfield (Sf), Bromfield (Cu, Sa) and Broomfield, a common name, "broom", Dockenfield (Ha) "dock", Mayfield (St) "madder", Mayfield (Sx) "mayweed". Few compounds of *feld* and a tree-name occur, but the first elements of Bockenfield (Nb) and Lindfield (Sx) are adjectives formed from the names of trees, "growing with beech" and "growing with lime-trees" respectively.

Sometimes the "open land" has been named from a near-by river: Blythe in Blithfield (St), Pant in Panfield (Ess) and Sheaf in Sheffield (WRY). The reference is to the soil in others such as Kelfield (ERY, L) "chalk", or to the type of cultivation as in Wingfield (Db) "pasture". The first element in the common Bradfield means "spacious", Chalfield (W) "cold", Micklefield (WRY) "big", Shenfield (Ess) and Fairfield (Db) "beautiful", and Whitfield and Whitefield, both occurring frequently, "white", which may refer to chalky land or is perhaps used in the sense "dry", hence "dry open land", the meaning in fact of Therfield (Hrt). Brafield (Nth) and Brayfield (Bk) have as first element Old English *brægen* "brain, crown of the head", presumably used in place-names of a "hill". That in Wakefield (Nth, WRY) may be the personal name Waca, found later in Hereward the *Wake*, but Professor Ekwall has suggested that it is rather Old English *wacu*, modern *wake*, as in Oldham *Wakes*. Wakefield would then mean "open land where the annual festival takes place".

Old English *mōr*, modern *moor*, used of wasteland, later develops the sense "high uncultivated land", especially in the North, and one of "marshland", particularly in the Midlands and South. It survives today frequently in the forms Moor, Moore and More, and one or other has often been added to a place-name, as in Ilkley Moor (WRY). *Moor* is not, however, common in names of important places, but the following may be noted: Barmoor (Nb) "where berries grow", Radmore (St) "red", Sedgemoor (So) "where sedge grows", Stainmore (NRY–We) "stony" and Wildmore (L) "uncultivated", as well as a few from the names of early owners—Chackmore (Bk) "Ceacca" and Cottesmore (R) "Cott".

In both simplex names and as the second element of a compound Old English *hæð* probably means "heath, heathland", the sense in the common Heath, the self-explanatory Blackheath (K, Sr), Small Heath (Wa) "narrow", and when it has been added to an older name as in Hampstead Heath (Mx) and Walton Heath (Sr).

Chapter Nineteen

———————— ★ ————————

STREET-NAMES

MOST of the names discussed in this chapter are of medieval origin. Later street-names are usually derived from the name of a local landowner or an important tenant and, though invaluable to the local historian, are comparatively easy to interpret as compared with medieval names. Many of these have been lost because of the constant rebuilding in the larger towns, but enough of them have survived to make it possible for us to obtain an idea of their general character. They often give useful information on the early history and development of the particular town, and especially on the different trades represented there and the location of them. It is impossible to give examples of street-names from all the medieval towns, for detailed surveys of many are not yet available, but in what follows as wide a selection as possible has been illustrated. Numerous other examples will be found in the volumes of the English Place-Name Society and in Ekwall's *Street-Names of the City of London.*

Most street-names end in *street* or *lane.* The distinction between the two seems to have been that the former denoted a wider and more important way than the latter, but not one which is, or perhaps even could be, consistently maintained. Of the two, *street* is by far the commoner, but in the North and North Midlands it is often replaced by *gate* (Old Norse *gata* "street"). This is not always easily distinguished from Old English *geat*, modern *gate*, "opening", the usual term for the entrance to a walled town, though as a rule the context will make it clear which is intended. Three other terms, *row, alley* and *hill*, are found less frequently in street-names. *Row* is used of a number of houses standing in a line, or of a street, particularly a narrow one, formed by two such lines of houses. It is more commonly met with in the North and Midlands than in the South, often with a first part denoting the trades carried on there. *Alley* seems to refer to a passage into a house, or to a narrow lane, and *hill* is usually self-explanatory.

Most street-names are descriptive, whether of situation, size or importance. High Street "chief or principal street" is particularly

194

common, and the comparable Highgate is also found in the North and North Midlands. King Street, however, as the name of an important street is usually modern, but an early example survives in Chippenham (W), while the first part of Coney Street (York) is from Scandinavian *kunungr* "king". In York, too, there is the Scandinavian compound Micklegate "great street". North, South, East and West Street are self-explanatory, as also are the similar Northgate, Southgate, Eastgate and Westgate. Nether Street and Upper Street, i.e. "lower" and "higher" street, occur in many towns, as well as Middle Street, which is paralleled by Middlegate (Newark and Penrith). Similarly, comparable with the common Broad Street is Broadgate, as in Lincoln, etc. Old Street, however, is uncommon, but there are many examples of New Street, which for the most part indicate an expansion of the town from its old centre. Here, too, may be included Newland(s) Street, a fairly common name, and Newland(s) (Lincoln and Nottingham), all named from land newly brought into cultivation on the outskirts of the town.

A street paved with stones is sometimes called Stoney Street, while Stonegate occurs in York. Comparable are High, Low and Middle Pavement (Nottingham) and The Pavement (York), as well as Chiswell Street (Finsbury) "flint or pebble street". Other reference to the surface is not common, though occasional examples of Clay Street are found, as at Colchester. Honey Lane is common in many small towns and villages, perhaps for a muddy or sticky way, but occasionally it may only mean that honey was produced there. There are also Wet Lane, Stinking Lane and Featherbed Lane, the last referring perhaps to a soft or muddy road. Other interesting names include Full Street (Derby) "foul street", Lurk Lane (Beverley) "dirty lane" and Summer Lane, which is fairly common for one usable only in summer. In London there is Addle Street, probably one "full of cow-dung", as well as two Pudding Lanes. These may simply have been lanes where puddings were sold, or perhaps sticky like a pudding, or, as Ekwall suggests, lanes down which *puddings* "butchers' offal" were taken for disposal in the Thames.

The common term for a cul-de-sac is Blind Lane, but Bag Lane and Pudding-bag Lane are also found, and in London there is Turnagain Lane, earlier *Wendagain* "turn back". A secluded way is often called Love Lane, examples of which occur in various English towns. Another name for a dark lane was Grope Lane, once common, but now surviving only occasionally, as in Bristol, and as Grape Lane (York). But apart from these examples the name has dropped out of

195

use, no doubt because of its suggestive connotations. A comparable name for a street of ill-repute may be Mutton Lane if *mutton* is used in the sense "loose woman, prostitute". It is not surprising that other similar ones, recorded frequently in medieval sources, have since been lost.

Streets and lanes named from their length or shape are common; Long Lane and Long Street are obvious examples, but more interesting is Endless Street (Salisbury), which leads out beyond the limits of the city. Twitchell was once frequently found for a narrow lane, but survives for example in Nottingham. Crooked Lane and Winding Lane are obvious enough, and Crink Lane (Southwell Nt) had several sharp turns, while Eastbight (Lincoln) is a street which runs east-west, then bends to the south at an angle of 90 degrees, and appropriately enough means "east angle or bend".

Other common names indicate the place to which they led, as with Bridge Street, and the corresponding Briggate (Leeds) and Bridge Gate, earlier *Briggate* (Derby); Castle Street, as well as Castlegate (York) and Castle Gate (Newark, Nottingham); Park Street, along with Little Park Street and Muchpark Street (Coventry), i.e. "little" and "big"; and Mill Street, Mill Lane and Mill Gate (Newark). In Hitchin, Portmill Lane led to the "town mill" and in Finsbury, Turnmill Street is named from a mill with a wheel. Equally common are streets which led to a well or spring, as in Well Street, and the Scandinavian Keldgate (Beverley). The self-explanatory Holywell Street occurs several times, and in Totnes there is Leechwell Street, apparently from a spring "where leeches are found", while three wells in Colchester have given their names to streets: Childwell Alley led to a "children's spring", Stanwell Street to a "stony well" and East and West Stockwell Street to a "spring marked by a tree-trunk". Conduit Street in Westminster and elsewhere was named from a water-channel, and Fishpool Street (St. Albans) from the abbey fish ponds. Other streets take their names from the stream or river towards which they led and so are self-explanatory, as also is the common Water Lane. Here, too, may be included Ferry Street (Lambeth), leading to a ferry across the Thames from which Horseferry Road (Westminster) is also named, and Heath Street (Barking), which led to a *hythe* or landing-place on the river.

Similarly, the numerous streets named from the village or town to which they led are obvious enough, but some of the "miscellaneous" destinations are of interest. Gallows Street is not uncommon today, along with Gallowgate (Newcastle upon Tyne and

Richmond NRY) and Gallowtree Gate (Leicester); but Gallows Street (Warwick) has replaced an earlier *Warrytreestreet* "street leading to the felons' tree, i.e. gallows", and Pillory Lane in London and elsewhere is self-explanatory. Litchdon Street (Barnstaple) was the way to the medieval "cemetery" and with this can be compared Lich Street (Worcester) literally "corpse street", leading to the cemetery belonging to Worcester Cathedral. In all probability Dead Lane, once common in many towns but now often lost, has a similar meaning. On the other hand Bury Street and Bury Lane, found in the South, usually represents Old English *burh* in one of its post-Conquest senses of "manor, manor-house".

It is natural that many old streets were named from churches or religious houses, frequently from their dedications, whether in the form St. Giles Street (Northampton), or simply as Magdalen Street (Colchester and Exeter). Names of this type, however, are usually self-explanatory, but Bow Street (Durham) is from the church of St. Mary le Bow, Gillygate (York) from a church dedicated to St. Giles and Sidwell Street (Exeter) from one dedicated to the virgin St. Sidwell. In London there is Gracechurch Street, literally "grass church", perhaps referring to the place where it was built, or possibly to a turf roof; Foster Lane and Sise Lane, from churches dedicated to St. Vedast and St. Sithe respectively. Here, too, belongs Ladygate (Beverley) "street leading to the church of Our Lady". The more common street-names with religious associations include Church Street and Chapel Street and the corresponding Scandinavian Kirkgate and Chapel Gate; Spital Street, from some medieval hospital; Abbey Street and Abbeygate (Leicester), as well as College Street, as in Northampton, where it was named from the college of the clergy of All Saints. Cross Street, too, is common, together with occasional examples of compounds such as High Cross Street (Leicester), note also High Cross (Truro), and from coloured crosses Red Cross Street (Leicester, Ln) and White Cross Street (Ln), though this last may simply denote a stone cross. Rood Lane "lane leading to the cross", however, is found only occasionally, as in Coventry and London, and in Newport (Wt) there is Holyrood Street "holy cross street".

Streets named from clerics include Bishop Street (Coventry), Canon Row (Westminster), Preston Street (Exeter) and Priestgate (Peterborough) both "street of the priests", Monk Street, Monkgate (York), and Mincing Lane (Ln) "lane of the nuns". More common are Friar(s) Street and Friar(s) Lane, as well as Friargate (Derby, Penrith) and Friary Street (Guildford), all from one or other of the mendicant orders. More specifically there is Whitefriargate (Hull) from the Carmelites, Blackfriargate (Hull) from the Dominicans, and Greyfriars (Gloucester), Greyfriar Gate (Nottingham) and Grey Friars Lane (Coventry) from the Franciscans, while Crouch Street (Colchester) and Crutched Friars (Ln) take their names from the order of the Crutched Friars or Friars of the Holy Cross. A further name which may be noted here is The Minories (Ln), from the abbey of the Minoresses, nuns of the second order of St. Francis, known also as the Poor Clares.

The Bedern (York) means "prayer house"; and Little Sanctuary (Westminster) was a precinct of the abbey in which refugees could seek protection. In London, the neighbouring Amen Lane, Ave Maria Lane and Creed Lane are all later names, perhaps imitating Paternoster Row, which, however, was *Paternosterer street* formerly, i.e. "street of the makers of rosaries".

People of the same nationality lived together in medieval towns, a fact reflected by such street-names as Lombard Street (Ln), Danesgate (Lincoln), Flemingate (Beverley), Frenchgate (Richmond NRY), French Row (St. Albans), as well as Petty France (Westminster) "little France". Jews were also usually segregated, as in Jewbury (York) "Jews' quarter", Jury Street (Warwick), Jewry Street (Ln, Winchester) and Old Jewry (Ln).

A further group is named from animals or birds which were kept or found there, hence Hengate (Beverley), Cock Lane (Ln), Culver Street (Salisbury) "doves", Huggin Lane (Ln) "hogs" and perhaps Boar Street (Mere W), though the common Boar Lane is more likely to refer to an inn sign. Here, too, may be noted Stodman Street (Newark), earlier *Stodmare Street*, where the stud-mare was kept and Loo Street (Plymouth), where there was a pigsty. Although Cat Street (Oxford) is referred to in a medieval document as "the street of the mouse catcher", the word was later taken to be a shortened form of *Catherine*, which was till recently the official name. The place where bull-baiting took place has given an occasional Bull Ring as in Beverley, Birmingham and Grimsby, while in areas affected by Scandinavian influence there is the common Hungate (Lincoln, Market Weighton, York) or Hounds Gate (Nottingham) "street where dogs are kept or found".

Some of these names may perhaps refer rather to streets where such animals or birds were sold, and this is the likely interpretation of Cowgate (Leicester, Peterborough), Rother Street (Stratford on Avon) "cattle" and Sheep Street (Stratford on Avon). Other appropriate commodities were (prepared or produced, and) sold in Bread Street (Ln), Bakehouse Street (Leicester), Fish Row (Salisbury), Fish Street Hill (Ln), Milk Street (Exeter, Ln), Oaten Hill (Canterbury), Oat Lane (Ln), Oatmeal Row (Salisbury), Pepper Alley (Southwark), Pepper Lane (Coventry), Pepper Street (Nottingham), Rye Street (Bishop's Stortford), Salt Lane (Salisbury) and Wheat Street (Nuneaton). Similarly, Lime Street (Ln) and Wood Street (Kingston on Thames, Ln) are obvious enough, but Woodgate (Leicester) is rather the way along which wood was transported into the town. Rather more difficult are Cowl Street (Evesham) "coal", Crock Street (Barnstaple) "pots", Hart Street (Ln) probably "hearthstones" and Whimple Street (Plymouth) "wimples". Gold and silver articles were sold in Gold Street (Northampton) and Silver Street (Lincoln, Ln) respectively. The latter is a particularly common street-name, and though the Lincoln and London examples are recorded from medieval times, most of the others appear only in later sources. Some of them at least may owe the name to the well-known London street. So many names show some kind of work going on that it is surprising to find Do Little Lane (Ln), a lane which apparently served simply as a passage from one street to another.

Most towns have their Market Place, but in many cases Place has replaced an earlier *stead*, a word of similar meaning. Occasionally there is Market Hill (Cambridge, Watford) but more often Market Street. Sometimes a particular commodity was sold there, as in Corn Market, a not uncommon name, Fishmarket (Hastings), Haymarket (Westminster), and Bigg Market (Newcastle upon Tyne) where barley was sold, while Butter Street (Alcester) was formerly *Buttermarket Street*. Here, too, may be included Butter Cross (Oakham, Winchester, Witney), a cross where butter was sold. There is also Beastmarket Hill (Nottingham) and Horse Market (Northampton), and the annual sale of horses in various towns is commemorated in Horse Fair (Banbury, Ripon), The Horsefair (Malmesbury) and Horsefair Street (Leicester).

Towns were sometimes given the right to hold markets on particular days of the week, often one on Saturday and another on some other weekday. There are frequent references to these in medieval sources, where *Saturday Market* and *Weekday Market* are common names. These rarely survive, but there is still Saturday Market and Wednesday Market in Beverley, and Weekday Cross (Nottingham) was originally called *Weekday Market*.

Old English *cēap* "market" is the source of Cheap or Westcheap (now Cheapside) and Eastcheap (Ln), as well as Cheap Street

199

(Newbury Brk), while Wincheap Street (Canterbury) is a very old name which seems to mean "waggon market". A derivative of *cēap*, Old English *cēping*, with the same meaning has given Mealcheapen Street (Worcester) "meal market" and Cross Cheaping (Coventry), named from a cross near which a market was held. Another and later derivative Middle English *chepere* "market man" is the source of Chipper Lane, earlier *Chipper Street* (Salisbury) "street of the market-men". Old English *port* "town" seems also occasionally to have meant "market place" and this sense is thought to occur in Newport (Lincoln) "new market place".

One of the most famous streets associated with the sale of food-stuffs is The Shambles (York), formerly *Fleshshambles* "flesh benches", so-called from the stalls for the sale of meat, set up in the open air, which can be compared with Fishamble Street in Dublin. Many other medieval towns had their Shambles and the name has survived in Chesterfield and Chippenham (W), though The Shambles (Worcester) used to be called Baxter Street and later Baker Street. The place where meat was sold was also called The Butchery (Ely) and there is also a Butchery Green (Hertford) and a Butchery Lane (Canterbury). Comparable names are Poultry (Ln, Nottingham) and Poultry Cross (Salisbury), where poultry was sold.

Often names indicating streets where various kinds of food or other articles were sold have as first element an occupational term. Many of those current in medieval times have since been lost, but others still remain, and the nature of the goods (produced and) sold is often obvious enough. Hence, there is Baxter's Row (Carlisle) and Baxter Gate (Hedon ERY) "bakers"; Butcher Row (Coventry, Exeter, Ludlow, Salisbury, Shrewsbury) and Fletcher Gate (Nottingham) "fleshers, i.e. butchers"; Fisher Street (Carlisle, Paignton), Fisher Row (Chesterfield), Fishergate (Nottingham, Preston La, York) and Fisher's Lane (Cambridge); Saltergate (Chesterfield, Lincoln) "salt-merchants", though this may denote a road used by salt-merchants; Spicer Street (St. Albans) and Spiceal Street (Birmingham) "spicers, i.e. grocers"; as well as Cook Street (Coventry), and Petty Cury (Cambridge), the last literally meaning "little kitchen".

Several are named from cloth-workers: wool-dealers were to be found in Woolmonger Street (Northampton), dressers or sellers of wool in Wolsdon Street (Plymouth), wool-combers in Cumbergate (Peterborough), makers and sellers of stockings in Hosier Lane (Ln) and Hosier Street (Reading), dealers in silks and velvets in Mercers Row (Northampton) and Mercery Lane (Canterbury), and a similar name to the last is Drapery (Northampton), where cloth and linen workers or dealers lived. Cloth fullers lived in Walkergate (Beverley) and Walker Lane (Derby), dyers in Lister Gate (Nottingham), while bleaching was done in Blake Street (York). Felt-makers carried on their businesses in Felter Lane (York), shoe-makers in Souttergate (Hedon ERY), tanners in Tanner Street (Barking) and Barker Gate (Nottingham), saddlers in Saddler Gate (Derby) and Saddler Street (Durham), and makers of pilches, i.e. outer garments made of skin, in Pilcher Gate (Nottingham). Here may be included Rack Street, from *rack* "frame for stretching cloth", and Tenter Yard, from *tenter* a word with a similar meaning, both found in some towns. Metal-workers, too, are well represented in street-names: smith, a general term for a worker in metals, is the source of Smith Street (Exeter, Warwick), goldsmith of Goldsmith Street (Exeter), bridlesmith of Bridlesmith Gate (Nottingham) and wheel-makers in Wheeler Gate (Nottingham). Billiter Street (Ln) was the home of bell-founders and Skeldergate (York) of shield-makers. Ironmonger Lane (Ln) and Ironmonger Row (Coventry) are self-explanatory and Iron Gate (Derby) also refers to workers in iron. Other trades recorded in surviving street-names include Coppergate (York) "joiners"; Crocker Street (Newport Wt) and Pottergate (Lincoln) both "potters". Coal-dealers are represented by Colliergate (York), and carters or carriers by Carter Gate (Nottingham, Scarborough), Carter Lane (Ln), as well as Catherine Street (Salisbury), of which the modern form is due to popular etymology. Waterbeer Street (Exeter) is "street of the water-bearers or carriers", a medieval name and not, as might be assumed, a modern depreciative name, while Birchin Lane (Ln) "lane of the barbers" seems to be the only surviving example of a street named from this trade. As is to be expected, few street-names are from agricultural workers, but exceptions include Blossom Street (York) and Blossomgate (Ripon) "street of the ploughmen".

A unique name is Bellar Gate (Nottingham) "street of the bell-man or town crier", but a few others refer to various sports or entertainments, hence Gluman Gate (Chesterfield) "street of the minstrels", Gigant Street (Salisbury) "fiddler(s)" and Bearward Street (Northampton) "bear-keeper", the trainer of performing bears or the keeper of bears to be baited. The meaning of Blowhorn Street (Marlborough) is uncertain, but perhaps a trumpeter lived or performed here. Bowling Alley is still fairly common and there is a Bowlalley Lane in Hull, while Threadneedle Street (Ln) perhaps takes it name from a children's game, and Pall Mall (Westminster) is almost certainly from the game of *paille maille* or *pelmel*, introduced into England during the reign of Charles I.

Chancery Lane (Ln) was formerly *Chancellor's Lane*, and earlier still was *Convers Lane*, from the Domus conversorum, home for converted Jews. Fetter Lane (Ln) preserves Middle English *faitor* "imposter, cheat", used particularly of beggars who sham illness or deformity. The exact significance of Maiden Lane (Ln), a name found also in other towns, is uncertain, but may well have had the meaning "prostitute".

Many of the later streets and lanes are named from the signs of inns or taverns, perhaps the most famous of which is the Elephant and Castle, an old coaching inn, now the name also of the cross-roads. Other names of lanes or streets derived from the sign of the Angel, Bear, Bell, Bush, Dun Cow, Greyhound, Harp, Hart, Ship, Star, Sun, Swan, White Horse and Woolpack can be found in various towns, and the list could be extended indefinitely.

A few miscellaneous names are worthy of note. Carfax (Oxford) "place where four roads or streets meet" is comparable with the self-explanatory Five Ways (Birmingham); Eden Street (Kingston on Thames) means "heathen street", but the reason for the name is unknown; Galliard Street (Sandwich) takes its name from *Galliots Bridge*, later *Galliard's Bridge*, of which the first element seems to be Middle English *galliot* "small galley or boat"; Land of Green Ginger (Hull) is thought to have been named from one of the old gardens in Hull, in which were grown pot-herbs with that name; Stepcote Hill (Exeter) is a narrow street with a series of steps and originally no doubt flanked by cottages; and Whip-ma Whop-ma Gate (York) may take its name from a whipping post and pillory at the end of the street.

A few are named from buildings: Old Bailey (Ln), The Baile (York), The Bailey (Worcester) and North and South Bailey (Durham) are all from Old French *baille* "outer defensive work of a castle, prison"; Barbican (Ln and elsewhere) referred to the outer fortification of a town; and the first part of Warser Gate (Nottingham) means "buildings by the wall", i.e. the Anglo-Saxon wall of the city. The Brittox (Devizes) was originally a place fortified with stockades, and Garret Hostel Lane (Cambridge) a watch-tower or look-out place in a hostel, on the site of what is now Trinity College.

Contemptuous nicknames for a poor or insignificant street include the common Rotten Row, literally "rat row", probably applied to a

202

row of tumbledown cottages, and Thieves Lane, a popular name for a street of ill-repute. Little London, a typical example of this kind, is usually late but appears as early as 1454 in Chichester. Others include Farthing Lane (Watford), the later Pennyfarthing Street (Salisbury), and Rynal Street (Evesham), which may mean literally "ruin hill". Paradise Street is often probably intended sarcastically, but no doubt was sometimes meant to be complimentary.

Chapter Twenty

--------- ★ ---------

MINOR NAMES AND FIELD-NAMES

THE names included here, along with field-names, are those of the smaller features of the landscape sufficiently important to be marked on the map. Even those minor names and field-names which are probably comparatively old are rarely recorded before the 16th century, but many in fact date from the period of the enclosure of the common land and the redistribution of the open fields in the 18th and 19th century. None the less, most country parishes contain some names surviving from at least the 13th or 14th century, though the size and shape of the particular field may now be very different. The names of the old open fields may still remain as North, South, East or West Field, though what was once the North Field may now be divided into Near and Far North Field, Lower and Upper North Field, or even Big and Little North Field.

A considerable number of the old terms for a smaller division of the land remain. *Acre* originally meant only a plot of arable land irrespective of its size, but early became used as a measurement of area. Names like Ten Acres or Fifteen Acres are common enough today, though a surprisingly high proportion of them bear little relation to the actual size of the present field. *Furlong* could mean "piece of land the length of a furrow", but more often refers to a division in the common field and is rarely found in field-names as a measurement of length. Modern names which include *Dole(s)* or *Doale(s)*, from Old English *dāl*, can be found in many parishes in the East Midlands, and *Dale(s)*, from Scandinavian *deill*, is common in some parts of the Danelaw. Each is used of a share of land in the common field. The singular form *Dale*, however, cannot always be distinguished from *dale* "valley", though usually the topography will show which word must be intended. Another common term is *Flat*, originally denoting a piece of flat ground, but in field-names the usual sense is "larger division in the common field".

A number of modern names commemorate the strips of land in the common fields. *Brade, Braid,* and in some districts *Broad,* come from Old English *brǣdu* "breadth", used in Middle English of a broad

204

strip of land, especially one in the common field. It is frequently found in the compound *Gorebroad* or *Goarbroad* "broad strip in a triangular corner of the common field", and *Shovelbroad* "strip of land as broad as a shovel", a name surviving also in a variety of forms including *Shovelboard*. The first element of *Gorebroad, Gore* "triangular piece of land", is sometimes used alone, or as the second element of a compound. The usual sense of *Balk, Baulk* in field-names is "strip of land left unploughed to mark the boundary between adjacent strips in the common field", while *Butt* is particularly common, often preceded by a numeral, and originally denoted a strip abutting on a boundary, a short strip or a ridge at right angles to another.

Head seems to have been more common earlier than it is today, and is frequently found in the compound *Headland(s)* used of strips of land left for turning the plough. *Hades* is also common, occasionally a nickname for poor land, but usually merely a variant form of *Heads* "head strips in the common field". *Land* itself "strip of arable land in the common field" is especially frequent both in the singular and plural, often preceded by a numeral, and references to as many as *Twenty Lands* have been noted in several counties, while *Sidelands*, synonymous with Headlands, is almost as common. *Ridge(s)* and *Rigg(s)* in field-names are normally used of cultivated strips of ground, again often with a numeral as in *Five Ridges* or *Six Riggs*. Though *Strip* and *Stripe* occur today for a narrow piece of land, they are rare in early field-names. A more frequent, but a more general, term for a strip of land, however, is *Shot, Shoot, Shutt* or *Shute*, all variant forms of the same word, usually denoting land on a boundary. This word also means "corner of land" and occurs in *Cockshut* and *Cockshoot* in an original sense "a shooting, darting of woodcocks", later also "a place where woodcocks shoot or dart".

Various terms for land for cultivation are common. Old English *brēc* "land broken up for cultivation" usually survives as *Breach* or *Breech*, sometimes as *Break, Brake* or even *Brick* or *Breck*. Consequently in the North and North Midlands it is easily confused with Scandinavian *brekka* "slope, hill", which gives modern forms such as *Breck* or *Brick*, but again the topography will usually decide between the two. It can also be sometimes confused with *Brake* "thicket". *Intake* and *Intack* "piece of land newly taken into cultivation" is often found in the Scandinavianized districts; it is frequent in medieval records and was commonly used at the time of the enclosures. *Mead, Meadow* and *Pasture* appear as field-names in almost every parish, though the last, apart from occasional examples in the 14th century, is rarely found before the 16th. Scandinavian *eng*

205

"meadow, pasture" is common in the Danelaw counties, often surviving in the plural form *Ings*. *Earth*, however, is uncommon in field-names, as it is in place-names, and when it does occur it usually means "ploughed land". *Fallow(s)*, with a similar meaning, is more frequent, and *Ground* is found in Enclosure and Tithe Awards with the sense "area of ground" or even "outlying field".

Old English *lēah* "wood, glade", a common element in place-names, is equally common in minor names and field-names in the sense "open land, meadow". The usual modern forms are *Lea*, *Lee* or *Ley*, but the plural *Leas*, *Lees* or *Leys*, referring to grassland or to cultivated land under grass or clover, occurs in many counties. These forms are difficult to separate from *Leas(e)* and *Leaz(e)*, representing Old English *lǣs* "pasture, meadowland", even when early forms are available. The dative singular *lǣswe* gives modern names such as *Leasowe*, *Leaser*, *Leasure* and even *Leizure* in many parts of the country. A strip or measure of grassland is sometimes called *Swathe*, common also in the plural and preceded by a numeral.

Wang and *Wong* could represent either Old English *wang* or Scandinavian *vangr*, but since the names are frequent only in the Danelaw counties the Scandinavian word is in most cases the likely source, and the meaning would be "infield" or "garden". "Vegetable garden" is the usual meaning of the field-name *Lawton* or *Laughton*, though when such names are old they may have the sense "herb-garden". *Bed*, however, almost always occurs in compounds with the names of plants or trees, but as a simplex name it means "piece of land where plants (or trees) grow".

Several place-name elements used in field-names in the original sense of "clearing" include Old English *rod*, with modern forms *Rood*, *Road*, and in the North *Royd*; Old English *rydding*, modern *Ridding* or even *Riding*, a very common name, and Old English *stubbing* with similar forms today. *Stocking* is occasionally used of the shape of a field as in *Stocking Leg*, but usually represents Old English *stoccing* "piece of land cleared of stumps". *Assart* "clearing in woodland", a French loan-word, and sometimes shortened to *Sart* is less frequent, however, as is *Fall*, a word of similar meaning.

Elements denoting plots of ground or enclosures are, of course, common. Of these, *Close* "enclosure", also a French loan-word, is found frequently, especially in Enclosure and Tithe Awards, but in most counties it is rare in Middle English sources. *Croft*, on the other hand, is as common in medieval field-names as today. It was originally used of a small enclosed field, but later, as in many modern names, it refers to a small enclosure of arable or pasture, especially one near a dwelling, while *Inland* is a similar term for land near a house or building. Similarly, *Eddish* "enclosure" occurs in some parishes, but in dialects has an additional meaning "stubble, aftermath", and so may, on occasion, have the same sense in field-names as *Fog* "aftermath, long grass left unmowed during winter". *Math*, itself, "mowing, cutting of grass" is not uncommon, and is used either of grass for mowing or of the place where it was cut, as in such a name as *Five Days Math*.

Lot "share; allotment of land", the self-explanatory *Piece*, and *Parcel* "piece of land" occur in almost every Enclosure or Tithe Award, as does *Plot*. This last, however, sometimes replaced the similar *Plat* or *Pleck* "small plot". *Place*, on the other hand, though found in earlier field-names, has often been lost today, but *Pingle* "small enclosure" is almost as common in some areas now as in the 13th or 14th century, and a variant form also survives as *Pightle* or even *Pickle*. *Yard* certainly sometimes has its usual modern sense of a small uncultivated area attached to a building and often surrounded by a wall, as in farm*yard*, but more often in field-names it has its earlier meaning "enclosure".

The commonest term for an "enclosure for animals" is *Fold*, but *Pen* is sometimes found, as well as a derivative *Penning*, while *Hitch* is used specifically of an enclosure of hurdles for sheep. In most parishes, however, the name *Pinfold* occurs for the pound in which stray animals were put. Many parishes also had their rabbit-warren, and the name for this, derived from the Middle English *coninger* or *coningre*, appears in a variety of forms in modern times, such as *Coninger, Conyer, Coneygree, Coneygry*. The similar *Coneyearth* occurs more frequently today as *Coneygarth*, especially in the Scandinavianized counties where it has been influenced by *garth* "enclosure", itself a common field-name in the North and North Midlands.

Some of the terms for topographical features which are not very common in place-names occur more often in minor and field-names, as for example *Bottom* and *Botham* "valley bottom", and *Bye* "corner of land in a river bend". Similarly with *Dimble* or *Dumble* "hollow" and *Dimple* or *Dumple* "deep hole", which are often confused in the modern forms, though the topography will often make it clear which is the correct etymology.

Most of the names so far discussed are common, though some have a particular regional distribution. Others are met with regularly but less frequently. So, we can expect to come across occasional examples of *Stitch* "piece of land", *Screed* "strip of land", the latter particularly in parts of the Danelaw, *Slang, Sling* and *Slinket* "long narrow field",

207

Spong "narrow piece", *String* "narrow strip (often of woodland)", *Sideling* "strip of land beside a stream" and *Tail* "narrow strip". Used as a noun *Long* denotes a long piece of land, while the derivative *Langet* or *Lanket* occurs in some areas with a similar meaning. *Hiron* and *Iron* usually refer to a spit of land in a river bend or to a corner of land. *Island* may denote a field surrounded by a wood, or one with trees in the middle, and *Roundabout(s)* has the same meanings.

Names denoting wet or marshy ground include *Featherbed, Forty* "island in·marshy land", though the latter is of course sometimes the numeral, *Gall* "spongy ground", along with *Bog, Gog* and *Quab* or *Quob*. *Slob* and *Lag* are used of a marshy field in some southern counties, and *Flash* or *Flosh* in the north, while *Honey, Pudding* and *Treacle* are descriptive terms for sticky or muddy land, and *Frog* is often apparently used in a similar way. A pool is sometimes called *Plash* or *Plaish*, while *Stank* is the term used for a stagnant pool and *Stew* for a fishpond. Other types of land do not seem to have such a variety of names. Rocky ground is sometimes called *Cloudy* and the noun *Cloud(s)* is also found for "rock(s)". *Cat's Brain* refers to mottled soil, often rough clay mixed with stones, or clay overlaid with marl, and *Marl* itself, as well as *Marled*, is a common descriptive term. *Checker* or *Chequer* also occurs for ground that has a variegated appearance.

Names such as *Distants, Hem, Sheath, Skirts* and *Meer, Mear* or *Mere* all denote land near a boundary, but the last of these may sometimes represent Old English *mere* "pool". *Ball*, too, sometimes has the meaning "boundary", since especially in the South-west it was used of a mound piled up as a boundary mark. Elsewhere, it usually has the dialectal meaning of "rounded hill, hillock".

Several terms for gates or openings are common, particularly *Lidgate*, surviving also as *Lidget, Ledget* "swing gate", and a name of similar meaning is *Clapgate*. *Cripplegate* usually refers to a low opening in a wall or fence which allows sheep to pass through. *Hatch* is used of a hatch-gate or wicket, and *Hatchet* and *Hacket* are weakened forms of *Hatch-gate*, while *Wicket* itself is by no means uncommon.

Several miscellaneous names, each occurring regularly, are worth noting. *Day(s) Work* was a field that could be ploughed in one day, and examples with numerals as high as *Twelve* have been found; *Farthing* usually means "fourth part" and *Half*, as a noun, is sometimes used in the sense "half share" or "half acre"; *Kitchen* refers to land cultivated for domestic purposes; *Hopping* means "hop-garden"; a name like *Lammas Close* or *Lammas Lands* illustrates the custom by which certain land became common pasturage between

August 1st and the following spring; *Pest* and *Pesthouse* are named from hospitals for those suffering from a plague; and *Rainbow* apparently often refers to the custom of ploughing parallel with the sides of a curved field. *Saintfoin* and *St. Foin* are forms of *Sainfoin*, a kind of grass; and *Several(s)* refers to land held in separate or private ownership, particularly that enclosed as opposed to common land. In Scandinavianized areas *Storth* is common for a plantation or land with brushwood. There are, in addition, some common field-names found regularly in some counties, the meaning of which is still obscure, as with *Fullock*, *Landew*, *Lion* and *Nattock*.

Many field-names, repeated in various parts of the country, are nicknames of a fanciful type. Sometimes they are complimentary, referring to productive land, as in names containing the words *Butter, Excellent, Fat, Good, Lucky* or *Sugar*. Other typical examples include *Dripping Pan, Fillcups, Fillpockets, Golden Valley, God's Garden, Heaven, Help Well, Klondike, Largess, Land of Promise, Long Gains, New Delight, Nonpareil, Paradise, Providence* and *Pound of Butter*, while *Mount Pleasant* may sometimes be complimentary, but is also used ironically. More often such names are derogatory, as with the large group containing the word *Lousy*, such as *Lousy Close*, and similarly with *Bare Bones, Bittersweet, Break Back, Cheat All, Clam Park, Cuckold's Haven, Devil's Own, Empty Purse, Greedy Guts, Hell Kitchen, Hungerhill, Labour-in-vain, Lifeless, Misbegoten, Mount Famine, Mount Misery, No-thankyou, Pickpocket, Pinchgut, Poverty Close, Purgatory, Quarrelsome, Rawbones, Small Beer, Small Drinks, Small Profits, Sodom Field, Spitewinter, Starknaked, Starveall, Starve Mouse, Thirsty Fields* and *Vinegar Hill*. Here, too, may be included *Goodman's Acre*, a bit of poor land left uncultivated and assigned to the Devil. Others refer to places in cold or exposed situations like the series containing *Cold—Cold Blow, Cold Comfort, Cold Hams, Cold Knuckles*—as well as *Bleak Hall* and *Windy Bank*.

A further group of nicknames describes the shape of the field, for example the very common *Shoulder of Mutton, Dogtail,* and *Boot*, as well as *Brandy Bottle, Butchers Cleaver, Buttocks, Cocked Hat, Dogleg, Fiddle, Halfmoon, Harp, Horseshoe, Knitting Needle, Leg of Mutton, Pancake, Rump of Beef, Sugar Loaf, Triangle* and *Wry Neck*. Small fields are often named ironically, as with *Hundred Acres, Thousand Acres, Million Roods, Handkerchief Piece, Wren Park, Mouse Park* and *Thimble Hall*. Some names containing *Penny* may also be of this type—*Halfpenny Bit, Threepenny Piece, Tenpenny Bit*—but in many names *penny* no doubt refers to the rent of the field.

A considerable number, named from distant countries and places, are called nicknames of remoteness, for these fields are usually a good

209

distance from the farm to which they belong, or are situated close to a parish boundary. So, *America, Barbadoes, Bohemia, Canada, China, Egypt, Gibraltar* and *Siberia* are common, as are names from North America, such as *Baltimore, Georgia, Labrador, New England, Newfoundland, New York, North Carolina, Nova Scotia, Pennsylvania, Philadelphia, Quebec* and *South Carolina*. Others which occur frequently include *Botany Bay, New South Wales, New Zealand, Van Diemens Land, Copenhagen, Dunkirk*, a very common minor and field-name, *Isle of Elba, Jericho, Jerusalem, Mount Sinai, Moscow, Nineveh* and so on. This type is not confined to those names adopted from abroad, but includes many from distant parts of England and the British Isles. Besides these, as nicknames for remote fields and places, we can add *Lands End, Utter Ends, Worlds End* and *Nomansland*.

Here, too, belongs a group named from famous battles or wars, such as *Waterloo, Crimea*, together with *Alma, Balaclava, Inkermann* and *Sebastopol*, and *Bunkers Hill* 1755. A few which occur only occasionally include *Blenheim* 1704, *Heights of Abraham* 1759, *Maida Hill* 1806, *Portobello* 1739 and *Spioncop* 1900.

Some names indicate that the rent from the field was used for a charitable purpose, as with *Poors*, for the parish poor, and *Charity*, for some local charity. But most such names have a religious association, sometimes general, as with *Corpus* or *Sacred*, sometimes a saint's name from the dedication of a local church or chapel, but more often simply *Church* or *Chapel*. In many cases the rent was assigned to some specific purpose, as is indicated by such words as *Chancel, Quire, Bell, Bellrope, Rope, Holybread, Vestry Light, Watchlight* and *Lamp*, which form parts of field-names. Indeed, *Lamplands* is especially common, denoting land whose rent was used for the upkeep of a lamp in the church. That allocated to individual clerics is indicated by *Parson, Priest* and *Vicar*, as well as *Glebe*, the land assigned to a parson as part of his benefice. But most interesting of all those with religious associations are names derived from the Rogation Ceremony of "beating the parish bounds", which took place during the week preceding Ascension Day, when the village officials, accompanied by the vicar, walked round the boundary of the parish to ensure that no boundary mark had been moved. At each halt at a mark, a passage of the Scripture was read or a prayer said. On many parish boundaries names in *Gospel* are found, while other names derived from this ceremony are *Amen*, as in *Amen Corner*, and *Paternoster*.

Reference to human folly, especially in building, is represented chiefly by names in *Folly*, such as *The Folly, Folly House* and so on.

Also interesting are *Cockayne* and *Cocken* from Middle English *cockaygne*, an imaginary country of luxury and idleness, and as a field- or minor name it is probably intended humorously.

There is also a group of names of the more fanciful type, which has not yet been properly explained. Here belong *Black Jacks*, *Blind Feet*, *Beans and Bacon*, *Brown Bread*, *Hen and Chickens*, *Noah's Ark*, *Smock Alley* and *Spicecake*.

Fanciful names, however, are by no means only of recent origin and similar ones can be found in early records. The following may be taken as typical of those so far discovered by the editors of the English Place-Name Society. Of the complimentary type are *Parodys* 1337 (Db) "paradise" and *Godesworlde* 1407 (Sx), while *le Sullen* 1369 (Sr), *Forsakenelond* 13th century (Ess), *Wabigan* 13th century (ERY) "woe-begone" and *le Schold in wityng* 1275 (Nt) "the scold in reproach", for a field difficult to work, are uncomplimentary. A number of others commemorate a now long-forgotten tragedy, as in *Dedemanyslane* 1370 (Ess) "dead man's lane" and *Dedquenesike* 13th (Nth) "dead woman's stream", while *Thertheoxlaydede* 13th century "where the ox lay dead" is what the editors of *The Place-Names of Buckinghamshire* have described as "a picture in miniature of a medieval farming tragedy".

COMMON ELEMENTS
IN ENGLISH PLACE-NAMES

(Chiefly those occurring in simplex names, and as the
first and second elements of compounds)

ME Middle English	ON Old Norse
ODan Old Danish	ONorw Old Norwegian
OE Old English	OW Old Welsh
OFr Old French	

COMMON MODERN FORMS		MEANING	SOURCE
Bank			
-bank		bank, ridge	ODan, ME banke
Bare			
Barrow	-beare	grove, wood	OE bearu, dative
-barrow	-ber		singular bearwe
-bear	-borough		
Barrow-			
Bar-	-berry	hill, mound,	OE beorg, ON berg
Berg-	-borough	tumulus	
-ber	-burgh		
Barton			
		barley farm, corn farm, outlying grange	OE beretūn
Batch-			
Betch-	-bage	stream, valley	OE bece, bæce
-bach	-beach		
-badge	-bech		
Beck-			
-beck		beck, stream	ON bekkr

212

COMMON MODERN FORMS		MEANING	SOURCE
Berwick Barwick		barley farm, outlying part of an estate	OE berewīc
Biggin Bigging	-biggin	building, house	ME bigging
Bold Bothel Bootle	-bold -bottle	dwelling, house	OE bold, bōtl, bōðl
Booth -booth -both		booth, temporary shelter	ODan bōth, ONorw búð
Botham- Bottom -bottom		bottom, valley bottom	OE botm, boðm
Breck -breck -brick		slope, hill	ON brekka
Bridge- Brig- -bridge	-brig	bridge	OE brycg
Brook- Brock- Brough-	-brook -broke	brook, stream	OE brōc
Brough Burgh Bury -borough	-burgh -bury	fortified place, etc. (p. 112ff.)	OE burh, burg, dative singular byrig, byrg
Burn- Brun- -borne	-bourne -burn	stream, spring	OE burna

213

COMMON ELEMENTS IN ENGLISH PLACE-NAMES

COMMON MODERN FORMS		MEANING	SOURCE
Burton Bourton Broughton		tūn near or belong- ing to a fortified place, fortified manor	OE burhtūn
-by		farmstead, village	ON bȳ
Camb Comb Cam-	Com-	comb, ridge	OE camb
-camp -combe		enclosed piece of land, field	OE camp
Carr -carr -car	-ker	brushwood; in ME marsh, bog	ON kjarr, ME ker
Caster- Chester- -caster	-cester -chester	city, (Roman) town, old fortification	OE ceaster, cæster
Church- Cheri- Chir-	-church	church	OE cirice
Clif- Cleve- -cliff	-cliffe -ley	cliff, bank, rock, steep bank	OE clif, ON klif
Clough- Clof- -cleugh	-clough	ravine, deep valley	OE clōh

214

COMMON MODERN FORMS		MEANING	SOURCE
Coat,			
Coate	Coton	cottage, shelter	OE cot, dative
Cote	Cotton		singular cote,
Coatham	-cot		dative plural cotum
Cottam	-cote		
Comb-			
Comp-	-coombe	coomb, valley	OE cumb
-combe			
Creech-			
Crich		hill, barrow	OW crūc
Crook			
Croft			
-croft		piece of enclosed land, small piece of arable	OE croft
Cross			
Cros-		cross	late OE cros (p. 61)
-cross			
Dale			
Dal-		dale, valley	OE dæl, ON dalr
-dale			
-dean			
-den		pasture, swine pasture	OE denn (chiefly K and Sx)
Dean			
Deane	-dean	valley	OE denu
Den-	-den		
Ditch-			
Dit-	-dyke	ditch, dyke	OE dīc
-ditch	-dish		

215

COMMON MODERN FORMS		MEANING	SOURCE
Down- Dun- -don	-den -ton	down, hill	OE dūn
E- Ea- -ey	-eau	stream, river	OE ēa
E- Ea- Ey-	-ey -y	island, etc. (p. 167f.)	OE ēg
Edge -edge		edge, ridge	OE ecg
Emmot Emmott		river confluence	OE ēamōt
-ergh -er		shieling, hill- pasture	ON erg
Fen Venn Fen-	-fen -ven	fen, marsh	OE fenn
Field Fel- -field	-ville	open land (p. 192f.)	OE feld
Fleet -fleet		estuary, stream	OE flēot
-font -hunt		spring, perhaps stream	OE funta, from OW

COMMON MODERN FORMS		MEANING	SOURCE
Ford- For- -ford	-forth	ford	OE ford
Frith Thrift		wood, woodland	OE (ge)fyrhð
Gate- Yate- gate -yate	-yatt -yet	gate, hole	OE geat
Gate -gate		way, road, street	ON gata
Graf- Grove- -grove	-grave	grove, thicket	OE grāf
-grave -greave		grave, pit, trench	OE græf
-greave -grave -greve		grove, thicket	OE grǣfe
Haigh Hale Hal- Hall- Haugh- -al	-ale -all -halgh -hall	nook, corner, recess, narrow valley, water-meadow	OE halh, dative singular hale
-ham		village, manor, homestead	OE hām

217

COMMON MODERN FORMS	MEANING	SOURCE
Ham -ham	enclosure	OE hamm, homm
Hampstead Hamstead -hamstead -hampstead	homestead	OE hāmstede
Hampton Hamton -hampton	home farm	OE hāmtūn
-hanger -honger	slope, wood on a slope	OE hangra
Hardwick	farm for a herd of animals	OE heordewīc
Haugh -haugh -hay -haw	enclosure	OE haga, ON hagi
Hay- -hay -hey	fence, enclosed piece of land	OE (ge)hæg
Head- -head -ide	head, headland	OE hēafod
Heath- Had- Hed- Hat- -heath	heath, heather	OE hǣð
Hill Hil- -hill Hel- -el Hul- -le	hill	OE hyll

COMMON MODERN FORMS		MEANING	SOURCE
Hole Hol- -hole	-al -all	hole, hollow	OE hol
Holme -holm -holme	-ham	small island	ON holmr, holmi ODan hulm
Holt -holt		holt, wood	OE holt
Hope Hop- -hop -hope	-op -up	dry land in fen, small valley blind valley	OE hop
Hough- Hol- Hoo- How- Hu-	-hoe -oe -ow	heel, hill spur	OE hōh, dative singular hōe
House -house -sham	-some -som	house	OE hūs, dative plural hūsum, ON hús
-how -howe -hoe	-oe	hill, mound, tumulus	ON haugr
Hulme -hulme		island, water- meadow	ODan hulm ON holmr, holmi
Hurst Hirst, -hurst	-hirst	hurst, hillock, knoll, copse	OE hyrst

COMMON MODERN FORMS		MEANING	SOURCE
Hythe Hive -hithe	-eth	port, haven	OE hȳð
Ing Ings -ing	-ings	meadow, pasture	ON eng
-ing		an ending in names meaning "place", "river" (p. 162)	OE -ing
-ings -ing		added to a personal name to form a folk-name (p. 63ff.)	OE -ingas
-ington etc.		with a personal name (p. 145f.)	OE -ing-, as in -ingtūn
Keld- Kel- -keld		spring	ON kelda
Kirk- Kir- -kirk		church	ON kirkja
Lac- Lack- -lake	-lock	stream, water-course	OE lacu
Lan- Llan- -land		enclosure, yard, church	OW lann, Cornish lan
Land- land-		land (p. 191f.)	OE land

COMMON MODERN FORMS		MEANING	SOURCE
Latch- Lach- Lash- Lech- Letch-	-lache -leach -ledge	stream, bog	OE læcc
Lea Lee Leigh -ley	-leigh -le -low	forest, wood, glade (p. 187ff.)	OE lēah
Leasowe Laisure Leizure	-lease, -lees	pasture	OE lǣs, dative singular lǣswe
-linch -lynch -ling	-linge	bank, ridge	OE hlinc
-lith -leth -ley		slope, hillside	OE hlið, ON hlíð
Load Lode -lade	-load -lode	water-course, track	OE (ge)lād
Lock- -lock		enclosure	OE loca
Lound Lund Lunt	-land	grove, copse, sometimes sacred grove	ON lundr
-low -ley		hill, mound, tumulus	OE hlāw

221

COMMON MODERN FORMS		MEANING	SOURCE
Mar- Mear- Mer- Meer-	-mere -more	boundary	OE (ge)mǣre
Mar- Mer- -mer	-mere -more	pool, lake, mere	OE mere
Marc- Mark- -mark		mark, boundary	OE mearc
Marsh- Mars- Mers-	-marsh	marsh	OE mersc
Meadow Made- Med- -mead	-mede -meadow	meadow	OE mǣd, dative singular mǣdwe
Mill- Mil- Miln-	Mel- -mill	mill	OE myln
Minster- Mister- -minster		monastery, church	OE mynster
-mond -mont		mound, hill	OFr, ME mont
Moor- Mor- More- Mur-	-moor -more	moor, waste-land, fen	OE mōr

222

COMMON MODERN FORMS		MEANING	SOURCE
-mouth		mouth of a river	OE mūða
Naze- Nas- Nes-	-ness	promontory, headland, cape	OE næss, ness, ON nes
Oare Ore, Or-	-or -ore	border, bank, river-bank	OE ōra
Over- Or- -or	-ore -over	bank, river-bank, edge, hill	OE ōfer
Over- -or -over		slope, hill	OE ofer
-path -peth		path, track	OE pæð, peð
Pen-		top, hill, end	OW penn
Pool- Pol- Poul-	-pole -pool	pool, stream	OE pōl
Port- Por- -port		harbour, town	OE port
-rick -ridge		strip of land, narrow road, perhaps also ridge	OE ric

COMMON MODERN FORMS		MEANING	SOURCE
Ridding Riding Ruding	-ridding -riding	clearing	OE rydding
Ridge- Ridg- Rudge-	-ridge	ridge	OE hrycg
Rig- -rigg		ridge	ON hryggr
Rise- Ris- -rice	-rise	brushwood	OE hrīs, ON hrís
-rith -reth -red		stream	OE rīð
Road Rodd Rode	-rod -royd	clearing	OE rod
Sand- -sand		sand	OE sand
Scale- scale- -skill		hut, temporary hut or shed	ON skáli
-scough -skew -scoe		wood	ON skógr
Sea- Sa- So-	-sea	sea, lake	OE sǣ, sā

COMMON MODERN FORMS		MEANING	SOURCE
-seat -side		shieling, hill- pasture	ON sætr
-sett		dwelling, place for animals	OE (ge)set
Shat- -shot -shott		corner, strip of land	OE scēat
Shaw -shaw		shaw, copse, grove, small wood	OE scaga, sceaga
Shelf- Shel- -shelf		rock, ledge, shelving land	OE scelf, scylf
-side -cett -sett		side, hill-slope, hill-side	OE sīde
-slack		shallow valley	ON slakki
Slade Sled- -slade	-slate	valley	OE slæd
Stain- Stan- Sten-	-stone	stone	ON steinn
-stall -stal		place, stall	OE stall

COMMON MODERN FORMS		MEANING	SOURCE
-stead -sted		place, site, religious site	OE stede
Stoke Stock- Stough-	-stoke -stock	place, religious place, secondary settlement	OE stoc
Stone- Stan- Ston-	-stone -ston	stone	OE stān
Stow Stowe -stow	-stowe -stoe	place, holy place, place of assembly	OE stōw
Strat- Stret- Strad- Streat-	Sturt- -street	Roman road, street	OE strǣt, strēt
Sty- Sti- -sty		path	OE stīg, ON stígr
Thorpe -thorpe		secondary settlement or farm	ODan þorp
Thorpe Throp Thrope Thrupp -throp	-thorp -drop -trop	farm, dependent farm, hamlet	OE þrop
Thwaite -thwaite		meadow, clearing	ON þveit

COMMON MODERN FORMS		MEANING	SOURCE
Toft -toft		site of a house, homestead	ODan toft
Tor -tor -ter		rock, rocky peak	OE torr
Town- Ton- -ton	-tone	enclosure, farmstead, village, manor (p. 141ff.)	OE tūn
Tree- Tre- Tro- -tree	-trey -try	tree	OE trēow, trēo
Wade -wade		ford	OE (ge)wæd
Wald- Walt- Wal- Wauld- Old-	-wold -wald -would	woodland, forest, high forest-land, later open upland	OE wald, weald
-wardine		enclosure	OE worðign
Wark -wark		work, fortification	OE (ge)weorc
-was		wet place, swamp	OE wæsse
Water- -water		water, lake, river	OE wæter

227

COMMON MODERN FORMS		MEANING	SOURCE
Wath			
-wath	-worth	ford	ON vað
-with			
Way-			
-way		way, road	OE weg
Well-			
Wel-	-well	well, spring, stream	OE welle, wielle,
Wal-	-wall		wælle
Wil-	-will		
Wick-			
Wig-	-wich	dwelling, farm,	OE wīc
Wych-	-week	dairy-farm, village,	
-wick		saltworks	
-with			
		wood	ON viðr
Wood-			
-wood		wood, forest,	OE wudu
		timber	
Worth			
-worth		enclosure	OE worð
-worthy			
		enclosure	OE worðig

BIBLIOGRAPHY

The most outstanding general works are:

E. EKWALL, *The Concise Oxford Dictionary of English Place-Names*, 4th edition, Oxford, 1960.

E. EKWALL, *English River Names*, Oxford, 1928.

The following are the county volumes of the English Place-Name Society (in alphabetical order of counties), published by The E.P.-N.S.:

A. MAWER and F. M. STENTON, *The Place-Names of Bedfordshire and Huntingdonshire*, 1926.

MARGARET GELLING, . . . *Berkshire*, 3 vols., 1973–76.

A. MAWER and F. M. STENTON, . . . *Buckinghamshire*, 1925.

P. H. REANEY, . . . *Cambridgeshire and the Isle of Ely*, 1943.

J. McN. DODGSON, . . . *Cheshire*, 4 vols., 1970–72 (fifth volume forthcoming).

A. M. ARMSTRONG, A. MAWER, F. M. STENTON and BRUCE DICKINS, . . . *Cumberland*, 3 vols., 1950–52.

K. CAMERON, . . . *Derbyshire*, 3 vols., 1959.

J. E. B. GOVER, A. MAWER and F. M. STENTON, . . . *Devon*, 2 vols., 1931–32.

A. D. MILLS, . . . *Dorset*, volume 1, 1977 (four further volumes to follow).

P. H. REANEY, . . . *Essex*, 1935.

A. H. SMITH, . . . *Gloucestershire*, 4 vols., 1964–65.

J. E. B. GOVER, A. MAWER and F. M. STENTON, . . . *Hertfordshire*, 1938.

J. E. B. GOVER, A. MAWER and F. M. STENTON with the collaboration of S. J. MADGE, . . . *Middlesex apart from the City of London*, 1942.

J. E. B. GOVER, A. MAWER and F. M. STENTON, . . . *Northamptonshire*, 1933.

J. E. B. GOVER, A. MAWER and F. M. STENTON, . . . *Nottinghamshire*, 1940.

MARGARET GELLING, based on the material collected by DORIS MARY STENTON, . . . *Oxfordshire*, 2 vols., 1953–54.

J. E. B. GOVER, A. MAWER and F. M. STENTON in collaboration with A. BONNER, . . . *Surrey*, 1934.

A. MAWER and F. M. STENTON with the assistance of J. E. B. GOVER, . . . *Sussex*, 2 vols., 1929–30.

229

J. E. B. GOVER, A. MAWER and F. M. STENTON in collaboration with F. T. S. HOUGHTON, . . . *Warwickshire*, 1936.

A. H. SMITH, . . . *Westmorland*, 2 vols., 1967.

J. E. B. GOVER, A. MAWER and F. M. STENTON, . . . *Wiltshire*, 1939.

A. MAWER and F. M. STENTON in collaboration with F. T. S. HOUGHTON, . . . *Worcestershire*, 1927.

A. H. SMITH, . . . *The East Riding of Yorkshire and York*, 1937.

A. H. SMITH, . . . *The North Riding of Yorkshire*, 1928.

A. H. SMITH, . . . *The West Riding of Yorkshire*, 8 vols., 1961–63.

and also two important works:

Introduction to the Survey of English Place-Names, edited by A. MAWER and F. M. STENTON, 1924.

A. H. SMITH, *English Place-Name Elements*, 2 vols., 1956.

Similar county volumes, but not including a treatment of field-names, are:

A. FÄGERSTEN, *The Place-Names of Dorset*, Uppsala, 1933.

J. K. WALLENBERG, *The Place-Names of Kent*, Uppsala, 1934, together with *Kentish Place-Names*, Uppsala, 1931.

E. EKWALL, *The Place-Names of Lancashire*, Manchester, 1922.

H. KÖKERITZ, *The Place-Names of the Isle of Wight*, Uppsala, 1940.

Other detailed surveys on various topics include:

O. S. ANDERSON (now ARNGART), *The English Hundred-Names*, 3 vols., Lund, 1934–36.

E. EKWALL, *Street-Names of the City of London*, Oxford, 1954.

B. G. CHARLES, *Non Celtic Place-Names in Wales*, London, 1938.

There are in addition several county volumes, dealing mainly with the names of the more important places, which are still useful but which will in time be replaced by comprehensive surveys by the English Place-Name Society:

A. T. BANNISTER, *The Place-Names of Herefordshire*, Cambridge, 1916.

A. MAWER, *The Place-Names of Northumberland and Durham*, Cambridge, 1920.

E. W. BOWCOCK, *Place-Names of Shropshire*, Shrewsbury, 1923.

W. H. DUIGNAN, *Notes on Staffordshire Place-Names*, London, 1902.

W. W. SKEAT, *The Place-Names of Suffolk*, Cambridge, 1913.

Some general books on English place-names are:

C. J. COPLEY, *Names and Places*, London, 1963; *English Place-Names and their Origins*, Newton Abbot, 1968.

J. FIELD, *English Field Names: A Dictionary*, Newton Abbot, 1972.

W. F. H. NICOLAISEN, MARGARET GELLING and MELVILLE RICHARDS, *The Names of Towns and Cities in Britain*, London, 1970.

P. H. REANEY, *The Origins of English Place-Names*, London, 1960.
F. T. WAINWRIGHT, *Archaeology & Place-Names & History*, London, 1962.

There are numerous important works, chiefly of a technical kind, on various aspects of the interpretation of English place-names, including:

BRUCE DICKINS, "Latin Additions to Place- and Parish-Names of England and Wales", in *Proceedings of the Leeds Philosophical and Literary Society (Literary and Historical Section)*, volume iii, 1935.
E. EKWALL, *Scandinavians and Celts in the North-West of England*, Lund, 1918.
E. EKWALL, *English Place-Names in -ing*, 2nd edition, Lund, 1962.
E. EKWALL, *Studies on English Place- and Personal Names*, Lund, 1931.
F. EKWALL, *Studies on England Place-Names*, Stockholm, 1936.
E. EKWALL, *Etymological Notes on English Place-Names*, Lund, 1959.
E. EKWALL, *Old English wic in Place-Names*, Uppsala, 1964.
R. FORSBERG, *A Contribution to a Dictionary of Old English Place-Names*, Uppsala, 1950.
MARGARET GELLING, "English Place-Names derived from the Compound wīchām", in *Medieval Archaeology*, volume xi, 1967.*
C. JOHANSSON, *Old English Place-Names and Field-Names containing lēah*, Stockholm, 1975.
S. KARLSTRÖM, *Old English Compound Place-Names in -ing*, Uppsala, 1927.
H. LINDKVIST, *Middle English Place-Names of Scandinavian Origin*, Uppsala, 1912.
K. I. SANDRED, *English Place-Names in -stead*, Uppsala, 1963.
K. I. SANDRED, "The Element hamm in English Place-Names. A Linguistic Investigation", in *Namn och Bygd*, volume 64, 1976.
R. TENGSTRAND, *A Contribution to the Study of Genitival Composition in Old English Place-Names*, Uppsala, 1940.
R. E. ZACHRISSON, *A Contribution to the Study of Anglo-Norman Influence on English Place-Names*, Lund, 1909.
R. E. ZACHRISSON, *Romans, Kelts and Saxons in Ancient Britain*, Uppsala, 1927.

Strongly recommended are the following, which deal with the evidence provided by place-names in various fields of study:

H. BRADLEY, "English Place-Names", in *Essays and Studies by Members of the English Association*, volume i, 1910.
K. CAMERON, "Eccles in English Place-Names", in *Christianity in Britain 300–700*, Leicester, 1968.*
K. CAMERON, *Scandinavian Settlement in the Territory of the Five Boroughs: The Place-Name Evidence*, Nottingham, 1965; "... Part II, Place Names in Thorp", in *Mediaeval Scandinavia*, volume 3, 1969; "... Part III, the Grimston-hybrids", in *England before the Conquest. Studies ... Presented to Dorothy Whitelock*, Cambridge, 1971.*

231

K. CAMERON, *The Significance of English Place-Names*, The British Academy, 1976.

B. COX, "The Significance of the Distribution of English Place-Names in *hām* in the Midlands and East Anglia", in *Journal of the English Place-Name Society*, volume 5, 1973.*

BRUCE DICKINS, "English Names and Old English Heathenism", in *Essays and Studies by Members of the English Association*, volume xix, 1933; and "Yorkshire Hobs" in *Transactions of the Yorkshire Dialect Society*, volume vii, 1942.

J. McN. DODGSON, "The Significance of the Distribution of English Place-Names in *-ingas, -inga-* in South-east England", in *Medieval Archaeology*, volume x, 1966.*

GILLIAN FELLOWS JENSEN, *Scandinavian Settlement Names in Yorkshire*, Copenhagen, 1972.

MARGARET GELLING, "Further Thoughts on Pagan Place-Names", in *Otium et Negotium. Studies . . . Presented to Olof von Feilitzen*, Stockholm, 1973.*

RHONA M. HUGGINS, "The Significance of the Place-Name *Wealdhām*", in *Medieval Archaeology*, volume xix, 1975.

J. KUURMAN, "An Examination of the *-ingas, -inga-* Place-Names in the East Midlands", in *Journal of the English Place-Name Society*, volume 7, 1975.

A. MAWER, *Problems of Place-Name Study*, Cambridge, 1929.

L. W. H. PAYLING, "Geology and Place-Names in Kesteven", in *Leeds Studies in English and Kindred Languages*, volume iv, 1935.

and an important group of articles by Sir Frank Stenton under the general title "The Historical Bearing of Place-Name Studies", published in *The Transactions of the Royal Historical Society*, Fourth Series:

"England in the Sixth Century", volume xxi, 1939.
"The English Occupation of Southern Britain", volume xxii, 1940.
"Anglo-Saxon Heathenism", volume xxiii, 1941.
"The Danish Settlement of Eastern England", volume xxiv, 1942.
"The Place of Women in Anglo-Saxon History", volume xxv, 1943.
"The Scandinavian Colonies in England and Normandy", volume xxvii, 1945.

All the works of reference followed by * have been reprinted in a collection of essays under the title *Place-Name Evidence for the Anglo-Saxon Invasion and Scandinavian Settlements*, E. P. N. S., 1975.

Three very important general works are:

R. G. COLLINGWOOD and J. N. L. MYERS, *Roman Britain and the English Settlements*, 2nd edition, Oxford, 1956.

K. JACKSON, *Language and History in Early Britain*, Edinburgh, 1953.

F. M. STENTON, *Anglo-Saxon England*, 3rd edition, Oxford, 1971.

Note also:

The *Anglo-Saxon Chronicle*, translated with an Introduction by G. N. GARMONSWAY, Everyman, 1960, in which the place-names are identified and a full index is given.

There are also three important articles dealing specifically with the interpretation of names of Celtic origin:

K. JACKSON, "On Some Romano-British Place-Names", in *The Journal of Roman Studies*, volume xxxviii, 1948.

I. A. RICHMOND and O. G. S. CRAWFORD, "The British Section of the Ravenna Cosmography", in *Archaeologia*, volume xciii, 1949.

A. L. F. RIVET and KENNETH JACKSON, "The British Section of the Antonine Itinerary", in *Britannia*, volume 1, 1970.

The following Maps published by the Ordnance Survey are excellent for reference and identification:

Ancient Britain, two sheets, 1951.
Map of Roman Britain, 3rd edition, 1956.
Map of Britain in the Dark Ages, 2nd edition, 1966.
Map of Britain before the Norman Conquest, 1973.

ADDENDUM TO CHAPTER 6

Note: In recent years a reassessment of the place-names of Scandinavian origin in eastern England has been taking place, and some significant findings have already emerged. There are various pieces of evidence which suggest that the Danes settled in existing English villages without altering the names. In the past, it was also believed that many of the Danish-named places in -*by* were older English villages renamed by the Danes. By comparing and contrasting these with adjacent English-named places in terms of land-utilisation I have been able to suggest that, though this has happened in some cases, the majority of the names derived from Old Danish *bȳ* represent new settlements on land little occupied at the time. Far too often the sites and situations of the places with names in -*by* were inferior for settlement to the English-named places for this not to have been the case. It would appear that, though Danish settlement here

233

was in origin essentially an army one, the Danes also came as colonisers in a real sense.

By using the same techniques, I was further able to confirm that the majority of the places with names derived from Old Danish *þorp* did in fact represent secondary or outlying settlements, though it may transpire that these were rather the result of Scandinavian influence than Scandinavian settlement itself. It may well be that *þorp* was taken over into the local vocabulary (as indeed we know it was) and as such was used to denote a secondary settlement *wherever* this took place in the area.

I was further able to confirm the theory that the hybrids in -*tūn* represented older English villages taken over and partially renamed by the Danes. But, again using the same techniques, my evidence suggested that such names belonged to the earliest stratum of Danish name-giving in the east Midlands, and it did not, as suggested on p. 82, represent extension of Danish settlement away from established (Danish) centres.

The techniques I developed were used by Dr. Gillian Fellows Jensen in a study of Scandinavian place-names in Yorkshire and her work confirmed the *broad* conclusions I had reached. At any rate, our joint work has provided a framework and a firm basis for future discussion. As a result, a new stratification of Danish name-giving, at least in Yorkshire and the east Midlands, suggests itself: that the earliest *identifiable* place-names are the hybrids in -*tūn*, representing Danish take-over of existing villages and partial renaming; the earliest *new* Danish settlement is represented by the names derived from *bȳ*; and a later stage is represented by those derived from *þorp*, with the proviso stated above. It must be clearly remembered that we are talking about *Danish-named* places. Of course, it is accepted that the Danes took over existing English villages without changing the name and that this must have happened in a good many instances.

The detailed evidence which lead to these conclusions is to be found in Kenneth Cameron, "Scandinavian Settlement in the Territory of the Five Boroughs: The Place-Name Evidence", ". . . Part II, Place-Names in Thorp", ". . . Part III, The Grimston-hybrids", all reprinted in *Place-Name Evidence for the Anglo-Saxon Invasion and Scandinavian Settlements*, E. P. N. S., 1975, and Gillian Fellows Jensen, *Scandinavian Settlement Names in Yorkshire*, Copenhagen, 1972. For a convenient summary of these, see Kenneth Cameron, *The Significance of English Place-Names*, British Academy, 1976.

INDEX

Place-names

For each individual place-name the reference is only to the page(s) on which the meaning or origin of that name is discussed.

235

Street-Names

Field-Names